BORN T

BORN TO DEAL

A Life with Horses

John Betteridge

Matador
9 De Montfort Mews
Leicester LE1 7FW, UK
Tel: (+44) 116 255 9311 / 9312
Email: books@troubador.co.uk
Web: www.troubador.co.uk/matador

ISBN 1 905237 41 3

Cover photograph: L–R
Fiona Shepherd Cross – Snowy River
Jane Walker-Okeover – Mystery
John Betteridge – Glendower
Sue Wilson – Herbie
Kate Cooper – Anni P

Typeset in 11pt Stempel Garamond by Troubador Publishing Ltd, Leicester, UK

Matador is an imprint of Troubador Publishing Ltd

Acknowledgements

This book could not have been published without the invaluable help of:

Annable Startin who deciphered my longhand.

John Loft for spending hours editing it.

My son and daughter, Tim and Sarah, for all their help, support and encouragement.

My very long suffering son-in-law Mark for all his invaluable input.

And lastly, my wife Linda without whom none of it would have been possible.

My heartfelt thanks to you all.

CONTENTS

Foreword
Michael Clayton   ix

Introduction   1

The Thirties   5

The Forties   8

The Fifties   34

The Sixties   59

The Seventies   94

The Eighties   140

The Nineties and Beyond   182

Epilogue   213

FOREWORD

Michael Clayton

There is an old Arab proverb that "the grave is ever open for the horseman...." It is a saying best forgotten as you are about to mount your horse. John Betteridge, in his biography, conjures up a much better saying which the horseman should remember every time he puts his foot into the stirrup to swing into the saddle: "If you don't have confidence you have nothing."

It is this precept that has helped John through a life-time of the joys and the perils of horsemanship. He elaborates on his theme thus: "It doesn't matter if you are any sort of a horseman, the one thing you need is confidence in your own ability."

Farming, horsemanship, hunting and the delights of dealing....all are fondly remembered in this story of a lifetime in rural Derbyshire. It should be preserved as a valuable sociological document on what it was really like to make your way in the much harder times faced by those who were born in the lean 1930's, through the second world war, and the post-war austerity years.

There is a freshness, and indeed an innocence, about that mid-20th Century period in a British countryside where vast change was on its way, but where there was still so much fun to be had from pleasures which seem basic compared with the diversity of "entertainments" on offer to the young of today.

John was the son of a horse-dealer, and therefore inherited a way of life where a "good deal" on a mount sold to a well-off customer augmented the basic income to be derived from pastoral farming on small acreages. He was a natural horseman, and quickly succeeded in show classes and in showjumping. His story evokes the fun of riding in a rustic show in wartime with none of the elaborate back-up facilities often taken for granted now on the show circuit.

At the end of the war John went to London to compete amid the awesome spaces of the White City arena. Clearly the confidence-factor was already working because John was by no means over-awed, and rode his pony, Johnny B, to win £30 and a silver cup as victor in the open juvenile class.

In manhood he continued a parallel career to farming as a show-jumper which meant that his horizons were widened far beyond his native Derbyshire. Meeting people has been just as important in his life as selling them horses. To succeed in his life-style you need fortitude as well as self-confidence. John records matter-of-factly that as a recently-married young man, with a new farm to run, in 1959 he had to undergo very serious back-surgery, having two discs taken out of his spine, involving four months in hospital and a year out of action.

The dreaded words "You will never ride again" were part of the medical verdict.

John did not allow such a dire prophecy to over-ride his natural confidence in himself – and it was not long before he returned to the saddle, to competitive showjumping, to the hunting field, and to his dealing. He is still riding to hounds over big fences at 70-plus.

Strengthened by his marriage to Linda, also a cheerful, extrovert personality, John has become one of the best-known dealers in the Midlands, and many a well-mounted horseman considered himself fortunate to be able to say, "Yes, I got this horse from John Betteridge...." John and Linda and their family adore their hunting, and their way of life in a beautiful rural setting which many would envy. Plough has not taken over from grass in Derbyshire to anywhere near the extent this has occurred in neighbouring Leicestershire.

Those of us who have had the good fortune to ride behind the Meynell hounds in their lovely country know how John makes clearing formidable hedges and timber, guarded by scoops, look so much simpler than it is when your own turn comes. He has the top-class showjumper's natural balance, excellent hands and timing, plus boldness tempered with a great eye for the country.

His life-story will be especially interesting for his contemporaries, but those born much later will derive benefit and enjoyment from a look back at horsemanship in an English countryside which was greener, far less spoilt – and where a man "with confidence in himself" could really go places on a horse.

Michael Clayton
Burghley-on-the-Hill, Rutland

INTRODUCTION

Sitting here meditating, after a heavy fall over an innocuous fence out hunting on Tuesday, 20th January, 1998, I wonder to myself if anyone would like to pass an hour or two reliving the life of a horse-dealer in a part-autobiography of John Betteridge.

* * *

Father told me that he took me, when I was two, to my first meet of the Meynell Hounds when they met at Findern in 1932. I rode in a basket saddle on a blue roan pony. On the strength of my appearance, I suppose, he sold it a few days later as a good hunting pony! Father came from a horse-dealing family. He told me his first mount was a donkey in 1895 which he and his brother were looking after for the seaside people. He was always very proud of the way that they had got this donkey so fit that his coat absolutely glistened. His first day hunting was with the Meynell at Calke Park Gates in 1895, where I was to hunt in 1943. I remember the occasion quite well. I was riding one of father's latest purchases - a trotter by Dan Direct. The drive to Calke Abbey must be at least a mile and a half. As the rest of the field were cantering and galloping, I was passing most of them at a trot! Trotters are normally good jumpers (Jappielou, the World Champion, was a part-bred trotter, even if he was French). This one didn't disappoint. He jumped superbly all day. It was interesting when we came to sell him to a fellow named Oscar Johnson from Walsall, a big friend of father's in his trotting days. I will never forget it. We had the stables at the Bulls Head, Repton. Father said, "Turn left out of the gates, jog down to the Square – and give a flash as you pass." I certainly did that. I was over the bridge into Willington before I pulled him up – about one-and-a-half miles away! Trotters do take a grip and he certainly did. Anyway, Oscar bought him, so I didn't do too bad a job. I suppose in telling that little tale, I have jumped a few years, so I had better go back to how one serves an apprenticeship in horse-dealing.

Father was a horseman when Lord Harrington had Elvaston Castle and the Estate. Most of the tenant farmers kept a brood mare. Lord Harrington was also Joint-Master of the South Notts and as he was always

1

needing hunters, he would go round his farmers, buy the hunter types – three-year-olds – and send them to various people, including Father, to break. End of July he would have the Elvaston Show and a special class for best broken three-year-old. When Father had won this class for the last two years, and wanted to win for the third time, he had to think up something special, so he taught this horse to lie down while he stood on its back and cracked a whip while it still lay down. People still talked about it for years. If I go down to Derby Market now, someone will still come up to me and tell me that tale: "I remember your father making that horse lie down and cracking a whip over it."

TROTTERS

Father had always been interested in trotters and felt that the English horse could be improved on. When they brought a load of American trotters over to London – Greenford Park was the venue for selling these horses – he and his brother decided they had better go for a look, and he bought a three-year-old colt named Blue Fox. I believe he was a lovely horse. He was bred at the Walnut Stud Farm in the Blue Grass county of Kentucky. Times are very important to trotters and in America he had a time of 2m.02s. for the mile, but the best he could do in this country was 2.10. The going was probably different over there. Anyway, he turned out to be a very good horse, winning lots of races from Pennybont in Wales, Hartington, Ashover and Manchester. Not only was he a very good horse, he was turning out to be a good stallion. He had eighty-four mares one season. His stud season always finished on 30th April, so he could get on with his racing. Father won the amateur cup at Greenford Park three years in succession. My sister still has that cup. Bill Gredley thought he was the first to have a horse who could do stud work and then run on the flat, but they were doing this in the 1920's. Another thing about trotters and pacers – a pacer is a horse that when it moves its near foreleg and near hindleg move together, while a trotter's fore and hind move diagonally. They do have to be very fit because they have to win two heats to get to the final. The harness is also very complicated. Pacers are fitted with hopples and to have them at the right tension is a highly skilled job. To describe them is just about as difficult as to fit them. A check-rein is also part of the equipment. It is a strap that goes from the saddle, along the neck, through the browband and down the face on to the bit. You tighten that to keep the head steady. Some people use a snooker cue from the girth to the bit to keep them running straight. Sheepskin nosebands used to be invaluable. TV commentators such as John Francome and Richard Pitman seem to think it is to make a horse keep its head down, but the real reason it is used is as a blind, which is the proper name for them. Long Eaton, Drolesden, Edenborough and quite a few other tracks were cinders. After a while holes came on the surface and filled with water. The horses would then jump these puddles and that would make them break into a canter, so that by the time you got them back to trot you had lost lengths. When you fitted a sheep-skin noseband, they would step into a puddle and not break the stride pattern. Another thing about trotting people is that they have different bets from most people. A chap walked into the stables — we lived in Ticknall then — and bet one hundred pounds Father hadn't got a horse that could trot three miles in nine minutes. At that time he had twelve horses in training and he picked a horse called Jack Fox. The bet was made on the Monday. He had to have a horse in Long Eaton Stadium on the Wednesday. Jack trotted the three miles in 7 minutes 22 seconds. He won the bet. Father had every horse fit to run for its life.

Father driving Jack Fox

THE THIRTIES

THE RIDING SCHOOL

Father was married in 1927 to Mary Flint, eldest daughter of William Stafford Flint, who farmed the Scaddows Farm, Ticknall, for fifty-five years. Ted Moult followed him. Mother was a very keen horsewoman – not that Grandad gave her any encouragement. My brother Harold was born in 1928 and I was born in 1930. In 1932 we moved from Ticknall to Findern where we had stables in the middle of the village and we lived in a bungalow on the Willington Road We cut down on the trotters and went for a riding school and more suitable horses. Mother loved teaching people to ride. Father did a lot more hunting. We had not been in Findern long when Col. Jenkins, housemaster of the Priory at Repton, who knew father from the First World War, asked him if he would move his riding school, which had really taken off, to Repton. Col. Jenkins wanted the boys in the O.T.C. to learn to ride if they were to become officers, and promised to send a minimum of forty boys per month – so we moved to live in Repton. I was still enjoying my hunting in the basket-saddle and both parents were enjoying their hunting, too – not a lot happened. In 1935 my sister Angela was born. That year I went to the Meynell Hunt Show at Tutbury – my first proper horse show – and won the Best Riding Pony (13.2 and under). I certainly gave it a good ride because it galloped absolutely flat out round the ring. Sir William Bass gave me the cup, and said Father "ought to make a jockey out of the boy" – but then came an announcement; it said there was an objection to the winner. Some people called Green had objected that the pony was over height and I'm afraid it was upheld. The pony – called Nanette – was 13.3 instead of 13.2.

Later, the Duchess of Devonshire rang Father wanting a pony for one of her daughters to hunt with the High Peak and Pony Club, so they bought Nanette and I have a nice photograph of her jumping a wall out hunting. In 1972 I got a call from the Duchess, asking me to find a horse for Lady Sophie. I sold her a lovely grey mare. I will tell you how I bought her and how I sold her later in the book, but for clients to come back after nearly forty years speaks for itself.

In 1933 my brother had an accident, bringing a load of hay back to the

5

yard. We think the horse saw the pitch-fork over the top of his blinkers and it frightened him. He ran away down the hill, tipped the cart over, and we all fell on top of Harold. He was taken to Bretby Orthopedic Hospital. He was in there for five years. He had T.B. of the hip which resulted in one of his legs being three inches shorter than the other and quite wizened in comparison. It certainly restricted his riding but not his determination to do things just as well as anyone with two good legs. We could not have wished for a better groom in the years to come, and I do feel he would have been a better jockey than me if he had had the chances I had.

In 1936 the hounds met in Repton and lost two hounds in the Shrubs. They tried different ways to catch them, but to no avail. So, about a week later, Sir Peter Farquhar brought all the hounds over to Repton again. Father lent horses to him and the Whip. They thought that the two missing hounds would join a hunt – which they did. Incidentally, Sir Peter Farquhar is the father of Ian Farquhar, Huntsman now in the Beaufort. Ian learnt his trade under Dermot Kelly when he was our amateur Whip.

PONY CLUB

In 1937 the Meynell Pony Club were chosen to do the ride at Olympia and Father and Mother, who were very keen Pony Clubbers, had quite a lot to do with it. I was a P.C. member from 1935 and in 1939 was attending rallies, including the Meynell Hunter Trials held at Brailsford.

Quote from the *Derbyshire Advertiser*: "Hunter Trials, fine day, good sport, gorgeous sunshine and perfect going and numerous young aspirants for jumping classes all combined to make a successful meeting for the Meynell Branch Hunter Trials held on Wednesday, 3rd May, 1939. The site chosen was by permission of Mr. C. S. Dalton, Capt. Strutt, and Major R. K. Knowles and there were six modest jumps for the junior events. There were many minor spills – the ponies apparently being aware that their jockeys had much to learn in the art of horsemanship. The water jump which was the last, and only about a foot wide, brought several young riders to grief. In the Open Class of the junior event, Lady Ann Cavendish was thrown two jumps from home and was somewhat shaken. Her riding companion, John Betteridge, quite a skilful young rider, galloped back to her rescue, and on pulling up suddenly, was thrown over his pony's head. He was down and out for a few minutes, but recovered in time to take part in the next event."

Looking through the prize-winners on that day, I notice the pair jumping – parent and brother or sister, was won by Mr. T. Birtwhistle and

Monica – later to become the trainer, Monica Dickinson.

I was looking forward to my first Pony Club camp to be held at Foston in September, but it was cancelled owing to the start of the Second World War. Never mind – we were still hunting! The hounds met at Repton. Father, Mother and I were out. We had a very good day – found in the Shrubs, ran through Carver's Rocks and on to Smiths Gorse – all over Scaddows Farm where Grandad and my uncles farmed. This is what I really do remember. There were about a dozen jockeys left. We were on a cinder path – down by the side of the Shrubs in those days – and Father turned to me and said, "In the future, if you go hunting and ride behind three better Joint Masters than you have been behind to-day, you will be a very lucky lad". They were Captain Kingscote, who was also Huntsman, Sir Ian Walker (later to add Okeover to his surname) and Stephen Player – all very good horsemen who rode many good horses.

THE FORTIES

In 1940 we had a lot of evacuees come to Repton. I made a lot of friends and a few of us keep in touch now. The Riding School was going strong. 7/6 per hour was the charge. Even I was helping by accompanying a few rides. We had a few more hunter liveries. Mr. Cecil Murray, who was later to become D.C. of the Meynell Pony Club – a position my wife was to take on fifty years later – and his friend Mr. Max Bemrose kept a couple of horses with us. (Incidentally we had dinner with his son not long ago at Victoria and George Shaw's in the High Peak Country near Bakewell – on 29th December, 1997, to be exact). At this time we were renting stables at The Bull's Head in Repton. Looking at it to-day, no-one would think that then it could stable up to twenty-five horses. There was also quite a large paddock. Despite that, we were getting more and more horses, so we took the stables and two fields at the Shakespeare pub about 200 yards away. Now we had room for about forty-five horses stabled.

Quite a lot of horse-shows were springing up. I think nearly every village was having one in aid of the Red Cross or some deserving war effort. Father and his friend Sam Hoult from Barrow-on-Trent were mustard in the gymkhana section. Mother was more for showing hacks. Her favourite was sold to Lord Scarsdale.

There were no lorries on the road then. The photos give an idea of how we used to get to the shows and gymkhanas in the early years of the war. They were taken on the way to Swadlincote and show Mother riding Rocket, with a friend and my sister, and Father driving the pony and cart that carried all the tack. In the last picture we have arrived and Rocket is jumping 4' 2". Notice the size of the crowd, and the wings leading in to the jump.

Hunting was still carrying on in a restricted way. I was now ten and what with taking rides for the riding school, I could ride all day. So I went hunting with Father more and more. As we always had to hack to the meet, it was a fairly early start. I remember meeting at Etwall by the church gate, opposite a pub, next to where the Darcy Clarkes lived. (A relation of theirs is Sue Wilson, who hunts with us now. I've sold her a horse too). I held the horses while Father went in for a drink and then brought me out a good big whisky. Another meet we went to was Radbourne Crossroads. That was a long way too from Repton, through Willington, Burnaston and Etwall (I think it would be about twelve miles), and then a hard day's hunting. On the way home that night, Father was riding a chestnut blood mare. Coming into Etwall, she cast a

Going to Swadlincote

Going to Swadlincote with the tack, etc.

Jumping at Swadlincote (note the wings and large crowd)

shoe. It hit the other leg and cut an artery. Blood spurted out. I remember it as though it was yesterday. Father went to the nearest house and got a bag of flour and stopped the bleeding by putting it on to the wound. It seemed a long way home that night. When we turned the corner in Etwall, we saw the long straight road to Burnaston. It looked never-ending and that night I vowed I would never ride down that road again. It is an easy vow to keep now. The road is under concrete at the Toyota factory! The mare called Bell Reign was turned out on Twyford meadows in the summer. She was found dead in the ditch. The Germans were bombing Derby and we thought bombs had caused her to have a heart attack.

BUYING IN

1941 was quite eventful. I had been riding 12.2 ponies: Snowball, a fiery grey pony, and Dainty, a chestnut mare that had been in the team to go to Olympia in 1937 with the Pony Club. Those two were sold to Joan Wilkins whose father had a paint factory in Derby. Later, they loaned Dainty back to us because she was a very good gymkhana pony. She was very hot but a true

Firefly at the Meynell Hunter Trials

professional when it came to flag races and bending races. She even knew when the music was going to stop in musical chairs. Another very good pony was called Nipper, a good jumping and hunting pony. When we had sold Snowball and Dainty we bought a lovely 13.2 pony called Algy, a chestnut gelding, with quite a lot of Arab in his breeding. He had been a very successful show pony before the war. He was bought from Summerfields, who were I think butchers in Castle Donnington, and we gave £50 for him. The next pony we bought was a novice jumping pony, that we called Firefly, very much a blood pony. We bought him, for £22, from a hunting mate of Father's – a chap called Frank Worrall from Aston-on-Trent, whose son was a successful show-jumping jockey. (At that time Billy Toye, Don Watson and Noel Pegg were similarly all good jockeys).

Father and I rode a horse a-piece over to Aston-on-Trent intending to lead this new pony back with us, but I could not resist having a ride on him, so, as we were coming out of Aston, we changed tack on to the new pony. We were going quite well through Chellaston, Swarkestone, over Ingleby, but then he shied suddenly. I fell off and sprained my ankle. It was the first of many times I was either to break it or sprain it! We still had to ride through Foremark and Milton to Repton – a good twelve miles. We certainly rode for many hours in those days, but there was very little traffic about.

For instance we bought two unbroken four-year-olds from Spencers of Kirk Langley: a liver chestnut mare we named Chocolate, about 15 hands, and a skewbald pony 14.2. We tied them together and drove them along the roads (We had gone on our bikes) all the way to Repton, through Mickleover, Findern and Willington, but on the way we bought another horse in Mickleover. He also was a liver chestnut, a gelding, bigger this time – 16.2.hh. We called him Rufus. We tied him to the other two because he also was unbroken. (Most farmers had brood mares at that time and could supply these unbroken horses). But there is a tale about Chocolate. She was a real B to break – and don't forget Father had won the best breaker for three years. It took hours to get a saddle on her. On a number of occasions when he did the girth up, she charged through the door, into the paddock and then bucked and bucked until the saddle came over her head. When it fell on to the ground, she savaged it like a dog shaking a rat, until it was in shreds! We never had one that could do that before or since.

In this year, 1941, Father and I went to the December Sales in Newmarket. I was on Christmas holiday at the time. War had been going for two years by then and the price of boodstock was on the floor, so we bought a lot of well-bred mares for as little as £20 each. However, we had taken a three-year-old colt called Lancewood, for I think J. A. C. Lilley, and he made 46 guineas. A lovely horse – he went on to become a good National Hunt stallion. As there was hardly a lorry about, everything went by train. The colt had gone by train and the mares came back by train, to the Repton and Willington Station. We still had to get them back to Repton which was a mile and a half on the road. A bit hairy at times, but as there was a good demand for them and they were sold, we made many more trips to Newmarket in the next few years – always on the train, and it was always cold. If the mares at the sale did not make twenty guineas, they were being taken around the corner and put down.

In the same year we had the Brealeys come to live in Repton, fifty yards from the stables. They were very interested in bloodstock. Stan, the father, was probably the best man in England at producing fighting cocks for the ring. Arthur, his son, was also very good and from a room in one of his outbuildings he probably would be selling fighting cocks in numbers. He would also go to people and give advice on how to get a cock ready. I used to go with him to places on quite a number of visits. I went with him to Gerald Balding's at Weyhill, I think that was the place. He had a contact who had been a jockey in Northumberland when Stan was up there. It was a lovely place – lawn and trees in the middle of a yard. I remember a chestnut horse there called Arctic Gold. Another place we went to was Chubb Leach in

Newmarket. In the loft was the cock-fighting pit. It was always covered over to make it look like a boxing ring for the lads. I rode out with them one morning. I was only a little lad.

Old Mr. Leach said, "What do you want to be?".

I said, "A jockey."

He then looked at my wrists and said, "You have too much bone to be a jockey, lad."

While we were in Newmarket, he bought two thoroughbreds at the sales to go flapping. That is horse-racing around an unlicensed track, such as a big field, but the field did not have to be very big. A chap called Stan Warren used to ride them. He was working for Fred Darling at that time and he looked after a very good filly called Sun Chariot. Stan and his brother Eric were riding a few winners on the flat at that time too. They were born and bred in Newhall, about seven miles from Repton.

Fashion in the 40s

Johnny Walker's first show at Burton

1942 was the year when we bought Johnny B and Johnny Walker.

Scotty was a grey pony, 13.2hh. We had seen him jump at a show near Leicester, ridden by a girl called Margaret Bradshaw, and thought he might suit us. He was advertised in *Horse and Hound* a few weeks later, produced by Ted Williams. We went by train to Syston where Ted Williams met us in a pony and trap. What jumps! Every fence was either tied up or nailed on, and underneath the parallel was a huge dyke. I had never ridden over such a frightening fence. He went all right, so we bought him – £145 he cost – and then Ted said, "I have a good horse here. Have a look at this one." He was black and white, a cobby sort, a lot of hair on his heels. We had seen him jump at Derby the week before, with Noyen Chamber's sister. (She owned a very good mare called Nan Tucker). Noyen was Ted's partner for years. Anyway, we bought the second pony for £100. That meant I had three jumping ponies now, a show pony and a games pony.

On the way home we decided we didn't like the name Scotty, so we called the grey Johnny B., thinking of a good trotter my uncle had called Wilben B, and the black and white pony we named Johnny Walker, after the black and white whisky.

The first show we went to with the three ponies was at Aston-on-Trent. I absolutely flew round on Johnny B. Ted came over to tell Father we ought to go a bit more steady. That was the beginning of September. We only did four more shows that year; indoor shows were unheard of in those days and the ponies were turned out in the winter. I hunted Johnny B a few times in the Spring.

We were still buying and selling horses. A person called Lady Everard advertised in the *Horse and Hound* every week, so we decided to go and see what she had to sell. As she lived just outside Leicester, we went by train and then caught a bus to the place. It was rather smart is all I can remember, but then it was fifty-six years ago. Father wanted a few horses for the riding school that could carry a small man or a woman. She told us she would have about a dozen for us to try. One advertised as a coloured horse, a good all-rounder, was the only one worth trying. I rode him. He seemed to go a bit, and was a bit of a kick model too, but he would do the job we wanted him for. We took him back into the yard where she took him from me. Instead of leading him to a stable, of which there were plenty, she took him to a headcollar on the wall and tied him up very short. Father haggled and ended up paying £45 for him.

The deal was that she would put him on the train for us and that would be the luck money. You never bought a horse unless you had luck money. It often came in the form of the bridle it was wearing, or a silver coin. The seller always gave the buyer something. Incidentally, we never had a horse vetted. We looked at eyes or heart room. We looked for lumps and bumps, and if we thought they were genuine hunting bumps, we didn't mind too much about them either.

On the train going home we wondered why he was always tied up to the wall. He didn't seem to have a stable of his own. When we collected this Appaloosa from the station, he seemed to be all right. We put him in the best box, with hay and water. We went to look at him after we thought he had time to settle. We soon knew why he had been tied tightly to the wall! I opened the door and just stepped inside the box. He turned round and flew at me with his mouth wide open – He was a man eater! We would have had no clients left! He was the worst example I have ever known. He went to Derby market for the best price we could get for it. First loss, best loss.

SHOW JUMPING

1943 was, I suppose, the year for consolidating the partnership with ponies. I hunted Johnny B. a few times. I remember one particular day around Rolleston. I followed Don Beard, who was home on leave and having a day's hunting, over some very big paddock rails. Don held the high-jump record for the United Kingdom. I don't know whether it was a world record, but it was gained at Olympia just before World War Two, at 7'6". He held it for about forty years until Nick Skelton jumped higher at Wembley or Olympia, sometime in the seventies, on a horse called Everest Elastic.

Don worked for a very big horse-dealer in those days, called Fred Foster. He specialised in selling hunters and show-jumpers, but he also farmed Marsh Farm, Etwall, and lived at Friary Farm, Etwall. My show-jumping style was suffering from too much hunting and gymkhana games. Mr. Foster had me there. He sat me on a chair, put a piece of string in my mouth, gave me a push in the back, and said, "You try and go forward if I am still holding on to your mouth." Styles in show-jumping were altering, don't forget. The instructions a few years before had been to sit back, and Father did just that, but we were changing. Now, we were encouraged to go forward with our hands and body – not to keep thinking there was a big ditch on the landing side of the fence

The jumps on the course (and they were called courses not tracks as they are known to-day) would consist of gorse or brush woven into hurdles. The high jump was sloping poles, covered in straw – less for the horse to hurt itself on. The vertical was another jump, sometimes a stile, with wooden scaffolding poles about twenty-five feet long to act as wings, followed by a double of sheep hurdles. A gate had three bars (for ponies hung about a foot off the ground). A water-jump had 14, 16, or 18 feet of water (or sawdust on a showground or a playing-field where holes could not be dug), with a bush in front. On every fence there was a half-inch piece of wood, known as a lath, which cost you half a fault if you had it down. A fence down with the front legs cost four faults, and with hind legs two. At the water the penalties were one, two, three or four faults, depending how many legs went in! These days, the penalties are not the same – four faults whichever leg does the damage and one fault however many legs go in the water. The jumps are much more sophisticated. Then, with the fences so very easy to knock down, horses sometimes needed to have a rap on their shins. Ponies didn't; they were careful enough. All the jumps were round the outside of the ring and the water jump down the middle. Before you jumped the water, you stopped and loosened the martingale so that the horse was able to use his neck. In those days there was no time-limit – you could take as long as you wanted. If you saw someone in the crowd, you could stop and have a word, and you always showed your horse the fences before the class started, when, if you had two rides, you would lead the other horse alongside, or if three rides, one on either side. (These horses were used to being led.) Because we all went by train the show would be probably within half a mile from the station. Should you be in the prizes, you took all the horses in the ring and had a gallop round.

I started at a new school in Derby called the Diocesan, basically for lads who couldn't win a scholarship or pass an entrance exam – mostly farmers' sons. I still keep in touch with quite a few of them. It was opposite Friargate House School for Girls, so I got to know quite a few of them as well.

1944 was the year we added two more show ponies to the string – Greta Garbo and Fortonian – both winners at Olympia before the war. Ivor Portlock, garage people from Birmingham, had already got some very good championship ponies – Slow Motion and Silver. We sold him Firefly for £300. Turning a £22 pony into £300 one was good dealing.

We were using the train for transport less and less. Although the war was still on, petrol seemed to be getting a bit easier, so we were using cattle-lorries to take the ponies to the shows. Parker's, from Swadlincote, were our transport people. Even their trucks were a bit primitive. No roof – just sides. I think the radius we could travel was about fifty miles. If the show was over fifty miles from Repton, we had to make arrangements to meet another lorry and go on in that. Such a show was at Leyland, near Preston. I think we went to Macclesfield in one lorry and changed to another to take us to the show at Leyland. We went there after Father had read in the *Horse and Hound* about how well the girl called Monica Birtwhistle was going. (As I have mentioned, we had first seen her in the ring at Brailsford in 1939). He thought he would like a bit more competition for us, and that was the basic reason why we went there – one hell of a long way. One of her ponies was called Silver Sand, a very good all-round pony. Later she was to become Monica Dickinson, a well-known trainer of racehorses with her husband, and mother of Michael, who went on to become private trainer to Robert Sangster. (My daughter, Sarah, became his secretary).

Another trip in 1944 was our first trip to Blackpool Three-Day Show, which took place in Stanley Park. We took six ponies, three show ponies and three jumping ponies. We had two railway horse-boxes because each box was made to carry three horses, all facing forwards. They were very well padded. In front of the horses was a groom's compartment. It was quite large, but filthy dirty and dusty, which was always the problem with trains. This trip was awful. All right going, when we loaded up at Repton and Willington, and on through Crewe and Preston to Blackpool. The express train there was very fast, but on the way back home they sent us round Pontefract and Leeds and not only did they send us the wrong way, but they stuck us down a siding at least a mile from the station and we couldn't get anything to eat or drink. Were we pleased to be home! Nevertheless we had a good show. We walked the ponies to the show-ground in Stanley Park. It was a mammoth task to get all the food and tack there. The stables were in a big hangar divided into small loose-boxes by small scaffolding poles, but we met lots of different show-jumping people. Alan Oliver had come from Buckinghamshire. I remember a lad the same age as me called Ian Hamilton from East Kilbride. We stayed friends for many years. What fun we had down to the pleasure beach after jumping – with rides on the "Grand National". To win a class was very difficult – very good ponies. The Makins had one called Springbok, ridden by Rosemary Auckland, who actually rang me a while ago to find her a horse to go hunting on. When Rosemary was too old for ponies, David Barker took over. Later he won the European Championships on Mister Softee and is at the time of writing Huntsman to the Meynell and South Staffs.

Another very good show we went to was the three-day Liverpool Show, held in Knowlsley Park, home of Lord Derby. This time we were able to go in Parker's lorry instead of by rail. Father and Mother could not drive, so we never had a lorry until I was old enough to drive. As I said, their lorry had no roof then, but when we were sleeping in it they put a tarpaulin over. You never drove under low trees or you would rip it and probably finish sleeping in a puddle. You cleaned the lorry out, put some clean straw on the floor, a horse blanket on top and slept on that. Hotel de Straw it was called. Facilities

Pom Pom winning the high jump at Matlock

were crude. An oil stove took ages to boil a kettle, or you got building bricks and made a fire inside them. As there was nothing else available, you had no choice. When the Primus stove came into fashion, it was a bit like living at the Ritz – providing you hadn't forgotten the pricker – a thing you had to have to clean the jet-hole out. Of course, you could have hot water in a few moments then. Later we had the Calor gas, freezers, showers, etc., but, in a way, we probably had more fun being Gentleman Gypsies than we ever had being ordinary people. As there were no stables at that sort of show, you had to start looking for a farm with stables within a few miles of the showground. If there was nothing available, you always carried a spare tarpaulin with you and tied one side to the top of the lorry, sloping it down to a fence or to stakes you drove into the ground, and you tied the ponies to the lorry. We parked in amongst the trees and got eaten by the gnats.

It was a private school I was going to, and as long as Father paid the fees they didn't seem to mind what time one took off. I was dealing in anything at school – air rifles, air pistols, cigarette lighters – anything that could be bought and sold. I made my first pony deal when I was fourteen. A lad called Harrison had a flat dray and did light haulage at the weekends. He had a nice chestnut pony about 12 hands but he wanted something a bit bigger. I told

Father that we could do a swap with our 13-hand coloured pony. I drew a bit of money as our pony was that much bigger. It was a reasonable deal Father wasn't too chuffed. He told me a lot would depend on what we made of the chestnut pony. The second deal I had a few weeks later came when I went to Lichfield and bought a pony for £12 – paid £1 to get it home – sold it that night to Matthews the butcher in Repton for his daughter for £19. A nice day's work.

The first Sheffield Butchers was held in Endcliffe Park in 1944, and there were thousands of people there. The show pieces were Johnny B and Johnny Walker. I went in for the Children's Jumping, and won. I won again in 1945 and 1946 and have the Challenge Cup to prove it. Michael Bennet won the Horse High Jump on Brer Rabbit.

We were carrying on buying ponies that had a jump in them. Bought a black pony from Percy Adcock called Nigger – jumped him a while and sold him to Billy Marsden of Sheffield. Another Sheffield family we got to know quite well were the Baldocks – Brian and Barry. We bought a pony called Diamond off them – sold that to Gerald Barnes from Alton in Hampshire (father of Tom and Mary). Mrs. Barnes helped out at Hickstead and the Horse of the Year Show for a number of years.

1945 was probably the year to remember. The European War ended in the

1945, Johnny B winning at the first White City after the war

19

May and the British Show Jumping National Championships took place at the White City Stadium on Saturday, 1st September, for the first time since before the War.

To get back to the dealing side, I left school in April, as soon as I was fifteen, with two new ponies to start the season with. As there were no indoor shows in those days, we started the season at Solihull, always on Easter Monday. One pony called Rocket – a nice 14.2hh bay pony who today would have been a very good working hunter pony – was all right, but no great story to tell about him. The other one – Pom-Pom, a roan pony, 13.2 – we jumped through that season but his best performance was winning the High Jump at Matlock at 5ft. 9 ins in 1947.

A chap named Cowley, whose prefix for his ponies was Holywell, held a sale in 1949 near Bridgewater which we went to – again by train. We noticed a roan pony which was the one I had jumped two years previously. In the sale he was down as a four-year-old. Father was quite cross. He told Cowley that the pony was six, but after looking in his mouth, we realised that when we had jumped Pom-Pom at Matlock over 5'9", he must have only been two years old.!

I remember one show in particular held in a park in Dudley. I always had to travel in the back of the lorry. The ponies travelled nose to tail as there were no partitions. We sat on a bale of straw and could look through the vent. This particular day, I could see, about a mile from the show, people walking four or five deep. It was estimated there were over 100,000 there that day. Probably one reason was that Winston Churchill was giving the prizes. I still have a silver cup he gave me – a very treasured memory.

There were hardly any mid-week shows, and no Sunday shows. We were all so religious.

The competition in Derbyshire was getting hotter. There was Doug Hibbert with two good ponies – Golden Boy and Lucky Strike. You had not won a class until he had been round! Shirley Edwards with Friary, and a bay pony, Star. (Shirley went on to represent Great Britain). A lad called Wileman, a butcher from Swadlincote, with Red Heather – a moody pony but on its day very difficult to beat.

Going against the clock had not been invented then. No shortened courses for us. We just jumped and jumped until they could go no higher – six or seven rounds before you got to a winner. I mentioned earlier that before the competition started you all went in to the ring and showed the ponies what they had to jump. A lot of ponies wore blinkers which kept their eyes focused on the fence. Also – if you wanted to give them a smack – they couldn't see it coming.

Another very interesting show was Long Eaton. That was quite a day to remember. A lot of Army chaps came from Derby and quite a few from Melton Mowbray. The racecourse had been turned into a gathering place for horses. I won the Best Pony – worth a tenner; the Juvenile Jumping – worth another tenner; and then we pulled out the games pony, Dainty, and won the Pig Sticking. (Four people galloped, carrying 10 ft. lances, and stabbed the bag). That was worth five pounds. The Bending Race was worth five pounds, like Musical Chairs and Flag Race. In total £40. Not a bad day's work!

Another show that year worth mentioning was held at Woolaton Park because it was the first Sunday show to be held and the local vicar said a few words. But to us jumping people, it was the first time we had seen coloured jumps – worse was to come – jumps with no wings. Practically every pony and horse spooked at these strange obstacles they were supposed to jump. I think they thought you had to go round them. (Malcolm Selby had two good ponies there – Shadow, who I bought off him about three years later, and Rocket).

WHITE CITY

About a fortnight later came a letter through the post inviting us to take Johnny B and Johnnie Walker to London to jump at the White City on 1st September 1945. This was going to be the biggest and best show-jumping event since before the war. There were just three juvenile classes, an Open and a High Jump. We went down in Parker's lorry with a crowd of people travelling in the back – still with a canvas top. We stayed the Friday night in Biggleswade. Every road seemed to lead to Biggleswade. We didn't sleep much. For one thing, it was too uncomfortable, and the other thing, everyone was too excited. A few had not been to London before. I will never forget the bomb damage. Hardly a house standing in some parts, but the White City didn't seem to be in too bad an order. It was the first time we had jumped in a stadium – a bit awe-inspiring. I knew quite a lot of the children riding, expecially from the North and Midlands. The first people we saw were the Selbys from Nottingham, with Shadow and Rocket, last seen at Woolaton park; Kathleen Dyson from Sheffield with Patch; and Peter Kaye from Yorkshire with The Collier. There was drama to start with. All the ponies were measured and Stirling Moss's pony, Ginger of White Cloud, measured out – 14.3 – a good inch over height – so that cut the field down to nineteen. I was third to go and jumped clear – so did Pat Moss on Brandy of White Cloud and Audrey Taylor on Spring. I was clear again while Pat and Audrey

Being presented to the King and Queen after Johnny B had won the first Royal
Windsor after the war

had a fence down each. They had to jump off for second and third place. According to my records they went another three rounds before Pat was second and Audrey third with Kathleen Dyson fourth. I had won £30 and a silver cup This show not only put show-jumping on the map again, but it put me on the map as well. There was a commentary on the wireless which all the folks at home were listening to. The Pathé Gazette News were there and that news-reel went all over the world. I had letters from as far away as Hong Kong saying how much they had enjoyed seeing show-jumping again. We stayed on to see the other classes. Major Nat Kindersley won the Open on Maguire, for which he won £100 and a silver cup. Ted Williams, riding for Bradshaws of Leicester was second, third and fourth, and Doug Dobson from Cheshire was fifth. Margaret Bradshaw, from whom we had bought Johnny B, won the High Jump at 6'4" on Silver Mint.

When we arrived home on Sunday, I think we had a better welcome than a Grand National winner gets nowadays. I think everyone who had been in the riding school over the past ten years was there to welcome us home, including Captain Kingscote, our Joint Master and Hunstman. Reporters from the *Burton Mail* and *Derby Evening Telegraph* photographers took photo after photo. All I wanted to do was have a hot bath. I had hardly had a wash since we left on Friday morning!

There were just a few more shows left that season. Most of the ploughing matches had jumping at their events – West Hallam, Brailsford – and we also did a few in Nottinghamshire, notably Flintham and Southwell.

AMONGST THE DEALERS

We were doing a lot more dealing now. A week could consist of Crewe or Mansfied on a Monday, Cambridge on Tuesday, Birmingham on Wednesday, Derby on Friday. Leicester always used to be held on a Saturday at the Repository in the middle of Leicester. It was a wonderful place, so clean. The horses were immaculate, and lovely clean show-men in white coats taking away the droppings. The tack was sold after the horses. Once we bought six, red white and blue, day-rugs and when we opened them up found they had the letter "B" on the corner of the rugs! I suppose the one big regret we always had was we were under-bidder on the day for a chestnut horse later to be named Red Admiral. Phil Oliver gave £155 guineas for him. We had bid £150. He turned out to be Alan Oliver's best horse. The battles Alan had at the White City with the D'Inzeo brothers were always memorable. The Leicester horse-sales were eventually moved to the Racecourse stables when the Repository was demolished to make room for an office block. To the likes of me it was never quite the same. It may have been cold and draughty, but it was still the best place to buy hunters and meet people. The April sales were like a Master of Foxhounds Association Meeting. Warner, Shepherd & Wade had got the sale nearly as safe as one could get a sale of horses. If you bought a horse sold sound in eyes, heart, wind and action and still looked at the small print, you would not be too far away from a genuine horse. John Craven was always there to vet them for you and with the warranted horses you would get a forty-eight-hour trial period. The sale had been moved from Saturday to Wednesday so it gave you a chance to hunt them on a Thursday, which I often did.

ROYAL WINDSOR AND OTHER SHOWS

1946 began with us in Mansfield market one day and there being sold three grey ponies, all 12.2. We called them Faith, Hope, and Charity because at that time teams of three looked like being a very popular class. I rode the one gelding, my sister rode Charity, and Faith was a spare ride for anyone at the show.

The Royal Windsor Show was held on the 1st June and was the highlight of the year We went down on the Friday, and stayed at a farm a couple of miles from the show. Father said, "I think Johnny B is a bit fresh. You had better ride him to the show. Follow the signs to the show." Of course, I got lost, found myself with not too much time left, riding down the main drive leading to Windsor Castle, but after a few enquiries, I found myself in Windsor Great Park.

I think I will quote what it said in the *Observer* on 2nd June, 1946: "Keen Jumping at Windsor Horse Show" by a special correspondent. "Windsor – June 1st. The King and Queen with the Princesses visited the Royal Windsor Horse Show today. When the weather improved after the appalling deluge yesterday, more than 4,000 people saw a programme that well merited their attention. In all classes the entries were of good quality. Winner, Mr. Betteridge, the well-known exhibitor of Repton, won the open children's jumping with Johnny B, winner at the White City last year and ridden by that fine performer Master Betteridge, who thus repeated his championship success. All the jumping at this show was for the first time under the direction and rules of the B.S.J.A. which had done much to improve the standard of jumping. Both Johnny B and Miss Pat Moss's Hairpin of White Cloud tied without fault, but Hairpin of White Cloud in the jump-off took off badly at the gate and knocked it down. Johnny B again completed a faultless course and the short one he put in at the wall showed real cleverness. How true it is that three-quarters of all success in the ring is gained outside. Schooling and timing are everything. There was a tendency to use the whip among many young competitors, who clearly did not know how to use it, or, most important, when it is to be used. More horses are stopped by bad riding than ever stop of their own accord."

What it does not say is that the first prize was a very nice silver cup which I still have. No money, though. Fancy going all that way to no prize money! Still, money couldn't buy everything. I did manage to shake hands and talk for quite a long time to the King and Queen and Princesses. I have wonderful photos to prove it. Afterwards, all people could say was, "What did they say to you?" I couldn't remember – my mind was a blank. (At the White City the year before I had won a cup, and £30).

The next big show was the Royal International held at the White City. From the details in *The Observer* there were two clear rounds – Audrey Taylor on Spring and me on Johnny B. Audrey went first and had a lath off the final fence for half a fault and I had the last fence down for two faults. In those days it was two for a fence down behind and four faults for a fence down in front. We were all naturally disappointed. For one thing it was the first fence he had had down that season, and the other thing was it was the first time, travelling South, we had been beaten. Audrey Taylor wrote a best-seller called "Half a Fault". It was about her career and got its title from the time she won at the Royal International by half a fault.

GROWING OUT OF THE PONIES

Later the following week, Father had a telephone call from Audrey's father (He was from the firm of Taylor Woodrow, civil engineering contractors): Would we sell Johnny B for his other daughter Gillian to ride? After a lot of soul-searching and discussion, we judged the sensible thing to do was to ask a big price, as I was 16 with only a couple of months to go, and my sister did not want him, as she was more into show-ponies than show-jumping. Anyway we asked £1000 for him and got £950 which was a price unheard of in those days. Unfortunately, Gillian didn't get on too well with him. Considering I was the only person to have ridden him over the last four years, it wasn't too much of a surprise. Anyway, Mr. Taylor invited me to go down and show them how to ride him. He met me off the train at St. Pancras and I stayed the night in his flat in Park Lane. The next day he took me to their home in Liphook in Hampshire. I did have a marvellous week. We went to the show in Aldershot, and took the ponies to the beach, but I expect the memorable moment was meeting Lionel Edwards, the painter. He was staying at the house to paint the ponies.

Then we sold Johnny Walker to Mr. Kay for Peter to ride. I think Father was more sorry to see him go than Johnny B. We made £600 of him. I can't remember whether Peter went on to horses, but I do know he went on to be a successful wrestler. He was often seen on the T.V. when wrestling was at its most popular.

Again I had a good Blackpool, winning the North of England Championship. Norman Swinnerton won the National Championship on Miss Margaret Lockhart's Jean, from Tamworth. Norman's wife went on to become Joint Master of the Atherstone.

This reminds me of something else that happened when I was sixteen. I had a day with the Atherstone, hacking from Repton through Bretby, Hartshorne, Ashby and three miles on from there. I was riding a big chestnut horse we had called Sportsman. We had bought him through my uncle who lived near Leicester and had show-jumped him a bit through the summer, but we soon knew he wasn't going to be good enough to go on with. Father said, "There is a chap looking for a horse to hunt with the Atherstone. See what he thinks". So I arrived at the meet after hacking a good ten miles, not too distressed. I thought I had better give a flash; so pulled out to jump a good hedge and did not bother to look. Guess what? On the landing side – barbed wire about four foot out and about four foot high. I hadn't noticed it, but the horse did when he was in mid-air. He saw the wire – made another movement to clear it. That led him to swing his head back and hit me in the mouth. It knocked out my front tooth – blood everywhere. It was a long way home that night!

After the ponies, 1947 was my first season on horses, but we were prepared for it as I had been riding horses for years. We were bringing on from novices two horses called Woodburn and The Doctor, but we soon found out we must buy something more experienced.

We heard Bay Lane was selling a few horses, including one called Huntsman, who had been ridden by Ted Williams (from whom we had bought the ponies). We eventually bought him for £1000 which was an awful lot of money in those days. In fact it is quite a lot of money today. Father always thought he was too old, but he was all right, even if he could have done better.

Harry Holmes, from Ilford, had bought a few horses from us, and he invited me down to travel the shows in Essex, including the County. We did not think the lorry – or my driving – was up to it, especially going through London, and so we loaded him on to the train at Repton and Willington Station, bound for St Pancras. Even the railway staff thought it was a bit unusual when I unloaded him on to the platform there. Harry met me with a lorry and brought me back after we had done the rounds in Essex. It had been a wonderful trip but I was very glad to see Repton church-spire come into view again. It was the last trip we made on the train.

We still had a few jumping ponies about to sell. Until we could sell one called Mount Royal, we had a girl called Jill Frost from Rugby to ride him. (Father Frost was into polo in quite a big way. Jill married George Rich, from Leicestershire, a well-known horse-dealer, especially for hunters. She eventually became Mrs. Fergie Sutherland and went to live in Ireland. Sutherland trained Imperial Call to win the Cheltenham Gold Cup in 1996). Jill had a good pony – a bay with a short tail named Lady Jane Grey. She certainly had the ride on Mount Royal – not for many times because some people called Tomlinson bought him. Tomlinson came for a ride on him and I remember him saying afterwards, "You just put him into gear and away he goes."

Another good pony we had was called Nip. We sold him to Gouldens, milk people from Walsall. Mr. Goulden was on the Walsall Show Committee for a number of years. Barry was the jockey's name. I believe he went on to be a vet in Canada.

Another very good pony we sold that year was a pony called Mr. Chips. One of the lads from out of the village rode him. I remember him jumping superbly well at Southport, and someone from Stockport saw him jump there and bought him. Their name will come to me one day.

After I had won the Juvenile Championship the year before, a lovely photo of Johnny B. and me appeared on the front of the Windsor schedule for '46, with the castle in the background. (That year the B.S.J.A. had gone back to using the white fences, plus very big wings).

That year, the Army started to disband their horse force and as we knew quite a lot of the chaps from Melton Mowbray and the racecourse in Derby (which is now the County Cricket Ground, and used to have the easiest mile in the country – all of it was downhill), it was no surprise when the phone started going, telling us that there were more champion jumpers going to Tattersalls in London to be sold, and would we give them a few quid for telling us about it. A fellow named Fred Wilder said he knew of a chestnut horse that was very special. (Fred had ridden a few horses for us. Later, a few years after the war, he went to ride for the Hon Mrs. Kidd as a jumping jockey and stud groom). We thought his tip was genuine so we caught the seven o'clock train from Derby to London, and then a taxi to Tattersalls. Basically we were looking for a type of horse to make a jumper of. What a place! The sale was held at the Elephant and Castle. The horses were stabled in stalls that were three storeys high. You and the horses walked up ramps to the next storey. When we walked into Tatts, as it was called, the very first person we saw was Dick Chambers, a butcher from by the cattle market in Derby! His son was about the same age as me. Not only was he there, but half Nottinghamshire, Leicestershire and Derbyshire were looking at the same horse. We bought him for 46 guineas. As the train did not leave London until gone midnight, Dick Chambers' party, Father and I decided to go to the Stoll Theatre to see Will Hay, a very well-known comedian at that time. It was great fun. The horse wasn't a lot of good so he went in the riding school until we sold him.

We were going to miss the Army buying horses from us. If one was really bad, they could make a pack horse of it. One we bought at Leicester was such a horse. Twopence he was called. He was a lovely-looking horse about 15.2, quite stocky. When he came back from Leicester, Father decided to go for a ride on him. I went with Father on a ride we called Robins Cross, a lane to a farm, very steep-sided. Without any warning, he shot up this bank about forty feet. Father jumped off, caught hold of a branch, let the horse go, and he rolled to the bottom. I caught him, Father remounted and thought we had better go home. At the bottom of Robins Cross is a watering place with a waterfall from a lake. Again without warning, he was scrambling up this waterfall into the lake. Father was shouting blue murder because he couldn't swim. The bank is very steep, so he only got threequarters of the way up. Father decided not to ride him any more and walked the mile and a half home. He was sold the next day to the Army – as a pack horse.

The other thing about 1947 was the months of snow – feet and feet of it. There was no hunting, no selling of horses. Money was going out and not much coming in – but that's horses.

SOUTHPORT AND THE SOCIAL SIDE

1948 was the year we bought the lorry. We had met a Mr. A.Kitson, a garage owner who had strings of jumping ponies and horses. As well as them, he had this green Austin truck, canvas top, but one problem – no third gear. He said, "You just go one, two, miss three, into four," and as no-one in our family had had anything to do with transport of any sort, we decided we could cope with it. But we couldn't! We soon had to have a new engine and gear box. I only had a provisional licence and not an experienced driver in sight! I remember driving on to the showground at Southport and a chap directing me where to back. I had only learnt to go forwards, so I said to Seamus Hayes, one of the great characters of the show-jumping fraternity, "Please could you back this lorry for me?" You had to be quite precise because, as I explained before, you had to get the tarpaulin just right from the top of the lorry to the fence, with the horses stabled underneath your home-made roof. (It wasn't until the next year that Woodhouses from Nottingham brought out their wooden portable loose-boxes). Actually that Southport show was about the best for us that season. Huntsman won the Southport Championship – a gold cup and £50 with the only clear round. He was fourteenth to go and, according to the programme I have, there were 115 entries.

What great entertainment we had at Southport Flower Show! As a crowd, we always went to the theatre. We really did see some great acts the years when we went: Tommy Cooper, Sandy Powell and some wonderful singers. Then it was fish and chips and the Scarrisbrick Hotel for drinks – Only I didn't drink – and then on to the Floral Hall, dancing until the early hours. This went on every night. One night in particular, about thirty to forty of us were walking back

Huntsman winning the Southport Championship

Seamus Hayes and I ready to go out at the
Bath and West

through the main ring where the course was set for the juveniles next day. We decided to have our own proper competition with a pound each in the kitty – winner take all. Ted Edgar was the stake holder. I was going round quite well, but unbeknown to me, Edgar had pulled the bush in front of the water. I could see when I was in the air I was never going to make it. Splash, right in the middle! And don't forget, we all had our best suits on. That is just one of the pranks we would get up to. The parties we had were unbelievable.

Derek Kent was a great party-goer. "Party tonight," he would say.

"Where?" we would say, innocently.

"In your box. I'll organise it."

One box we never had a party in was Edgar's. His lorry was always spick and span, never a thing out of place. He was never going to have his little palace made untidy by loads of jumping lads and lassies.

Southport was a great social occasion. A lot of people would come down from Scotland – the Jamiesons, Jimmy Snodgrass, Jack Barrie, the Turnbull girls and W. Mclung (Doug Iggledon used to ride for him. Eventually he went to ride for someone in Ireland). Quite a lot from the South came until the big British show at Timpkin started.

BLUE SMOKE

There's a true little story, one with a moral, that began in Southport in 1947. Some people from Shropshire named Parton – Shall I say? – asked us if we would have a young horse to school. They had bought it in Ireland, along with some bullocks. They farmed in a big way. We took this horse – a four-year-old grey, about 16 hands, and very, very green. He didn't know how to canter. We started him jumping on the lungeing rein and he did have a most enormous jump. He was a lovely-natured horse, just right for me coming off ponies. Anyway, we rang them up to say we would like to buy him and offered them £300, which was quite a good price for a horse which had never been to a show, or even learnt to canter. Ordinary horses in the market were making about £150. They came over and assured us money would't buy him; they just wanted occasionally to go to a show to see him jump. We were to pay all expenses and have all the prize money, which wouldn't be much considering he had never been to a show. But they seemed nice people, so we took their word that everything would be all right.

It was the first time I had ridden for anyone other than Father, although I had had a number of offers. The best, I suppose, was from Mr. Bunn from Selsey-on-Sea, to ride a string of his jumpers. Some very good horses there were too. His son Douglas was away at Cambridge University. I had to turn it down as Father and Mother didn't want me to leave home. (I wonder what sort of life I would have had if I had taken that job?).

Father spent a lot of time riding and schooling the grey horse which we went on to call Blue Smoke. He was a "clear-round machine". The B.S.J.A. had brought out a new class called Special Jumping Class for Young Riders born in 1930 or 1931. Father won quite a lot of money backing Blue Smoke to win this. There were bookmakers about in those days, expecially at Southport. He went especially well there, but the show where he really made his name was Christchurch in Hampshire. We took Huntsman and Blue Smoke. It took us two days to get there but it was a wonderful time. We set off early in the morning, stopped for a bite to eat just outside Oxford, on through Newbury – never been to the New Forest before – and we stayed the night at Brockenhurst or Lyndhurst. I just can't remember which, but I do remember it was a big Riding School. The day was quite windy. I know Aherlow won the Open – worth £200 to the winner – and I won the Novice on Blue Smoke. After that, there were people clammering to buy him, especially when they got to know we did not own him. Mr. Palethorpe was able to buy him for Jill. We never stood a chance to buy him for me. The Partons just came with a head-collar and little trailer and took him. They just would not listen to us pleading with them to give us chance to buy him. I don't really know what powers I have, but as he went down the yard, I said, "That horse will never win another class".

A year after Mr. Palethorpe had bought him for Jill he came to me asking if I would take the curse off him. I just said that I could not do that. He never

Blue Smoke winning the Novice at Christchurch

did win another class, and worse still, I never knew what happened to him. So the moral to this story is – Have something in writing. Word of mouth is just not good enough. We did learn a very hard lesson in life with that one, but it never happened again. We insisted on part-ownership, or we did not ride, except on our terms. Anyway, that's life.

We used to keep a lot of horses on the Trent Meadows. The land was farmed at a basic level by the farmers in the hills beyond Repton. It was prone to flooding, so they used to herd their cattle back home about September. With the land not being too far away, we could put our horses in those fields and keep our eye on the Trent. After the snow, we got caught out. One day the river was all right – in full flood the next and we had to have a big rescue operation. The lads from Repton School were the bravest I have ever seen, but we could not find one chesnut horse called Polo. We had it at livery for Flavia Phillips, who was in the W.A.A.F. at the time, stationed at Burnaston Airfield – aunt of Captain Mark Phillips, the eventer. We found him a few days later on a little island down river.

Some of the boys at Repton became great friends: Colin Hamilton, who lived in Jersey, was very keen on his horses. He came to the yard to go riding, very proudly showing off a pair of jodhpurs his mother had made for him. We went for a ride over the fields to Grandad's at Scaddows Farm, Ticknall. It would be about six miles. With about a mile to go, a little hole came in the knee. We stopped at Grandad's for tea and after about an hour on the way home, a hole came in the other knee. A bit further on towards home, they fell to pieces! What a laugh we had. After all the trouble his mother went to, I suppose they lasted about an hour and a half! After he left Repton, I believe he went farming in Devon. Another lad came from Devon, Bill Sprott. He went into farming and had a racehorse or two. I must mention David Cashmore too. I still see quite a lot of him. He is the D.C. of the South Staffs Pony Club. Such grand chaps! I thought that if ever I got married and had a son, he would go to Repton.

Another exceptionally good jockey who was in the W.A.A.F. at the same time as Flavia Phillips, stationed at Burnaston, was Joan Blacker, sister to Monkey Blacker, steeplechase jockey and show-jumping jockey, rider of the show-jumper Workboy, an ex- racehorse.

1949 saw us still buying a lot of horses. One week, Father was ill in bed and, as he had a number of orders for horses, he said to me to go to Leicester and find some horses to fill these orders. So, with an open cheque, off I went. I had bought a few when I saw this quite well-bred gelding, by Mr. Toots, named Dingle Bay – full brother to a very good chaser called Cool Customer. I thought at the time he could do a few jobs. Anyway, after I bought him I started having second thoughts: I must have bought enough for one day. When I got home, I went to see Father in bed.

"What have you bought? he asked.

"This and that" I said – left it a minute – took a deep breath – "And a racehorse."

"A racehorse? We want no racehorses," he said and shot up in bed. That was a quick cure! The air was blue.

THE FIFTIES

THE START OF OUR RACING

Father soon came round, however, and actually got quite interested. I hunted the horse a few times and found he was a very good hunter and superb jumper. Father took out a permit to train, and so we made a start with our first racehorse. Knowing he was of show-jumping stock, we thought we had better school him. We had no hurdles so we asked Mr. Morley if we could gallop on his Trent Meadows – a big flat field. Racing people think that they have just invented interval training, but we did it fifty years ago. Anyway, we were fortunate enough to have this field that was more than half a mile round and put two 45-gallon oil-drums with a pole across the tops, and galloped him flat out at this. Looking back, it's a wonder how I did not break my neck – with no ground-line or anything like that for the horse to be aware of. The first race we took him to was a novice hurdle at Leicester. A friend of mine having a ride there was Derek Leslie, who had turned professional. (He later rode the favourite for the National). He told me that if Dingle Bay had been hunting he would jump well. Derek must have been right for he ran a terrific race considering neither of us had done it before. He finished fourth, so we decided that as he was such a good jumper, we would put him over fences.

We took him back to Leicester on the 13th February, 1950. There were twelve runners, including Pearly Prince who was later to have a good run in the National. Dingle Bay ran well again and finished fourth. We were all very pleased. Father decided we would run him once more over two miles. He finished fifth. Then Father decided he needed three miles, so we entered him in a three-mile Handicap Chase at Southwell. He was weighted 9 stone 7 lbs., which I could do then quite easily. He didn't quite make the trip. As I had always wanted to ride over the National fences, I entered him for the Beecher Chase at Liverpool, which was a race for novices. As we did not have the best schooling fences, or the best gallops, we entered him for a two-mile novice chase at Nottingham a week before Aintree. It cut up to three runners, which was ideal as the favourite was a horse of Rimmell's called Ballindine – a big chestnut horse, but a poor jumper. I was told to keep well clear of that one, but unfortunately it found me at the water jump down the back straight and cannoned into me just on take-off and knocked us for six. We hit the floor an almighty bump. The horse got up before I did and galloped off towards the stables, scraping his side on a door going into a stable. I'm afraid that was the end of his racing days and my riding over the National fences. Not only was I very disappointed, so were the rest of the family, but the horse came all right. We turned him into a show-jumper. Looking at some of the old Southport programmes, I see he was entered for Open jumping there. I remember him jumping particularly well at Canwell one year in an A.I.T. What a good eventer he would have made.

I suppose our show-jumping season was made by Huntsman winning the Open Jumping at Wokingham. There were over a hundred competitors, all very good.

DOING THE SHOWS

As we all had our own horseboxes now, we could travel more easily, and what we were doing, along with a lot of Northern people, was to tour the West Country. One of the shows was at Swang near Bridgewater on a Saturday. A wonderful show that, and £50 prize-money to the winner. The Roe family who farmed at Swang ran it for the West Somerset Foxhounds in conjunction with the Quantock Farmers' Pack, of which Mr. Roe was M.F.H. His father would ride all day long seeing everything on his bay cob. What a journey to get there – Burton, Warwick, Stratford, Cheltenham, Gloucester, Bristol, Bridgewater. But then we seemed to have all the time in the world, driving through lovely countryside. It was a delightful drive through Bristol, round by the Docks, over a small bridge, up and around a steep hill. At the top you stopped and looked right over Bristol – a marvellous sight. We would probably take the horses out for a graze (It was like a common ground) and then load up again. The cafes were not like they are to-day, but proper transport cafes, with fat bacon, eggs, sausage, fried bread, all out of a greasy frying pans, washed down by a large mug of tea. You either ate and drank there, or not at all. We would stop again going into Bridgewater for a Somerset cider out of the barrel. It was special for me as I was quite a teetotaller. What had made me so was a pretty hard day's jumping at Sutton Coldfield when it was boiling hot. I was terribly thirsty but all I could get was a glass of beer, and it was warm. It tasted horrible and I spat it out and after that I was pretty well teetotal. I did not dislike pubs, just the smoke inside, although I was a heavy smoker.

From Swang we went on to the show at Shepton Mallet where a chap called Creed ran the show. We bought a grey pony off him. He said the standing martingale should be so many inches long – in other words it carried its head very high. It was no good. From there on to stay at the Garth Hunt Kennels for their show, and then on to Wokingham and its real old agricultural show – a wonderful event with thousands of people. The win there was very special – beating the likes of Wilf White on Nizefella, Tom Taylor with Jorrocks and Alan Oliver's string.

The big talking-point at Wokingham was that Wilf White had just been bid £6000 for Nizefella. He wouldn't take it though. His argument was that Nicefella was still a young horse and he would win £1000 a year. In six years he could have a good time winning that sort of money and would still have his horse. Which is exactly what happened. Still, he was lucky in the respect that he had a sound horse for all those years.

From there we all went in convoy to the Hampshire Hunt Hunter Trials where there were three good show-jumping events. They were held on Mr. and Mrs. Gerald Barnes' farm at Alton where we always stayed for a few days, as Wokingham was on the Saturday and this show was in mid-week. We had supper with them as we knew them quite well having sold them a pony called Diamond, which had come from the Baldocks of Sheffield. It was the most lovely farm with nice old boxes. Gerald Barnes would find a horse for those who wanted to go cubbing – which I did. Those were really idyllic days. We played pontoon most days and nights. What wonderful friends the Barnes have been to the show-jumping people. They were so hospitable to me. When they retired, they helped at Hickstead on the collecting ring, at Harringay in the little room by where the horses went in, and at Wembley where they were not only in charge of the collecting ring, but in charge of giving out the badges – not a nice job. They also bred some very good jockeys. Their Tom and Mary were exceptionally good. Both represented their country on a horse called Sudden.

The end of our travelling was the Hampshire Hunter Trials, as it was called – our last show of the season after which we turned the jumpers out, although quite a few people went to Harringay for the first big indoor show of the season. It was called the Horse of the Year Show, but we thought we had done enough and we turned our horses out.

One day we found Huntsman dead in the field. It was a terrible loss. For one thing he was by then too old to be insured. I knew in my mind we could not afford another horse like him. He had been a good horse to us, but I would say to anyone buying a horse for a junior coming off ponies: Don't buy one so old. It just does not work. I could name other parents who have done it. It did not work out for them and take my word for it, it does not work for anyone.

JUMPING AND RACING

Anyway, things could only get better and I was getting calls to ride National Hunt horses. Through going to those meetings I made friends with one of the older jockeys named Nicky Pinch, who rode for a Mr. Doney of Amberley, father of John Doney, the course builder, whose main job was producing show-jumpers. He used to stay with us when they had runners at Southwell, Nottingham, or other local courses. In return I went to stay with Mr. Doney at his place just outside Stroud and I had some wonderful holidays there. When you opened the gates off the common probably fifty or sixty horses would come into the yard. A girl called Rachel Carpenter was there at the time. She later rode some jumpers for him, and later still went as a companion to the Hon. Mrs. Kidd. We bought a nice grey horse from him called Araby which jumped a bit, but not a champion. He had been in a circus and could do the Spanish Walk, kneel and lie down. We then bought a pony called Swank which was sold on to the Baldocks of Sheffield.

We first met the Morleys from Mickleover when Nicky Pinch brought a pony down to Fred Foster's yard in Etwall for Ann Morley to try. The pony, called Dandy, was one of Doney's, a very good one that jumped in Open classes all his life. He was a black pony, about 14.1hh. I saw him jump 6'4" in the high jump at White City. When Nicky was showing him off, he jumped a triple bar from the wrong side. He made a good pony for Ann, though perhaps a bit on the careless side. She did win a very good class with him on Easter Monday at Solihull. Mrs. Morley was over the moon.

I said to her, "Make the most of it. It may be a while before you win another." And it did prove to be quite a while! I would never say that to anyone again.

They bought another one called Lady Jane Grey. I used to take Ann about a bit in the lorry when her father's lorry-driver was away on cattle business. Mr. Morley said to me one day, "I want you to take Ann to Windsor Horse Show. I'm busy and I need our lorry." I said our lorry wasn't really good enough to take all that way, but he just laughed it off and said he'd put the petrol in for me. The lorry was not really ill, but it was not very well either. For one thing it still had no third gear; I just used to go one, two, four. Anyway we all three got in the lorry. Mrs. Morley sat in the passenger seat and I explained to her that the bit of string was to stop the door from opening. She was to hang on to that. The other bit of string was to stop the battery from dropping on to the road. We got as far as Biggleswade before she said, "My arms are dropping off."

"But Mrs. Morley," I answered, "never mind, my dear. We won't be long before we get there now!"

We were actually making for the Star and Garter in Windsor where we were to stable. We had quite a nice time.

1951 was a momentous year. I was twenty-one. We had a wonderful party for it. Jumping people came from all over Englad and I still have a few twenty-first presents to look at now. They have stood the test of time. I have a letter from Wilf White appologising for not being able to come.

RIDING FOR MR. KITSON

Show-jumping prizes were hard to come by without Huntsman, Blue Smoke, etc. We had one or two novices. Dingley Bay was going reasonably well; he was an ex-racehorse now. Out of the blue, Arthur Kitson, the garage-owner who had sold us that first lorry, rang to ask if I would ride two of his horses for him – Mercury and Angus. He would pay livery and all expenses. At least we would have them on a different footing from how we had Blue Smoke, more business-like. I had only the fourth string because at that time he had Ernie Jewitt, Alex, a Welshman, Jack Littlewood and Jack Turner. He also had a string of ponies. His main business was lorries, and he had a fleet of buses. Before them, he used to tell me, he had horse-drawn buses and used to take coach-loads of people to Doncaster Races. In Sheffield, his garage and body-building works were opposite the Sheffield Wednesday Football Club Ground. I won a few classes on Mercury and qualified for Harringay. My big win of the year was there – the Horse and Hound Gold Cup on the Saturday night. It was a very good win and what a party we had afterwards. I wonder if they still have them today. We always took the wind-up gramophone with us and any excuse for a dance. When rock 'n roll came into fashion, I remember Ted Edgar saying to Chris Jackson, "Come on. You're not at the Hunt Ball now." (Chris was later killed in a car crash). They were marvellous times. We were amateurs in every way. No-one took show-jumping seriously in those days.

Mr. Kitson thought that as we had won the Horse and Hound Cup, we ought to go to the Horse and Hound Ball at the Grosvenor House. Mr. and Mrs. Morley came with us and we all stayed overnight at the Grosvenor. I remember having a bath and the water out of the taps seemed to come at about five gallons a second, but to stand on the balcony, looking down on the dance-floor and seeing those sights and colours was something to remember for the rest of my life.

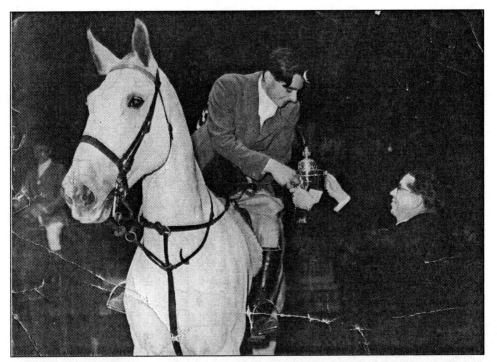

Mr Case, the Editor, handing me the Horse and Hound Cup

A CHANGE OF DIRECTION

Another important thing happened that year. As I said earlier, I always wanted to be a horse-dealer, but Mother would warn: "Horse-dealing is fowl one day and feathers the next," and as my brother, after his accident, couldn't really ride, he wanted a farm as well, so we bought a small farm just outside Burton-upon-Trent. It was right next-door to Cadley Hill Colliery. (The miners were a tremendous bunch of chaps. You were never short of help when they were about). There were no electrics, and probably not the most salubrious surroundings, but it had twenty-five acres of good ground, a four-bedroomed house, four loose boxes, and a cow-shed for about twenty-five cows. My brother had been to Broomfield Agricultural College for a year – he was one of the first students to go. I had been working for Grandad at Scaddows Farm instead of doing National Service, so between us we had a fair idea of how to farm.

Then, quite out of the blue, Michael Sadler from Burton, who was our vet at that time, came to the farm one day after the show-jumping season, saying that Charlie Hall from Tadcaster was looking for an amateur National Hunt jockey, and he could get me the job if I wanted it. Mr. Sadler was a well-known vet in racing circles, expecially for firing horses. It was rumoured he used to go over to Vincent O'Brien's to oversee his horses. Anyway, my brother said he could manage the farm, and, with the best wishes of the family, I caught the train to Tadcaster.

I didn't get many rides – there were too many professionals on his books – but I did learn a lot about horses. He had a wonderful head lad, Ben – I wouldn't know him by any other name. He knew horses, and all about feeling legs. He was very willing to share his knowledge with me. We would often stay up burning the midnight oil. Colin Dukes was the first jockey when I was there. Another lad was David Gill whose daughter we had met through show-jumping.

Mr. Hall trained for the Caleys from the Holderness country. They asked me if I would ride their point-to-pointer for them. One very good horse I rode for them was First Bid. I rode him in all his early races. The people who farmed next to the Halls were called Chapman. They had a number of point-to-pointers and I would ride a gallop for them, hoping to get a ride, but Guy Cunard was their jockey and I suppose you were never going to jock him off. What a character he was! He was a very very dedicated jockey who would stop at nothing to win a race.

First Bid having his first race at the Derwent

THE SHOW-JUMPING ROUND

When Mr Kitson sold Mercury to go to Canada as a working hunter, he went over to see him settled in and had to rely on the people who bought him to fund him while he was over there as in those days you could only take £5 abroad with you. After he had sold Mercury, he asked me if I would go and live with him in Sheffield and ride as first jockey to him. After a lot of soul-searching and talking over the move with the rest of the family – it would be a big wrench for Father, who was still my greatest fan – I went to Sheffield. I had a very good wage, 10% of my winnings, and I could keep a horse of my own. At that time, I had a good mare called Duchess which I had bought from Peter Gregory, a butcher in Derby. It was interesting work; I went up about the middle of March to get the horses fit, but they were old jumpers who knew their job. We always aimed to be ready for Easter Monday, which was usually Dore Show. After that, one geared oneself for the agricultural shows with the Newark Show being the first of the big ones. Before that we had smaller shows, like Darrington and then Fairburn, starting about 5 o'clock at night, and had two or three per week, where we jumped for sweepstake money. Everyone who jumped put a certain amount of money up front as entry fees. After Newark, there was Oxford, on the aerodrome, and then, every week-night up until the middle of September, there would be a two or three day show, normally Tuesday, Wednesday and Thursday. We travelled home on Friday, ready to jump on Saturday somewhere. Never on a Sunday, that was a day off.

We had a very nice lorry – not like to-day's lorries, but we did not complain. They were just for getting us from A to B. Humans were quite secondary to horses. Mr. Kitson generally drove himself to the three-day shows and stayed at hotels, but when we went to one-day shows, he would travel with me, and when we were in the money, he would take out his little note-book and reckon up who owed who.

We riders often divided the prize money. At smaller shows it would be £30, £15, £10 and £5, For instance, if I jumped a clear round and Seamus Hayes jumped a clear round (He rode for Tommy Makin) and we tied with a clear round apiece, we would divide first and second, making £45, and we would then have £22.50 each. It just made sure you had a bit each. Mr. Kitson would divide the prize money with anyone. All he wanted was his horses to go well. We had a straightening up at Harringay and he knew down to the last penny who he owed money to, and who owed him money, but he enjoyed it.

That went on until Harvey Smith came along and said, "What money I win, I'm keeping." So that was the end of dividing up the money. A shame really, as it did give the not-so-good ones a bit of a chance to go home with a quid or two.

I think Mr Kitson's favourite horse was Roger. If he was travelling back with me and we had seen a horse had been sold for quite a lot of money, he would say, "How much must Roger be worth then?"

There are lots of tales I could tell, but two events stand out as far as I am concerned. One was that I won the main class at Peterborough – £50 to the winner and the John Cobb Gold Cup. I wonder if they still have that class. I had been there for three days – I was twenty-two then – and Mr. Kitson said to me, "My word, lad, you have done well to-day. Here's 10/- (or 50p. to-day). Get yourself some fish and chips on the way home." But I had the last laugh.

I won, again on Roger, the Coronation Cup at Chester. £200 to the winner. I was putting the horses away ready to travel back to Sheffield – we didn't have grooms then, you got someone to help with the horses – when Mr. Kitson came over to the lorry and said, "My word, you have done well to-day. I would like to give you a little present. Anything you would like?"

I said, "My scarlet coat is getting a bit tatty."

"Go and get yourself another one, and send the bill to me," he offered.

So I went and got one. In fact I got measured for one at Bernard Weatherills. To say he went spare was an understatement! It came to as much as I had won, but it was very smart and it did fit well. All the time I rode for him, we never had a cross word. I rode some very good horses – Pippin, Lorna Doone – but one thing about him, he would always fork out for a good horse. He only liked the best. I made some wonderful friends.

I had been living with the Kitsons, but I thought I ought to move out. All we talked about was horses and show-jumping; I wanted a bit of a change, so I found myself living in digs. My landlady was a Mrs. Powell who looked after me superbly – nearly as well as my mother. Talking about friends, I remember the Barbers, Ann and Robin – and later Jean, whom he met when we were skating on a pond. Robin saw this girl and that was that. We gave him a wonderful stag-night, travelling the pubs around Baslow and the outskirts of Sheffield in his horsebox. After about forty of the party had been unloaded down the ramp, Robin shut it up (I was the driver) but somebody had left the passenger door half open, and Robin walked straight into it. He cut his face badly, and looked a mess the next day at his wedding!

They were halcyon days! Someone asked me if we went out often. I said fourteen nights a week. I was the only one with a motorised vehicle – it was a Ford van, but with luxurious seats and cushions in the back. One night we were going up one of the steep hills in Sheffield, four or five in the back, when

I changed gear rather quickly – the back doors flew open, and out they all went, including their cushions, finishing up in the road.

In the early fifties, the big agricultural shows did not have a permanent ground. The Royal was down at Newton Abbott one year – one hell of a way to travel from Sheffield – but what I do remember from that show was the evening meal that Bill Hanson took us to that night at the hotel he must have been staying in at Torquay. It was a fabulous place. Pamela Macgregor Morris was one of the party. She was the main show-jumping correspondent for *Horse and Hound*.. The dining-room had a sea view and to see the lights dancing on the water and having this marvellous meal was really something. I was terribly lucky. When Bill died of cancer the following year, it was a great, great loss, not only to me, but to the whole of the show-jumping world, and what a loss to his wife Patricia, a lovely Irish girl. They weren't very old. Afterwards, I saw Patricia a few times when I went to Newmarket Bloodstock Sales. She had gone back to live in Ireland, was into breeding thoroughbred stock and sold her yearlings at Newmarket. She never married again.

The year before, I had won a huge great cup at the Coventry Show, so I drove through the night from Newton Abbott to Coventry to have a crack at winning it again. Luckily enough, I jumped the only clear round.

I said to Sir John Black, who was chairman of Standard Motors at that time, "I've travelled through the night from Newton Abbott to win this cup again. Is there any chance of my keeping it for good?"

He had a quick word with one or two, and said it was all right. I could! It is an absolute monster. Sometimes it pays to have a bit of cheek.

I travelled up to Glasgow to the White City Stadium, a very impressive place. As we usually got there the day before the show started, we generally went out that night. About a dozen of us were going out to paint the town red. As we were going through the gates, a security guard came over and said, "I shouldn't go into town if I were you. You might not get back. There's gang warfare going on at the moment." So as discretion is the better part of valour, we turned round and made our own party.

I had taken the mare Duchess, which was mine, up to Scotland. She went very well up there, and the Turnbulls came over and said they would like to buy her from me. As they had got my old jumping pony, Johnny Walker, the black and white pony, from Mr.Kay, they asked if I would like him in part-exchange. Would I? They had the mare and I took the pony. Of course, it was a case of one's heart ruling one's head because I was never going to sell him again. We loaded him into the lorry and I took him straight down to home. I had rung ahead and said I was coming, and asked if they would get a stable ready.

When I pulled into the yard, I said to Father, "I've got a present for you." I dropped the ramp and walked the pony down into the yard. To see his face when he knew I had given him Johnny Walker was something I can't describe. He kept him on the farm and rode him but we never jumped him again, although I feel he would have been able to – he was then a fit seventeen-year-old.

That year I was jumping a big chestnut horse, called Angus, and Urky Newton came over to me and asked if I would sell him. She wanted a horse for her husband Lance to hunt. Anyway, she bought him and that started a friendship which lasted over forty years. She was very good to me. She would ring me in Sheffield and ask if I would like to come and hunt a horse for her tomorrow, Saturday. What wonderful horses I rode: a bay horse named Cedar Hill that went on to win some very good races; and another horse named Ragdale, a good sort of chestnut horse. I would go down on the Friday night, hunt all day with the Belvoir and return to Sheffield on Saturday. What a wonderful person she was. We were hunting one day and she said, "I was dreaming about you last night. We were galloping down to this canal and we jumped it together, just as though we were pair jumping." Once, Urky rang to see if I had an all-rounder for Pat, her step-daughter, to hunt and show-jump.

Angus jumping in Gloucestershire (note the "wings" of the fence)

I said I had a chestnut mare called Margo which I had bought in Scotland (I think it was from Jim Barrie) but I couldn't say how it would hunt, or – as they say in Leicestershire – jump a ditch towards. As it was the Belvoir Hunter Trials, Urky asked me to stay with them and see how she went in them. I didn't even know if she had ever hunter-trialled before, but that day she won the Heart of England Hunter Trials worth £50 to the winner and Urky bought her for Pat to go on, along with a very good chestnut that Pat already had, called Waving Corn. Pat travelled all the big shows and was a very popular, pretty girl. She went on to be one of the top point-to-point jockeys, not only riding for her father, but also riding a lot of winners for Frank Gilman. (She certainly had some very good parties at Skillington). She went on to marry Alan Hinch, a farmer, who later became joint Master of the Fernie.

I think I was a factor in introducing John Walmsley to Ann Morley, later to become Mrs. Walmsley. How that came about was Mr. Morley thought that Nugget needed a stronger rider than Ann was, so he asked me if I would ride him a few times. I rode him when the Derby County Show was held in Markeaton Park. I went well enough on him – he was quite a difficult ride – he had a choppy stride going into a fence, and was very powerful. Mr. Kitson was not very pleased with me riding for someone else and he said so, so I had a word with Mr. Morley and suggested John Walmsley ride him. He went very well for John and romance blossomed.

RIDING FOR MR. POWELL

At the end of 1954, I was offered the job of riding for Mr. Powell of Macclesfield. I knew him quite well because earlier I had sold him a very good jumping pony called Shadow, which I had bought off Michael Selby from Nottingham. (Actually, I had taken Shadow in part exchange with him for a Grade C jumper I called Woodburn – a very nice bay horse. Michael Selby had another pony called Rocket. I don't know much about him, but when they stabled at a show they only used to book one stable, and both ponies lived in that one stable). Mr. Powell offered me twice the wages and 25% of my winnings. I knew I had only novices to ride, but good ones, so that if I had luck, I was going to be a lot better off, with a percentage on what we sold as well.

In the following Spring, I went up to live with Mr and Mrs Powell, Shirley and Stewart. That did not work out any better than when I lived with the Kitsons, so I found myself some digs just outside Macclesfield with a very motherly soul. When I went jumping for the day, she would pack me up so much lunch I just could not eat it all, and, so as not to hurt her feelings, I would have to throw some of it away. But she was very good to me, considering I often had to leave early and get back late. The difference I was finding was that while I had been at Mr. Kitson's I had three or four to exercise, here I had probably fourteen or fifteen rides a day – but then Mr Powell had a field full of horses. A lot came from Kernans of Ireland.

Stewart had the team of ponies – Shadow, Dickey, and Lady Jane Grey – and Shirley had her horse, Winston C and a novice. Geoff Hornsey had Riverside and a novice or two. Then there was me, I had John Peel who came from Tony Dickinson (Funny how that name crops up through my life!) and Musket, who John Walmsley used to ride, a nice little dun gelding. John Peel was a very good sort of horse, but a bit on the careless side.

Mr. Powell had had his eye on Bett Schwabe's Blakedon, who had started refusing with her. At Liverpool show, in 1955 I think it was, Mr. Powell thought I had better have a ride on him. We had three horse-boxes at the show and he borrowed another lorry and made a corale out of these boxes – sat me on the horse – he could go nowhere – got out his hunting crop, or long tom as they are called in racing circles, and said to me, "Just sit tight. Don't do anything." He started cracking this whip behind him and about drove poor Blakedon crazy. Then he bought him, and he never once stopped with me. He certainly learnt his lesson, but Mr. Powell was a great one for not letting us carry a whip. He maintained if a horse was looking back at you, he could not be looking at the fence ahead.

He bought a grey horse called A.M. and another grey horse called Blue Prince that came from Ireland, so, with Blakedon, I had a team of greys besides a team of novices. A very good novice I had was a horse called H.B., supposedly half brother to Masserella's Hunstman. I don't think he was, but he was a "clear-round machine" up to 4'6", with 4'7" his limit. He was a very good horse across country. Riding round the farm, one never had to open a gate. He went as a Huntsman's horse to the North Staffs.

Mr. Powell was a great man to ride for. He was always on about, "What a good horse this one will be next year!". I think his favourite show was Southport. He and Mrs. Powell used to take a caravan. I think it was her only outing of the year.

At one Southport, a farmer from Lincolnshire, Billy Lunn, known as Mushy, lost a very good black mare. She broke a leg, and so we had a collection for him. I have no idea how much he got. I must ask him sometime – forty years later. He still travels the shows and I think he breeds horses now.

Mr. Durham is someone else I would associate with Southport. He

Mr Powell with his team of greys

would always greet you, "Now brother, how are you?" He had a few good horses, such as Sailor Boy and Bald Ben, ridden by his son Peter. His grand-daughter has done very well with a horse called Welham. I tried to buy it at Derby County Show. She won some very good classes on it, but thought it might go better for a man, so she put up one of the best jockeys in the world – John Whittaker – who jumped him in the Olympics and the Volvo World Cup final. How her grandfather would have enjoyed that!

Southport was Wednesday, Thursday and Friday, and it was always on to Poynton for Saturday. Mr. Pashley, who owned Golden Rocket, used to be there for the whole week and would be there early on Saturday morning to wave everyone in. John Roberts and his father Ciggy, as he was called, always made a full week of it too. John is still jumping; he must be sixty-something now. He has had some very good horses through his hands since those days. His daughter, too, has represented England a few times, both on ponies and horses.

Another good show started up – the Caledonian Show at Falkirk. It was a good warm-up for Harringay. The first year they did not get the going right. They put soil down that had been stored outside for a few weeks previous to the show, which was held in an ice-rink. The soil had got wet through and when they put it down the surface was like a bog. The organisers worked all through the night to get it better.

47

It was a long way from Macclesfield and there were still no motorways. We went through Lancaster, Kendall, and over Shap. I could not believe it when someone said they had come two hundred miles down. I think we had gone two hundred miles up!

They were a very sociable people, the Scots. Amongst them I must mention the Buchans. Jimmy was a very good jockey and so was Anna, his sister. Jimmy died while he was quite young. So did Raymond Poskit, another very strong jockey of that time. They still have an Equestrian Centre just outside Lincoln named after him.

My best year at Falkirk was 1958. I won the test or puissance, whichever you like to call it, on Blakedon who was now becoming a good horse. We had already won two good classes at the Royal when it was held in Bristol.

Another show I ought to mention is the Royal Welsh that was always held on different grounds, often Rhyl or Aberystwyth. It always clashed with the Royal International. On one occasion we were watching it on television in a pub. At ten o'clock the landlord called " That's it, lads. Out you all go. It's closing time." They were just into the jump-off in the King George V Gold Cup and Ted Edgar was leading. The landlord decided if he didn't want his pub wrecked he had better stay open.

Another year it was Cynthia Warburton's twenty-first birthday. She used to ride Tiger Lily, a nice little dun horse, always beautifully turned out, like her Morris Minor that was also gleaming. A lovely girl, she went on to marry Terry Wharton, a horse-dealer out of Yorkshire.

Another year about six o'clock in the morning the hunter people at the show, who always had to get up early, were shouting that the river was overflowing. I didn't take any notice. About an hour later someone was knocking on the door, crying, "You'd better get up. The stables are flooded." The show-ground was awash!. The water was gushing down between the boxes at about four feet deep. It was all hands to the wheel. The show went on; they moved the show jumps to the highest point of the ring, and put up a course of five fences. It was quite exciting splashing through the water to get to a fence.

Another good show was at Brighton. Harringay had been the furthest south I had travelled before that. We had some fun there, too. The show was held on a ground about two miles out of Brighton. It was a lovely flat arena, big stands, and the fences were so easy they seemed to have take-off poles in front at every fence – a jolly sight different from Hibaldstow where one day I jumped ten fences, and eight of them gates. There was no ground-line in front of them! I got to know a lot of new people, such as Dicky Stillwell and his bevy of beauties – I can't remember many names – but there was Jane Liley;

Judy Shepherd, a great friend, and still is when I catch up with her. (She later became Mrs. Brian Crago); and Sue Cohen, later to become Mrs.Fred Welch. We organised a cabaret one night. Seamus sang, "There's no business like show-business" – he was very good. I have never ever seen so many autograph-hunters as there were at the show. I sat on a bale outside the lorry and I bet there was a queue twenty yards long. I got writer's cramp, but one couldn't disappoint them.

As Harringay, the last show of the season, finished on the Saturday of the first week in October, I was at home in Castle Gresley on the Sunday night.

WINTER RACING

I enjoyed my racing too much to hang about in Macclesfield. with Mr Powell. I was at Leicester sales when George Warby asked me if I would ride two for him at Warwick. It was the beginning of December and very icy and they had put some kind of sand or grit on the landing side. The horse I was riding, called Master Builder, fell at the last, and the sand and grit did my face no good at all.

Earlier, I had been riding a few point-to-pointers for Frank Allen, who was farming at Willington at the time. There was Windy City, bought at a sale just outside Warwick, and another horse. Windy City went well enough when I had ridden him at the Meynell, and was placed, but he ran a cracking race at the High Peak and was third. The horse summered well and Frank Allen started running him under National Hunt rules. It looked as if I had been jocked off, but he wasn't running very well – fell a couple of times – so he asked me it I would ride him at Warwick. It was in a two-mile novice chase. What happened but he galloped straight through the first and broke his neck! I was brought back in the ambulance with a back-injury which was never really going to recover. The horse was not insured. Frank had not signed the papers. They were still on his desk. Warwick was not a very lucky place for me.

RACING FOR MYSELF

I used to go home to do my racing, but I was having a few falls too many. I found I was doing the schooling but when they were ready for off, I wasn't riding. So, in 1956, I decided I would buy a racehorse myself. I went to Ascot

Sales towards the end of March and bought a very nice 16.2 bay gelding called Easy Manner, a five-year-old by Wood Cot. He had run a few times round Fontwell, over two miles one furlong. I took out a permit to train and entered him for a novice hurdle at Huntingdon on Whit Monday – about the last day of the season. Anyway, he was half fit when I bought him, so when he got to Huntingdon, he looked well, and felt well to me.

It was a while since I had ridden in a hurdle race. There were seventeen runners. I had walked the course, thank goodness, and, with seventeen runners, created an 'A' plan to try and lie up about fourth or fifth, and see how I was going . Two out, I could not believe what I was seeing. Everything else was struggling, so I let him go on and he won pulling up, by twenty lengths at twenty-to-one. I had a few quid on, but nothing to amount to much. That day, I had told one or two people that I thought he would go well, including Mr. Milner, the saddler from Leicester, who had a stand at the sales there for years. Some time later, at the sales, he came round to find me and said, "–That tip you gave me at Huntingdon. I've got a present for you." He gave me a blue travelling rug, a hood with my name on, and a paddock sheet,

Easy Manner

also blue with a red binding and my name on it. He was quite a friend of mine and of my father. Another day at the sales he said to me, "You'll never see a horse-dealer in a Rolls Royce." How true! I often think of him telling me that.

In hindsight, what fools we were over that novice hurdle. We should never have won that race. It was a novice and the end of the season when there was nowhere else to go. We should have kept him a novice till the beginning of the following season, but we didn't. As he had run a few times before we bought him, he could be handicapped.

For the first run of the 1957 season, he ran in a two-mile handicap hurdle at Birmingham. He was weighted at 10 stone 5 pounds. As I still claimed 7 lbs. as an inexperienced jockey, I had to do 9st.12 lbs. Well, I sweated and starved from my show-jumping weight, which was 11st.5lbs., and as I was six foot tall it was taking some doing – but I was determined not to carry any overweight.

On race-day, which was a Tuesday, I came out of the Turkish baths in Derby at 9st.6 lbs. The Turkish baths only takes the liquid out of your body, so I knew that I dare not have a drink until after the race. I weighed out at just 9st.12 lbs. The plan was to go off in front and make all the running. With such a light weight, we thought he could win like that. He jumped the last in front but they came and swamped us. Eric Cousins, the trainer who I had had a few rides for and who started Robert Sangster off with his racehorses, said, "I had a bet on you to-day, but when I saw you go off in front, I knew my money was on a non-trier." He was wrong – I had not taken all that weight off to ride a non-trier. I was so hungry when I finished, that I had a pork pie as soon as I could, not realising my stomach was so small I could not eat all that food. I was so ill that I had to go to the medical room and lie down.

That Autumn, my brother had bought a chesnut mare which had run once and won a three-year-old selling hurdle at Worcester. Not a bright thing for my brother to do, as it was very difficult to do any good considering you have to run them three times before you can get them handicapped. Imperial Lady was her name – a nice mare, not very big, and not a lot of her, but at least she was something to gallop with Easy Manner.

(Angela, my sister, was riding a gallop one day when the stirrup leather broke. She had a terrible fall – bad tack! She made quite a hole in the gallop – my sister that is!).

The first time we ran Imperial Lady was over hurdles at Haydock and she fell at about the fifth. We thought we had schooled her plenty, but she just missed it. The next time we went to Haydock, Easy Manner was in a handicap hurdle, weighted at 10st. 4lbs. He was ready we knew, because he was getting naughty in the box, and he was looking magnificent. Charlie

51

Hall, who I had been with at Towton, near Tadcaster, came to me in the paddock and said how well the horse looked, and I said I had got him ready on his lines. Anyway, we all had a tremendous amount of money on him. I backed him with the local bookie before we went to the races, and on the course, the Tote and the Tote Daily Double. I was going to ride him as I had done at Huntingdon — lie about fourth or fifth and kick on about two out. I don't think I have ever jumped a hurdle so fast as the one turning into the straight. For all that, I knew the money was safe. The official distance he won by was four lengths; it could have been further. There have never been more pound notes on the table than there were that night! The Tote paid 50 – 1, the Bookmakers 33 – 1 (Just great!) and the Tote Double paid a lot too.

A fortnight later we took him to Nottingham. We thought the ground would be the same. It was wet. I had £100 on him, but, going past the stables, I knew we would win nothing. He could not run in that going. At Haydock it had been sloshy: at Nottingham it was holding.

We gave him until Easter Saturday, 1958, at Uttoxeter, and by then he had recovered. He had gone up in the weights to 12 stone. He looked really well, so we backed him, and again he won by four lengths. We had landed another coup!

The next time out was at Bangor in the fifth race – the Bronington Handicap Hurdle Race of two miles – the winner to get 300 sovs., the second 60 sovs and the third 30 out of the plate. The entry was 3 sovs. and 3 sovs if declared to run.

No 1 on the card – Mr. J. Betteridge – Easy Manner, 6 yrs. 12.0. B.G. by Wood Cot out of Late Coup – Royal blue, light blue sleeves, maroon sash and quartered cap, trained by J. Betteridge, ridden by J. Betteridge (Not often you see that to-day – owned, trained and ridden by the same person.) I had never seen the horse look better. He was gleaming on his coat. I had never been to Bangor before – more like a point-to-point course I thought, but the money was down. It all went well. I got a super run up the inner just turning into the straight and won by four lengths. We didn't know how good this horse was.

I had in the meantime bought another bay gelding, Kings Star, by Kings Legend, who had run well on the flat without winning. He ran second at Southwell and seemed to be running on, so we sent him to a two-and-a-half mile hurdle. Again he was second and seemed to be running on, but by now Mr. Powell was screaming that I should be back there riding his show-jumpers, so we turned the racehorses out and I went back to Mr Powell at Macclesfield.

BACK WITH THE SHOW-JUMPERS

The show-jumpers were just coming good horses. They were in their third and fourth seasons and it takes that time to make a jumper. Blakedon was good by now. He was really enjoying himself. I remember, when the Cheshire Show was on the Roodee, they put up a nearly unjumpable treble, but he could jump it. One of my favourite shows was the Shrewsbury Flower Show. Not only was there very good jumping, but the outside circus was also going on all day and there were the flower tents to have a walk round in the evening. The trouble those people went to! I can smell the scent of all those flowers now. There was always The Shropshire Young Farmers' dance on the Wednesday night. It was a lot of fun. One year I took Diana Wycherley (later to become Mrs. Bill Foulkes). I don't think Billy was too pleased. He went on to become champion amateur jockey under National Hunt rules and Joint-Master of the Meynell.

Another show-jumping jockey at that time, from a little further into Wales, was Roy Edwards. Not only were he and his sisters to become well-known in the show-jumping world, but Roy was later to ride the winner of the Champion Hurdle. His sister Sheila became Mrs. Crow, mother of Alistair, champion point-to-point jockey. His sister Lucy became champion ladies' point-to-point jockey.

Talking about lady jockeys reminds me not to leave out Jennifer Renfree. At Harringay that year, 1957, Jennifer was in the Horse Personalities of the year. I was always interested in pretty girls, and was she pretty! Anyway, I made myself known to her and we were talking racing for a few hours. Next day she brought her racing form-book and came and sat with me. She knew more about me than I knew myself! She said I wasn't running the Kings Star horse far enough. If he was by Kings Legend he would need at least three miles. We had more fun at Harringay that year, though I did not really expect to see her again. I was on the look-out for a three-year hurdler, and as we had bought Easy Manner there, the Ascot Sales on the 1st November was the place to go. The first person I saw was Jennifer. Mr Renfree bought a horse called Blackwrath by Vulcan, and she asked me to go back with them for a few days. That turned out to be a week! I met her mother – they made a typical Cornish couple – and her brother Jimmy who was to become champion amateur National Hunt jockey. I travelled home on the train, but I was to go down a few more times that winter, and she invited me to go and watch her ride Lonesome Boy at the East Cornwall point-to-point – over banks – very interesting and exciting – but not for me. A lovely girl and lovely family. She was very clever. She went on to marry David Barons and they trained the winner of the Grand National, the Whitbread Gold Cup and loads of other races.

LAST VENTURE OVER HURDLES

I went to the next Ascot sales and bought the three-year-old I was looking for – Royal Bloom, by Kingstone a sire of jumpers, that had been second at Bath over six furlongs and second at Nottingham over one mile and two furlongs. He was just what I wanted. We got him ready to run at Huntingdon in a three-year-old hurdle. He was set to carry 10st. 7 lbs., and no way could I get down to that weight. I had been show-jumping all summer and my weight had gone up to 11 st. 7 lbs – not 10 st. 7 lb. We got Derek Leslie to ride him. He looked superb and we schooled him plenty. It was a disappointment – Derek pulled him up before he jumped the last. Father had really taken to this horse and spent a good hour each night strapping, or cleaning him – Call it what you like.

The next run was to be at Haydock. The race at Huntingdon had done him good. We ran Imperial Lady on the Friday at Haydock and she was second in a Selling Hurdle and not beaten by far. We knew she couldn't live with Royal Bloom, so we thought the stable was in form. We had a decent bet on him. Derek rode him again, going superbly, running first to half way up the straight and going easy. We thought, "This is more like the horse we know at home." Suddenly, he went out like a light. Derek's explanation was: "He doesn't stay. He's got speed to burn but doesn't stay. I should send him back to Ascot. Let him go for what he makes."

Father was so disappointed. He had worked so hard on him — but that's life!

Another horse I bought at Ascot was a horse called Bim Bom who had won the Brocklesby Stakes at Doncaster for Captain Elsey. He was by Chanteur who had won the Derby. A nice little horse, butty sort. We ran him a few times. He had never run over hurdles before we had him, but he jumped well, so in 1959 we laid him out for a race at Uttoxeter. At Market Rasen on Saturday, 7th March, he was set to carry 12 st. 1 lb. I rode him, claimed 7 lbs. – he carried. 11 st. 8 lbs. No way could I win with that weight when against a lot of horses in the same class

At Uttoxeter, on the 31st March, he was weighted at 10 st. I could not do that weight any more. The weight was piling on – 10 st. 10 lbs. was the least I could do, even after starving myself stupid. In fact it was getting to be a problem and I had to get Roy Edwards to ride him. (I think by then he had turned professional). I had a substantial bet with Mr. Ash, who I knew quite well, as his daughter used to be a show-jumping jockey. A very nice family. My orders to Roy were: "Be in the first two till you come into the straight. Then make the best of your way home." He carried out the orders to a tee. Then, a hundred yards from the post, he dropped his hands, patted him down his neck. Bim Bom thought he had done enough, stopped as though he had been shot, and another came upsides. By the time he had got him going again, it was too late. He was beaten by a head and the money was lost.

Easy Manner had gone to the top of the handicap. He ran quite well in the Imperial Cup. He carried 11 st. 7 lbs. (John Oaksey rode the winner). With all that weight, the hill at Sandown had told on him, so we schooled him over fences, and he did jump well. When I had a fall at Harringay and broke my ankle, Don Underwood drove me to hospital. (There didn't seem to many ambulances about in those days.) It meant I wasn't able to ride him, so we got Roy Edwards to ride him at Nottingham as it was first time over fences. The orders were: "Don't win this under any circumstances. We want him for another day." It was very foggy. They should really not have been racing. It was an ideal day for not being too busy. I had had a talk to Roy Whiston, and we thought his horse ought to win, so I had a few quid on that. At race-time, it was such a foggy day you could just see the last fence. Who should jump it in front but Easy Manner! He was pulling up. The jockey certainly never rode for me again. People thought I had backed him. With that race he got a leg which most of them do. Anyway he never ran again.

Another horse to break down on his first trip over three miles, at Bangor, was Kings Star, the bay gelding we had been working up to longer distance. He ran a tremendous race – lasting well – suddenly his legs went and he could hardly get back to the boxes. I couldn't be doing with any more lame horses, so I gave him away to a farmer called Norman Renshaw over at Tutbury. He stood him every day in a fast-running stream. He came right after a year, and won four or five long-distance hurdles. Norman never once invited me either to ride him or to have a bet on him.

Mention of Don Underwood driving me to hospital reminds me of an incident that was funny at the time. How it will write up, I don't know but I'll give it a try. Don was with quite a crowd of us that went to the Windmill Theatre. Jacky Turner was the first to break the silence as all these beautiful girls came on stage with very little on. He shouted, "First time I have seen them with stars on." Then in walked this chap from the City – bowler hat, rolled umbrella – with a very pretty girl, and they sat down in front of me. After a while he put his arm round her, and it must have taken twenty minutes for him to be just going to give her a kiss, when I leaned forward, gave her a peck, and said "Beat you!" He immediately got up, and said to the girl, "Come on darling, we aren't stopping in here with this rough crowd". And off he went.

UPHEAVALS

In 1958 at Macclesfield Show I got pains in my back. I told Mr Powell about them. He laughed it off saying I had just got a cold in my back, and would be all right – I wasn't, and at Falkirk later that year I had to have pain-killing injections to keep me going. At Harringay, Bertie Hill, the three-day event rider, said, when I told him, "We have a back specialist who lives in Redruth. Come and stay with us and let him look at you." As soon as Harringay was over I went down and had a week, but my back didn't seem any better. Then I heard of a chap in Glasgow. He didn't do any good either, but with not riding it seemed to be getting a bit better.

The Coal Board decided they would like to expand their coalmine at Cadley Hill and use our land. Our farm was about twenty-five acres. We were milking and had a bit of arable. It was a going concern, especially with what I brought in from the racing and the show-jumping. Everything went in the kitty. We had brought the farm in 1951 for three thousand pounds. Now we negotiated with the Coal Board for a price of six thousand five hundred pounds and to be out of the farm in a year. It seemed a long time then. We thought the change would be easy but believe me it was not. With the Coal Board owning such a lot of farms in the area we thought they would be sure to let us have one to let. We put in for a few farms and seemed to be on a short list, but never quite got there. Just when we decided we had better start looking to buy, we had a letter from the Coal Board saying that the twelve months was up. They wanted to get on with enlarging the pit and we had a month to vacate the place, as they were coming to knock the buildings and the house down.

The first farm we looked at after that was at Ambergate. It stood halfway up a hill, with the house on one side of a road and the farm buildings on the other. It was about seventy acres, which would be quite a step up for us. We decided to give seven thousand pounds for it at the forthcoming auction, but it went past our limit, leaving us the under-bidders at seven thousand eight hundred pounds. Naturally, we were very disappointed, not least because we had to be out in a fortnight, with all the stock and nowhere to go.

As we were coming out of the sale-room in Derby, a chap came over and said to me, "You were wanting a farm but that one you were bidding for was never worth that sort of money. Now I will sell you my farm at South Normanton." We made arrangements to see it the next day, Saturday, at ten o'clock. When we got there we could see it didn't suit us. The farmhouse and buildings were in the middle of South Normanton, also in a mining part of the world, but there was a pub on each corner, and I could see me never getting any sleep on a Saturday night.

When I said to him, "It just isn't really us," he seemed to accept it.

Then he said, "There's a friend of mine wants to sell his farm over at Stanton Hill. I'll give him a ring and let him know we're coming."

It was about seven miles. On the way, as we were going into Stanton Hill, I remember saying to Mother, "This is Brass Band country". After going down a very bumpy road, we came upon this quite nice farm – a good four-bedroomed house, a good nearly-new cowshed, with room for twenty-nine milkers, an older shed that could hold another twelve milkers, and about one hundred and thirty acres of good ground, but very rough. There were fifteen milking cows, a quite new tractor and various implements. There was a phone but no electricity, only Tilley lamps and oil lamps in the house. We asked what sort of money wanted for it. His answer (Don't forget this was 1959) was four thousand five hundred pounds for the farm and two thousand pounds for the cows and everything, lock stock and barrel. It was eleven o'clock when we first saw the farm. By one o'clock we had bought it. My brother stayed overnight with Mr Shepherd, who actually moved out on Monday morning. He only took with him a suitcase and his dog. We moved into the farm, that was known as Springwood Farm, Stanton Hill, on Monday afternoon.

It was a far bigger farm than we had ever envisaged buying. We tried to sell twenty acres but no one wanted to buy. A good job they didn't because in a year it was actually us who were buying more land. My mother and father had been more than capable of managing a smallholding but this was a bigger farm. It was quite an ambition to fill the cowshed with twenty-nine milkers but in less than two years we had not only filled that shed, we had filled the other one as well.

I had to tell Mr Powell I couldn't ride for him any more, as I had to stay and help the family to farm this place. He came over to see me but he couldn't change my mind and so he sold the horses. Mr Kitson brought Blakedon for Jackie Turner and Carol Beard rode A.M.. Mr Powell came over again and gave me commission out of the sale of the horses. He said if I stood Blakedon in that field he could claim he had made more money out of him than we had given for the farm. And then Peter Richardson's father sold Yorkshireman to

57

Mr Cawthaw and bought his farm with the money he made out of him. So there are the guide-lines: in those days a very good Grade A was more than the price of a farm, and the price of a good Grade A would still buy a good farm today.

THE SIXTIES

OUT OF ACTION

As I said earlier, I kept having pains in my back. One day when I was doing some tractoring they came on terribly strong. I managed to get back to the house and said I had better go to the hospital. There, they had a look at me and said, "You will be staying with us for a while. You had better ring your family and let them know where you are." They came over in the car and brought me my clothes. The doctors said, "You will never ride again. You might not walk again either."

I was to stay in the Bolsover Ward, Mansfield General Hospital for the next four months. They operated on my back and took out two discs. I still have the scar to show for it.

Hospital was a new experience. I remember one chap who had come from Hull. He was a fisherman on a trawler and promised he would take me with him out into the North Sea trawling but he never made it. He died under the anaesthetic. He was only quite young. There was certainly a lot of banter too, especially with me about. With me being a farmer, on a Monday they would say, "It's time you were getting up. It's Market Day today. What are you taking?" – they knowing full well I could not move. I was put on traction; that meant you had your legs taped together and weights attached to your legs hanging over the edge of the bed to stretch your body. When I went for my operation I was six feet tall and when I came out of hospital I was six feet two. One of the worst things to happen came when they took the tapes off my legs. The hair had grown through and they pulled a lot of skin off along with the tapes. It hurt my legs; they kept sticking together. I must say the nurses were brilliant. I slept all day and talked all night. I thought it quite a good arrangement.

After four months they said I could go home, but first of all they put me in a plaster cast from my neck down to my hips. Once I had got this on, of course I had too much to eat and of course the plaster cast would not give. I thought I was going to burst. I was out of action for twelve months – In fact for all of 1960. The nurses were all very kind. One or two came to see me and took me out. One very special day I was taken to Hardwick Hall which was a real treat.

My father and brother were having to manage without me but the farm was running very well, and I must say the miners were marvellously helpful; any excuse and they would be there. They really enjoyed themselves working outside and would all work for free as long as they had a barrel of beer to go at. You would give one a pint and before you could pull another one he would say, "That hardly touched my throat."

Meanwhile, I don't think Jackie Turner was going too well with Blakedon and Mr Kitson sold him on to Lady Zinna Cummins for Fred Welch to ride. Mr Kitson was heard to say, "When I bought Blakedon there were tears in Mr Powell's eyes" but later on he said, "After I had had him three months I was crying my eyes out." A.M. wasn't going any better for Carol Beard. He gave her a crunching fall, breaking her pelvis and generally making a mess of her. At least Blakedon went well for Freddy. We had no use now for Imperial Lady, so we sold her to Roy Whiston who had some success with her. As well as having to put an end to our show-jumping we had moved to an area where it was impossible to get racehorses ready, although that didn't prevent the miners from gambling on anything. Even Doctor Woodside was a great racing man. If I went to see him, which I did quite often with my back, he would sooner talk about racing than about me.

BACK IN THE SADDLE

As I said I was under the doctor for just a year and by then was walking better. Of course all the experts had said I would never ride again, but one day when everyone had gone out, I caught old Johnny Walker, who was now about twenty-five years old, and heaved myself up on him. He was marvellous. He knew I wasn't very well, but I was riding again, and to speak the truth after a few strides I was in no pain either. It felt super. Of course I had to tell them when they got back, and the air was very blue, especially from Mother, but after a day or two, in not much pain, I resumed riding regularly again. I was still in plaster from my neck to my hips, not very comfortable, but I got by, and then it was not too long before I had all the plaster off. What a relief! I kept getting a bit of pain but I could cope. I was still going to see the specialist. He said he had touched the sciatic nerve when he operated and that it would take time to settle down.

We were getting the farm up and running. There was a twenty-acre field that was fairly overgrown and a three-acre wood that was very overgrown. You could not get into it. We thought the thing to do was buy some pigs and an old wooden hut and put an electric fence round all of it. The pigs made a wonderful job of clearing it up. We then started to clear all the hawthorns but there were some old oak trees as well. As there was a place just outside Alfreton where they made explosives, I got a permit from the local government offices and permission to blow up those trees.

The first one we did, I put in four sticks of the dynamite, then a detonator, and a long piece of fuse-wire, which must have been twenty feet long, lit the fuse and, of course, stood well back. We did not realise that the roots on the tree were fairly rotten. We thought it might just blow it a few feet out of the ground. We suddenly heard a massive explosion and saw this quite big tree disappear into the sky. Where it came down I don't know. At least I did learn from that not to use so much explosive and to see that the tree had roots to hold it down. After a while I did get very blasé with everything to do with explosives and fuse-wire. I even got down to using a foot of fuse-wire instead of twenty. When one day I went to do another tree, the dynamite was sweating that much it had stuck together. I was very lucky. I could have blown myself up – and the farm as well.

RIDING FOR MR. BALL

I remember one day in 1961 a very smart car came into the yard when I was milking. A tall well-dressed man got out and came into the cowshed and spoke to me:

"Are you John Betteridge?"

"Yes, that's me."

"I would like to buy a top-class show-jumper and I would like you to ride it for me. I've got two novices already; one I think is quite good."

To say I was taken a-back would be putting it mildly. I said I would have to talk it over with the family. If he left me his phone number I would let him know.

After a conference, the family came to the conclusion that if I could get a good deal then I should go for it. So I rang him up and arranged to meet him at his place, which was only in Mansfield about six miles away. The arrangement he suggested was that he would keep the horses; all I would have to do was drive the lorry to the shows, and go to his place twice a week to ride the horses. For this I would get one hundred and fifty pounds a week as a retainer and twenty-five percent of my winnings. He had a few Premium stallions, including one called Dover Light which was getting some quite good stock. I would have nothing to do with them as the grooms who did them also did the jumpers. I only had to ride them.

Mr Ball had said when he came down to the farm that he wanted to buy a good horse; so when I heard that Yorkshireman was on the market I told him all about the horse, how Richardson, a farmer from Yorkshire, had sold him to Cawthaw for Ted Williams to ride, and Richardson had bought his farm with the money he had made out of him. At the time a girl in Gloucester was riding him. Anyway we made arrangements to go and see him. It was early April – something good always happens to me around my birthday. Mr Ball drove down in his Rolls-Royce. I had not been in one before.

I had a ride on him and thought I could do it – so we bought him for four thousand pounds. What made me confident in him was that we had bought Johnny B and Johnny Walker from Ted Williams.

The first show was the Newark and Notts. People were quite surprised to see me back on the circuit. He went quite well, but at the next show, the Staffs County, I won the leading rider. A new pair of breeches was the prize – a very useful present.

Mr Ball thought we ought to have another top horse so we bought a horse called Grand Manan from the Hon. Mrs. Kidd. A good horse but not for me. I could not ride him. David Broome had ridden him and done very well on him but whereas I shortened a stride using my right hand David had used his left. I won a class or two on him but nothing much, so he was soon on his way.

The Hon. Mrs. Kidd threw some wonderful parties when the Bath and West Show was held, not far from where she lived. At one of them I was talking to Johnny, her son, in Tom Hudson's horse-box, a converted furniture-van so big that you could probably have got fifty people in it. I told him I thought his horses had improved lately.

"They have," he said. "I've been doing what you lads do."

"Oh, what's that?" I asked him.

"I have an iron pole and put it across about six inches higher than the fence. They only touch it once. Never again."

All I said was, "That's what they do, is it?"

Of the novices I took over, one was a nice grey horse about 15.2 named Carburettor, a lovely little horse, and going well enough; the other big horse, named Sputnik, was a useless show-jumper, but quite good-looking. I thought he could be on his way as a hunter. So I talked to Mr Henson, Geno to his friends, who had done about one hundred days of hunting the previous season, and was, I thought, the senior Joint-master of the Blankney at that time. He said, "Bring the horse up, have a day with us and we'll see how he goes."

It was the cubbing season. When he said, "Follow me," he led me over to see quite a big dyke, probably about twenty feet across the top from bank to bank and very steep. Anyway I went back about one hundred yards all set to jump this dyke. When I was going a good gallop, Mr Henson cut in front of me, waving his arms and shouting, "You can't jump it like that." Afterwards he explained, "You don't exactly jump them. What you do is walk down one side, jump across the bottom and climb up the other side."

I had a nice day out just the same, although he said the horse was a bit on the common side for him.

Mr Ball was in the lorry business. He said he was going to make me a purpose-built horse-box. He had done two horse-boxes before but I can say I had a bit of input in to this one. With them being so different today, our scheme is difficult to explain, but basically ours had four horses in stalls facing forward, with an exit-ramp in front at the side as well as the usual ramp at the back and human needs were looked after with mattresses hinged to the sides that let down across the rear partitions and dining-table and eating area in the front two partitions. There was even an extra bed on the cock loft, or as some call it the canopy, over the cab. Shades of open trucks, tarpaulins, and sleeping on straw!

I think the first show I took the horse-box to was the Bath and West where I had a reasonable show, and after it was over Derek Kent and I helped Annelie Drummond-Hay to jump a white gate. Then, along with her faithful groom Merlin Meakin, we all went out for a meal in Bridgewater that night. Annelie went on to win the *Sunday Times* cup at Wembley that year when it was probably the biggest and most difficult course I have seen in show-jumping.

FARMING

After Wembley I returned to the farm as usual. I have to say that not a lot happened. We were not really in a hunting country, but to keep my hand in I had an occasional day with the Barlow, where Ted Hill was the Huntsman. Very good he was too and to hear him blow a horn was magic – not surprising from a man who won the horn-blowing competition at the Horse and Hound Ball more than once.

On the farming side, my brother was into buying pedigree Friesian cows. Much against my will, we were giving up to three hundred pounds for a pedigree Friesian against one hundred and fifty pounds for a commercial cow, but as he was putting more in to the farm than I was I had to go along with him.

As he wanted to rear his own bull he had semen from the well-known sire, Dalton Black Magic. We used a very nice cow that we had given quite a bit of money for. And we had a bull calf out of her. My brother was excited – this was going to be the start of something big. My brother was a good feeder and the bull was the apple of his eye. When it was getting older, he decided that he ought to show it at Bakewell in the Young Pedigree Friesian Bull class, along with another nice cow that we had. About two months before Bakewell show we started exercising this bull, bedding him down with the best white straw. He had a rug on every night and was not allowed to get a stain of any sort on him. He looked as fit as a racehorse – in fact he had been managed along the same lines, plenty of work, plenty of the best food and plenty of grooming. The great day arrived. We set off to the show with the young bull and the young cow. They looked magnificent when we unloaded them outside the cattle tent (Don't forget we had never shown any cattle before; in fact we had not even looked down the cattle lines). When we were called into the ring, my brother was leading up and our bull was outstanding. The judge could not help but give him first prize — Not bad for anyone seeing it was their first time for showing cattle! Then it was the turn of the cow. She also looked outstanding, but she was not placed, pulled out really right down the line. So when the judge had finished his day's work we asked him if he would give us some advice on showing cattle. When we showed him the cow he had been judging he said, "This is a nice cow. I can't remember seeing this one." So we decided there and then that would be our last day's showing if that was how it went After all that work and the cow that looked magnificent not to be noticed! We decided we were not up to taking the pain of showing cows so that was our first and last shot at it. At least we went out with a winner.

A GREAT YEAR FOR JUMPING

March 1962 was not long in coming. This was when we started to get the horses ready. One always geared oneself for Newark and Notts, never a very lucky show for me, but it was there I once saw Foxhunter jump for Norman Holmes and could tell then that he was a bit special. The next we knew was that Colonel Harry Llewellyn had bought him and the rest is history. As usual, the show that followed Newark was the Oxford County. I learnt one great lesson there: I looked round the collecting ring and thought to myself, "With Yorkshireman I am better than anybody here," and that gave me so much confidence in myself I could only go on and win. It doesn't matter what kind of sporstman you are, the one thing you need is confidence in your own

Yorkshireman after winning
the first prize of £500 given in
this country

ability. It is a great thing to have. If you do not have confidence, you have nothing.

The next week was Stafford County and I won the leading rider – another pair of breeches! The Bath and West was next and I won the leading rider again. The prize should have been a saddle, but I thought, "Why should I have tack to put on other people's horses?" so I asked if I could swap the prize for something that would do me a bit of good. I plumped for a nice riding mac and a super long-length sheepskin coat that I still have.

I did all the big agricultural shows, each one coming in the same week each year. One of my favourites was the Cheshire County Show on the Roodee. Yorkshireman was jumping out of his skin.. I was riding with so much confidence that to have a fence down now was unthinkable.

I suppose the highlight of 1962 was the winning of the first five hundred pound prize ever given in this country. It was in the class called the Champion of Champions, at the Royal Lancashire Show at Blackpool. One had to qualify to jump. The North of England was one qualifier, the Royal Lancashire was another and the Blackpool Show Championship was the other. Out of those three classes they had twenty qualifying and there were some very good horses that had come for that sort of money. I was about fifteenth to go and I knew Yorkshireman wasn't the fastest against the clock. So, after watching a few go, I decided that the only way I could do any good was to gallop to the first and second fences. A few of the other riders I thought were a bit negative, so I really did set sail. As I came out of the ring we had gone into the lead, and, believe me, watching the next few to go was agonising — but I won the Champion of Champions!

The five hundred pounds to the winner was the largest amount of prize money ever given in Great Britain. The second received only sixty pounds. The B.S.J.A influenced it after that, ensuring the lower prize money had to reflect the value of the first prize.

At the party that night we drank twenty-eight bottles of champagne. When I rang Mr Ball to tell him we had won and ought to celebrate in champagne, he said, "Send me the bill." So I did.

The next day was Blackburn Show. It was absolutely throwing it down with rain, so I decided not to jump. I had had enough, but I did jump on the Saturday when there was two hundred and fifty pounds for the winner. I had the first fence down — That's jumping!

An idea came to me at the Blackburn Show and I think that show-jumping would have been the better for it. I maintain that had all the sponsorship money gone into prize money instead of individual pockets it would have done the game a lot of good. For one thing, the money would have filtered down to the grooms.

I did not jump at Blackburn on the Friday. I had got my money for that week up front and a lot of people who were sponsored felt the same way: Why bother getting wet through when you didn't have to? If you had a fence down you were never going to win so you didn't bother carrying on, you just pulled out, doffed your cap and retired. If, however, you had to get your expenses you would have had to jump for the lower places to earn your wages for that week.

Another highlight of the year was jumping for the King George V Gold Cup at the Royal International held at the White City. What a week! It rained from the moment we unloaded and never stopped until we loaded up again. You had to be placed in one of the classes taking place before the Wednesday night when the big competition was held. I just managed to qualify. On the night it was bucketing down. As I watched the course, under floodlights, I thought it was big, but when I got into the ring and looked down the last line of fences, which included the biggest combination I have ever seen, I thought it was massive. I have never seen so many poles in a fence in my life as in that combination. It *was* massive. And the one before it was the usual Railway Gates with the big red disc in the middle. It was a Champions' course for a Championship Class. Yorkshireman jumped his heart out for one down, which I put down to him pulling a shoe off. I felt him do it turning into the combination, but he was the only one on four faults. He jumped well and was placed fourth. It was a very memorable show.

The European Championships were being held there and that year our huntsman David Barker won the championship on John Masserella's Mister Softee. I think he appreciated the going. It was the first time I had met Ronnie Masserella. Down there he seemed to be in charge of Mister Softee, and from then on he became the team trainer and adviser on the selection of the British Show-jumping Team – a job he still holds some thirty-five years later.

Another interesting feature that year was the American team who were over here to compete. They had probably been before but it was the first time I had seen them close up. They were always turned out immaculately. The horses, all thoroughbreds, probably bought off the racetrack, were so beautifully schooled and so well turned out. They bought their own vet and blacksmith, their own fodder for the horses. The vet seemed to be giving the horses endless injections.

The Russians were also over that year and the contrasts between them and the Americans were remarkable but I shall do my best to describe them. For example, the American saddle-room was a sight to behold. What they had done was to put two wooden loose-boxes into one. They had lined the sides with blue curtains and had tied the curtains back at the door with plain snaffle bits. Each horse had two grooms. The Russian quarters were filthy in comparison. As they were communists the grooms had the same status as the jockeys and the top officials. They all stayed in the hostel on the show ground, whereas the American grooms stayed in the hostel, and the riders and officials in the best hotels. The Russians had not brought anything with them and so they relied on handouts. They found the courses far bigger than any they had attempted before. Nevertheless they were very nice people. I was to meet one later in life but I will write about that at the appropriate time – if I remember.

1962 had been one of my best show-jumping years. I finished as the fourth leading jockey and Yorkshireman won two thousand two hundred pounds..

FARM SECRETARY REQUIRED

As usual I finished with jumping at Wembley and then continued with my farming. Although I lived at home, show-jumping took me away an awful lot. It was quite difficult to change from one to the other. A big contest in front of large audiences one week, and driving a tractor up and down a field the next week but I managed – I had to. Luckily my brother loved show-jumping and was a big fan of mine. He always said if I really wanted to make the headlines I should go and ride for someone down South. That was where you got the most publicity, but I never made the move. It was not to be.

At the time it was very good for farming. The pedigree Friesians were taking off and we had a lot of registering of calves to do. We were having all our feed and fertiliser from a firm situated in Worksop calling themselves the North Notts Farmers. One day one of the reps suggested that as the farm was doing so well we should be able to spend more time outside instead of poring over paper if we had a secretary. The rep said that North Notts Farmers had started a new scheme for farms like ours that were getting to be quite big business and were providing the first travelling farm secretary. She would go to farms one day a month or week, for a morning or an afternoon, or however long she was needed. It sounded good and we agreed to join the scheme. Anyway, along came Linda Winston, a blonde five-foot-five with a rounded figure. She had been educated at Harrogate Ladies' College. When she decided to forget the secretary bit for a while we talked horses. She kept a horse on a farm where she was secretary once a week, and she rode every morning before going to work. She happened to be in digs in Worksop and the horse was kept about five miles away at Fred Salmon's Farm (Fred went on to be Joint-master of the High Peak Harriers). She had actually seen me competing at Bakewell Show that year on Yorkshireman and thought that he was by far the best turned out, his coat was absolutely gleaming. So we found we had a bit more in common than paperwork. I found out she had no one in attendance at that particular time — and she accepted when I asked if I could take her out on Saturday night.

She lived in Hope and that was miles away from Stanton Hill. – nearly too far I thought, but I could not go back on my word. The address was Fulwood Holmes, Hope, and in case I got lost in those hills I said I had better have a phone number. Sure enough, on Saturday I did get lost and had to find a telephone kiosk in Hope. As I opened the door of the kiosk that happened to be by the side of the church, the bells started ringing. It was a bit frightening. I wondered if it could be an omen. The bells rang in a pleasant evening for us, however. I remember I bought a bottle of Blue Nun and when I see a bottle of that it always reminds me of our first evening out. After that we did see a lot of each other. Linda would either come over to Springwood or I would go to Worksop and help with her horse. She was into showing and had competed at Bakewell when I had been there, so she was more than a competent jockey. She had also hunted with the High Peak. Before long we were going to get engaged before Easter but Mother thought it bad luck to get engaged during Lent, so we put it off till May, in other words till the start of the show-jumping season. I had always said to myself that the massive silver cup I had talked my way into keeping at Coventry a few years earlier would do to buy an engagement ring – I could sell it and put the money towards it. But we still have the silver cup. Linda wasn't having it sold. Instead I sold a pony to the Owens, who had a jewellery shop in Ilkeston, and the engagement ring was part of that deal.

NEW WIFE AND NEW FARM

We did have a very good summer. Linda went to loads of shows with me and Mother came too. We got married on the 17th of October 1964 at the Church at Hope and the reception was in Bamford, where my brother-in-law now lives. Alan Oliver was Best Man. Lots of show-jumpers came: Trevor Banks, the Lanni's, the Barbers, Cynthia Warburton of Tiger Lily fame, and Roy Simpson and Jean his partner, as you would say nowadays.

Roy lived at Selston, not far from Springwood, and owned a very big black and white horse called Champ that had done a bit of show-jumping for him. He came over one day to see if I would have a ride on him. When I had jumped a few fences I knew he really had a big jump that could make one feel very brave. After I had jumped him at a few local shows, we decided to take him to Southport Flower Show, partly to see how he would jump a Championship course, but probably for our own enjoyment; we felt we needed a holiday. He jumped very well on the first two days but on the third day he jumped out of his skin and qualified for the championship at night. Any one who remembers the lights at Southport will know that when the wind blew so did the lights. They were on wires suspended about forty feet from the ground and when the wind blew as you were approaching a fence the light moved and the jump would be in darkness. This happened to Champ and me and it terrified him. He just stood there too frightened to move, petrified – call it what you like. I could feel his heart beating through the saddle flaps. He just would not move so I had to retire.

To add to our troubles with Champ, we had to retire Yorkshireman because his feet had gone. Mr Ball wanted to buy more jumpers but I didn't want him to buy them for me. I had to tell him that now I was married I wished to stay married. I would have to give it up. I had seen so many of my friends' marriages go wrong. In a sport like ours where you are so high one day and so low the next day, you need a lot of comfort – I don't know how else to put it – or you drink too much. And so, at thirty-three, I would give up what someone has called the big time. I might ride a novice occasionally but I would sleep at home every night.

We moved into our first little house at Stainsby near Hardwick Hall. It was very nice before the motorway was built. Although I did not think so to start with, Linda was very sure it was for us. She will probably tell you she was not the best cook in England. The gravy was so lumpy we had to strain it. The first people we invited for dinner were the bank manager and his wife. They were to be with us for seven-thirty. At eight-thirty he rang to say he was very sorry but he and his wife couldn't make it. Thank God; he would never have lent us another penny! Linda learnt after that and has turned out to be a very good cook – except she still can't make round cakes, always square ones. Peter Wragg was farm-manager at Hardwick Hall and a neighbour. He and his wife Rosalind became very good friends of ours. Rosalind loved horses and hunted with the Barlow.

We spent our honeymoon in different places. The first night was at the Haycock, Wansford, then down to Newmarket to the sales, on to Sandown races, and after that it was Newbury to see Mill House and Jay Trump run his first race in England. Jay Trump then went on to win the Grand National. We stayed our last night just outside Oxford.

When we got back from honeymoon the house seemed to welcome us. Rosalind and Peter had made it very comfortable. The fire was going. It was home.

I bought a motorised bike to get me to the farm, which was about four miles away. I did not mind getting up in the morning. and I always did the morning milking. My brother did the evening milking, or one of the miners who helped us. They were very good. They just loved being on the farm and could turn their hand to anything. The bike started to let me down a bit, especially on the way home. I had to wrap up well for the four-mile run. It was likely to refuse to go with a couple of miles still to do and I had to walk with probably two overcoats on, dressed for the North pole, and pushing the bike. I was so exhausted when I got home, I just lay on the floor and went to sleep.

As my brother thought we needed somewhere to rear the young stock and ought to grow corn as well, Linda and I were looking for a farm to rent. At some time during our prospecting for a place Linda told me we were expecting to have a baby. We would have to be settled in before October.

We were runners-up for two Coal Board farms but we did not get them. We were told we ought to get in touch with a man called Marshall who did the letting of farms on the Radbourne, Kedleston, and Ednaston Estates. After sending him our C.V. we soon got a letter back asking us to view a farm over toward Muggington, about six miles from Derby. We did not like the look of that one, made a hasty departure, and wrote and thanked him very much. By return of post he sent the particulars of Shuckton Manor Farm – one hundred and twenty acres, just the size we were looking for. When we got there, talk about rough! The farmyard was three feet deep in muck; part of the cowshed had blown down; the hedges had not been touched for fifty years; the drive was a mess; the water was brought up to a concrete reservoir by a windmill that looked as if it had seen better days and from there to the house, where there was no electricity and no other water laid on. It was very run down. Linda and I were deliberating whether we wanted to live here or bypass this one, when Mr Marshall came over and said, "Would you be interested in this farm?" When we both said we would, he asked us to be at Radbourne Hall on the Tuesday at two o'clock – Champion Hurdle day. We drove up and met Major and Mrs Chandos-Pole, the owners of the Radbourne Estate, who seemed very nice. They asked us if we could be by the phone at four-thirty. The phone rang punctually, and they said we were the new tenants for Shuckton Manor Farm. It was as easy as that.

I must admit they did a lot to the farm and buildings, taking away the part of the cow-shed which had fallen down and putting up a new all-purpose building forty-five feet by thirty feet, which was going to act as a grain-store and cattle-shed. It had cost a thousand pounds and I was expected to pay ten percent back per year. They were also going to put us on mains water when it was available.

Although we had seen the farm in March it was August when we moved in. Linda shortly afterwards gave her notice to the North Notts Farmers. It was not until 25th of September that we took over the land, as it had been let to Trevor Dalton, but he only had the plough-ground. It had been a wonderful hot summer, so we made as much hay as we could and I was able to take all the young stock from Springwood, which relieved a lot of space for more cows there. With that we decided we could put a new set-up at Springwood and up went a new cubicle shed to hold one hundred cows and the barns and the milking parlour to go with it.

On October the 18th, '65, Sarah was born, a day after our first wedding anniversary.

Strangely, it was a very lonely time. We did not seem to know anyone, although we were both born and bred in Derbyshire. In fact we nearly put a notice on the bottom of the drive. Linda joined the Young Wives and the W.I so that she got out and about. One lady used to come and see us quite often on behalf of the Meynell Hunt. In those days as you were tenants of the Radbourne Estate you were made to welcome the hounds if you wanted to or not, although we of course were very pro. Although it didn't help that no-one told you when they were coming. The first you knew was when the heifers started running about. It must have been quite easy to be a Master of Foxhounds in the Sixties. Everywhere you went belonged to some big Estate.

As I said earlier I was to grow corn and rear the heifers. We decided that the new farm was only good enough to grow barley. Winter barley had not really made its mark on farming yet and as it was too light a ground for wheat, we grew continuous spring barley. It suited me to farm this way.

LIFE WITH THE MEYNELL

It strikes me now that as our lives became more and more centred on the Meynell Hunt, my story should be centred on it too. There is no point in giving a complete history from 1966 to 1998, but I ought to give some sort of record of people who played the most important parts in its story and an idea of all the work done to make hunting possible, chiefly by holding all sorts of events and gatherings to raise money for the Hunt Funds and for the sake of jollity and friendship. From now on each year will begin with some notice of what was happening in the affairs of the Meynell and, later, the South Staffordshire Hunt.

1966

In the '65-'66 season we moved to Shuckton Manor, when Dermot Kelly was the Joint-Master and Huntsman. Mr Hodgson was the other Joint-Master with Johnny O'Shea as the Kennel Huntsman. That season Johnny moved to the Cheshire to be Huntsman and was succeeded by Cliff Standing for the '66-'67 season. According to my recollection, the Hunt Supporters' Club came in to being in then and Dr Bowden was the first Chairman. Although farmers did not have to pay anything, when Linda made her first contribution to the Meynell Hunt she gave ten pounds. For others the going rate was sixty pounds for one day a week, ninety pounds for two days and a hundred and twenty pounds for three. Associate Pony Club Members paid twenty pounds but that did not apply to Pony Club kids. Farmers whose sole occupation was farming and whose land lay within the borders of the Meynell Hunt had to pay a five-pound subscription. If you broke a gate out hunting it would cost you ten pounds.

In 1965 Linda had been not only a member of the Young Wives and the W.I, but had also been asked by a hunt-follower to help at the Hunt Fair, which was the big fund-raiser of the day. It was held at the Queen Street Baths, Derby. Everyone involved had his or her own little stall. Linda's was shoes. The helpers always had a look round first and she always came away with some very special things. Linda was helped by Judy Jones from Alton, who hunted along with her husband George. They were always nicely mounted and they always gave a good meet and a good tea afterwards, but then they gave up hunting and behaved very oddly. They turned anti-hunting Yet that is what several hunting people have done.

Linda had been giving more and more help to the Meynell Hunt and the

Dermot Kelly moving off riding Socks at Kirk Langley, Linda on Napoleon and Sarah in my arms

Meynell Pony Club, when she was rung up by Mrs Farquhar, the chairman's wife and sister of Mrs Ley, to see if she would like a gift horse, the one and only Napoleon that was very well known in the Meynell hunting field but was now suffering from occasional azoturia. A lovely little horse, cobby, about 15.1hh, and luckily we found a cure: Epsom kidney powders given one night before hunting and plenty of cantering. Whenever I went out and about people were telling me how well Linda was going and how brave she was. It took a bit of believing because at home I would put up a couple of hurdles in the front field and I had a real job to persuade her to jump them.

The hurdles were there because my brother and I had bought a Flat horse from a trainer named Russ Hobson, for whom Linda had worked as secretary. A lovely dark brown gelding that looked like a typical hurdler. I took out another permit to train. We got John Docker to ride him, who in my opinion was the best amateur around at that time, and also in my opinion should have turned professional. He was the right build, the right height and a horseman. Our first run was at Nottingham. The horse ran all right but was not really in love with the game. We thought we might give him another run. He wasn't looking as well as he did and I couldn't understand what was wrong with him so I called Mr Sadler the vet from Burton-on-Trent. He diagnosed that the horse was being slowly poisoned by the red shavings we were using. They had been treated with something close to a poison and when he lay down the fumes were going up his nose, into his system. The vet declared you should never put a horse on red shavings. I changed him over to white ones and he soon started to pick up. Then we sold him.

1966-67

Mr Hodgson retired from the Joint-Mastership after a year. In this season, Richard Perkins took his place as a Joint-Master. The Hunt Supporters made a donation of fifteen hundred pounds to the Meynell Hunt. The Masters' grant was four thousand, nine hundred and fifty eight pounds. Major Gourlay was Hunt Secretary. His expense-allowance was five hundred pounds, and the Assistant's was fifty pounds.

They hunted seventy days after the opening meet. A total of sixty-one and a half brace were killed which was very satisfactory.

Linda and I worked our week-ends so that she would go hunting on Saturdays and I would baby-sit, and the next Saturday I would watch Derby County and she would have Sarah. (What great players! I have watched Roy McFarland, probably the best centre-half Derby have ever had, and seen their greatest manager, Brian Clough). As Linda was now going hunting regularly, she subscribed in the 1966-67 season and was loving it. She knew lots of people. She was asked to go on the Supporters' Committee. One day, Rob Hutchinson, probably one of the keenest hunting-farmers there has ever been, said to me, "Linda's going well. I could do with you having a ride for me on a horse I've got." I agreed, providing all I had to do was get on it at the meet. So, on that Saturday Mother came over to look after Sarah while Linda and I went hunting and I discovered she really was going well. And that seems to prove that people as well as horses are different when they get a pack of hounds in front of them.

I was sitting in the lounge one Saturday when a chap called Mr Towle knocked on the door. I think just then he had probably had a bit of a fall-out with his daughter and that was why a decent novice that he had was idling in the field. He and his wife enjoyed show-jumping. He had a horse-box that I could use and he would pay all the expenses. It will come as no surprise that we decided to have a go. I didn't pull up any trees with that novice, but it got us out and about a bit. One thing that was quite interesting was Sarah's enjoyment of show-jumping. I remember at a show at Radbourne she was in the pram by the side of the ring and watched every horse go. It kept her very quiet.

The farm was quite prosperous, but I was finding that in our system I was only really busy in the spring and autumn because we only grew spring barley and reared the young stock and in the autumn I drove the combine. In our first year at Shuckton I did the combining over at Springwood and left the combine there all winter. Next year I did Springwood first and Shuckton afterwards, keeping the combine at home, so that we had only one 25-mile journey between the two farms every year.

MY SERVICES REQUIRED BY BERNARD SWAIN

Roy and Jean Simpson came over one day. Roy said his friend Bernard Swain had bred some nice horses and wanted someone to break them for him. He wondered if I would be interested. I said if the money was right I would be. After Bernard had been to discuss the money side, he brought over a grey mare and a chestnut gelding. She was a four-year-old that had already bred a foal. He believed that it was a possibility to breed from a well-grown two-year old. The chestnut now was a lovely horse, 16.2hh, and took no breaking. He had a lovely temperament and could jump, a real natural. What an eventer he would have made!

For a day out I went to Doncaster Sales and got talking to a friend of mine, Mr Smith, who was into show-jumping, and later became one of the top show-jumping judges. As I knew him well enough, I asked him why he was there and he told me he was looking for a point-to-pointer for his son John (who later on in life became Manager of York racecourse). I told him I had a very nice horse at home, which I thought could be made into anything. He got in touch with Bernard and they came over and looked at him. Bernard asked four hundred pounds, and Mr Smith bought him for three hundred and fifty, with a provision that he was to get another fifty pounds when he had won a race. He did not have to wait long as he won his first race on Easter Tuesday at the High Peak races at Flagg. I was there to see him run. He was called Tudor Playboy by Beau Tudor, one of Mr Ball's H.I.S stallions. Ridden by son John, he went on to win nine out of ten races. Mr Smith used to take him hunting on a Monday with the Quorn. He stayed with the Smiths all his life and was put down at the age of twenty-five. So he had a good life all because of a lucky meeting at Doncaster.

Bernard had bought the loveliest horse in Dublin. It was fourth in the middleweight four-year-old class in Dublin that year and he sent it to me to school on a bit. It was very good-looking and the most athletic horse you have ever seen. I put him on a line to lunge over a fence, a thing I always did with a horse I had not seen him jump before. Disappointed is not really be the right word. Devastated would be better. He could hardly get one leg off the ground. I put up a parallel about two feet high and one foot wide. He tried to step on the first part to lever himself off so that he could jump the second part. The moral of this story is: See a horse jump something if you want to buy it. Looks are nothing to go on.

Bernard did send me another horse, called Darren, which we had a bit of fun with. When Darren was being ridden by the Whip, Bernard had seen it jump a huge post-and-rails when he was out with the Grove and Rufford. He came to me in March and I took him to a few friends who had show-jumper and he did show a lot of promise. Linda did the exercising while I got on with the farming. We took him to a few shows in April and he was going really well. At Newark in May, he jumped a clear round and was in the money. We had by now bought ourselves a Land Rover and trailer. When I was loading him up one day, Sarah crawled to the end of the ramp as I led him in. Suddenly he backed out – right over her, without touching her!

We did have a very enjoyable season with Darren, able to go to a few decent shows because he was very brave. He was a special novice. We qualified for the regional Foxhunter Final at Birmingham by winning a Foxhunter at Holmesfield, and to keep him in trim were going to take him to a little country show where the fences were not very imposing. Two days before the event I gave him a jump at home over some really fixed stuff with the assistance of the lad who helped me on the farm. He really was too brave for his own good. When I pulled him out of the trailer on the Saturday he really did look well – a bright bay middleweight about 16.2. I took him over a jump or two in the collecting-ring and he was giving everything about three feet. I thought we had really overdone him. The time came for us to go into the ring. What with the newly painted fences, the huge crowd and the really big substantial course, he gave the first fence about two feet. It was a very long course built by Ixer the Fixer. Every fence we jumped he was coming down nearer to earth until the last fence, which he cleared by just one inch. However, his was the only clear round of the day out of sixty starters, and that qualified us for Wembley – not bad for a first season novice.

When we got to Wembley everything went right. We jumped a clear round in the morning and considering he had had no experience of indoor jumping it was very good. Everything went right, as I said, until the final at night. It was raining stair-rods and in the collecting-ring there was one person hogging the practice fence. They were calling me to go in when I gave him a jump. The fence was very big and he fell through it. He went into the ring frightened to death. I had a lot of trouble over the first three fences. He had the first down and only just managed to jump the next two, but after that he settled down and jumped well. Just one of those things I'm afraid. Luck was not on our side – but that's show-jumping. As Bernard Swain was not really a great show-jumping fan, he decided that Darren would go hunting. That was the last we saw of him. How good he would have been we shall never know.

1967-68

The season was a disaster as far as hunting was concerned, except that cub hunting was very good. With an early start, the hounds were out on thirty-five days and killed forty-five brace which was the most for many years. We had many good hunts in October with the hounds hunting exceptionally well. However, because of the Foot and Mouth, the Opening Meet was cancelled and the hounds did not hunt again that season. I hope we never have a repeat of that.

The Hunt Ball that year was held at Shirley House, home of Major and Mrs Ley. Linda and I went and really enjoyed ourselves. It was probably one of the nicest hunt balls we had been to and made a profit of four hundred pounds. The Hunt Fair was going from strength to strength. Linda had not yet been promoted from shoes. People had realised what bargains could be had and the Fair raised another four hundred pounds. The Hunt Supporters were running lots of functions, such as wine and cheese evenings and supporters' suppers and that year they made a contribution of seventeen hundred pounds to the funds.

The best thing that happened in 1968 was that we had an addition to the family. Timothy was born in the August. What a fine boy he was!

ONE THING LEADS TO ANOTHER

When I had been at Wembley with Darren I ran into an old friend of mine, Fred Harthill of Pennwood, and told him I was looking for a horse to hunt. That was just up Fred's street and he told us to go over, but when we got home I had to ring him for instructions how to get there. He had just come back from Balinasloe – with thirty to forty horses of one sort or another. I always found Fred very straight to deal with and although ninety-five percent of the horses he bought had a little something not quite right the price always reflected that. This chestnut horse we were looking at had a curb.

"I wouldn't bother about that if the price was right," I said to Fred, "but are you sure this horse has hunted?"

"Take it and try it," was his answer. He probably would not have said that to many people but I had known him from when he was a show-jumper himself. When we had first been to Pennwood he had just a few stables and a little indoor school. It was obvious he had done very well from those early dealings. Later he opened his tack shop, which was run by his son, and that also grew and grew.

Anyway, I took the horse home and called him Springwood. As it was the season of the foot and mouth I only managed to cub him a few times, but could tell he had hunted before. I show-jumped him a bit and took him on hunter-trials. In the end I sold him to a client of mine down at Hickstead when I was doing the bookmaking for Ladbrokes. And that leads me into another story – how I came to run the betting on show-jumping for Ladbrokes.

RUNNING A BOOK

I have always liked to gamble. I told Linda that I could be a bookmaker and thought I should learn more about it – only with their money and not mine. When I heard that Ladbrokes were doing the bookmaking at the Royal Windsor Horse Show, I thought there might be an opportunity for me there.

My only transport then was our very old long-wheel-base Landrover, which was about clapped out but it had just gone through its MOT. I put on my best grey suit and set off for Windsor. Speeding down the M1 at about forty-five miles an hour, I suddenly heard the police sirens. I pulled on to the hard shoulder and luckily they could not find too much wrong with it. I had to produce everything at the local police station. Anyway, I still got to Windsor – What a shock! There were Rolls-Royces, Bentleys, and you name it all there. I parked in amongst all these cars. To say it was embarrassing would not be quite the right word. As I had got my best suit on I just could not belong to a vehicle like the old blue Landrover. So I slid gently out on to my hands and knees, closed the door, without bothering to lock it, thinking the thief would be ashamed to be seen anywhere near it, and crept round until I came to an expensive-looking vehicle. Then I stood up.

I paid to go into the show. Among the friends I met were Liz and Ted Edgar. I told them what I was thinking of doing there and they encouraged me, saying it would be a good thing for show-jumping. I waited until the jumping started and then looked round for someone shouting the odds, as one sees on a racecourse, but no, they were in a tent with the Ladbrokes sign outside and all the prices on a board inside. I had a look and could see in a minute that they had not got a clue about show-jumping form. The horses I thought should win were 50/1 and the horses that stood no chance were 5/1. I had a few quid on what I thought would win and Harvey Smith came in and had a bet on a couple of horses. Between us we won more than our expenses.

Who should come in as they were paying out but Raymond Brookes-Ward who I had known for many years. I quietly suggested to him that I ought to run this book for Ladbrokes. As I was checking my winnings he said to Ron Pollard, " I want to introduce you to John Betteridge. He's the chap you ought to have on your side."

Ron, in my mind, was Mr Ladbroke. He was the one who made the book and put out the prices on Miss World contestants, which party would win the General Election, if there would be snow on Christmas Day, and all the other things you could gamble on. Ron was, and still is, a really nice fellow. We got on very well from the start. He said, "Raymond said you want to work for us," and I told him I thought it would be very good for show-jumping and I would like to see it run on the right lines. He wanted to know a bit about me and I think I impressed him.

"We have one more class tonight. You tell me what you think will win, we'll make that favourite and who will be second and so on down to tenth place."

In the event I wasn't far away. He said he was very impressed and asked if I would I go to London to meet Cyril Stein who was the Managing Director of Ladbrokes. Could I make it the following Wednesday, about eleven-thirty?

It was dark when I made my way back to the Land Rover. There was no need to go on my hands and knees as just about everyone else had gone.

Ron had said that Ladbrokes would pay all my expenses, so on Wednesday I had my breakfast on the train, and took a taxi to the offices. I just made it by eleven-thirty. Ron was there and took me straight through. He introduced me to Mr Stein. We had a chat and then he told Ron to show me how to make a book, and that took a bit of learning. Making a book was all about percentages and to make it pay you had to be one hundred and ten percent, but I didn't bother too much. Ron said that one of his girls would help me. As I was representing Ladbrokes I must always dress well and stay at the best hotels – which suited me fine – but we always had to keep a low profile. At Hickstead for example we had a tent behind the Grandstand and out of the TV coverage.

There were a few dishonest people who would back a horse after it had jumped a clear round, but we soon sussed that out. We had someone at the ringside to signal to us what was going on. I thought we were doing very well, not only did we do every Hickstead but quite a lot of other shows as well. Very few people recognised me as someone who knew about show-jumping. With my suit on I could pass as someone from the London office but one Hickstead I nearly overdid it. I was in the bar the night before the jumping Derby and as we could not bet on Sunday I had to do the betting on Saturday. When Brian Dye came in and asked me for a price on his own horse for the Derby I gave him 33/1.

"What about a finish in the top ten then?"

"You're on!"

That was more to his liking and he put on thirty pounds for a finish in the top ten at the same odds, 33 to 1.

Mr Stein and Ron Pollard came down to see how things were going and liked the bets, apart from the one I had made with Brian Dye. Mr Stein thought it was the kind of bet Ron, but not the likes of me, would have made.

When the time came for Brian to enter the ring the three of us knew that this was the big one as far as we were concerned. If Brian was placed in the top ten and won his bet I would have to pay out nine hundred and ninety pounds, plus his thirty-pound stake back. He started off by jumping out of his skin over the first few. I was having palpitations. He had a fence down. Then some more. Luckily for me he finished eleventh.

Another quite frightening day came after I had put out the prices and a few people walked in to the tent. One chap said, "I want five hundred pounds to win on Mallory Spen's horse." Its price was 4/1. It was a speed class and it was the favourite, and I thought it would win, but the bet went down for him anyway. Yet back he came, "I want five hundred on the second favourite." That went down for him too. Even then he came back, "I want three hundred on …....." (I forget which one it was) and it was at 10/1. I obliged (that's what you call it when you accept a bet from a punter), but that went down as well. I never saw him again.

I enjoyed it; we weren't making a great profit, but just holding our own. I was learning the trade, and considered I was doing a service. I felt the business was very straight. It happens to be very difficult to stop a show-jumper from winning, because often the more you look as though you are pulling them the better they jump.

However, the B.S.J.A wrote to Ladbrokes to say that they were going to suspend betting on show-jumping. I rang Mike Ansell and had a long talk to him on the telephone telling him that I thought the betting was doing no harm to the jumping game. If it was I would never be in it. I had two small children and wanted them to go into show-jumping and would be quite happy if they did, but it made no difference. They stopped it and there was no more I could do. It had been a nice little earner for me during the summer and I enjoyed it too.

A Fox from Bodens Thorns

This story was given to Anne Feversham by Sir Peter Farquhar, Bart., D.S.O., Master and Huntsman of the Meynell from 1934 – 1938, Joint Master and Huntsman of the Whaddon Chase from 1934 – 1938, and Master and Huntsman of the Portman from 1947 – 1959.

It was in 1931 when I took over the Mastership of the Meynell Hounds – this was the time of the great depression, and agriculture, in common with all other industries, was going through a bad patch.

The Meynell country was then, as it is today, largely a grass country made up of dairy farms, many of less than a hundred acres. Most of these small dairy farmers were barely keeping their heads above water and I well remember the care we took not to add to their troubles by causing damage in the hunting-field.

The depression was also having its effect upon the Hunt finances – many large landowners, who normally supported the Hunt generously, were foregoing their rents in order to help their tenants, and in consequence were obliged to curtail their subscriptions, whilst some of the smaller subscribers had been forced to give up hunting altogether.

It was therefore with considerable difficulty that we were able to keep the Hunt going at all during those lean years.

There was, however, one Member of the Hunt who remained a tower of strength to me throughout that period. He was a retired Derby business-man who had made a large fortune in something or other during the Great War, but, unlike many of his ilk, he was a genuine sportsman, if ever there was one. Foxhunting in general, and the Meynell hounds in particular, were the passion of his life and his generosity was unbounded. Not only was his subscription magnificent, but one had only to mention in a casual way that a new boiler, or some other adjunct to the Kennel, was required, and it would appear miraculously before the week was out. It was not only on account of his generosity to the Hunt, but because of his intense interest in the sport and anxiety to be of assistance to me in every possible way, that I became much drawn to him and despite the difference in our ages we became close friends.

One day I learned that a certain covert in the country, which had been famous in former times, was coming up for sale. This covert had been much neglected; there was no "bottom" in it and in consequence it had of late years been hardly worth drawing. On my mentioning the matter to my friend, he at once offered to attend the sale and, if possible, purchase the covert himself. He was as good as his word and more, for not only did he purchase the covert, but immediately replanted it with privet and other low-growing shrubs which provide good holding cover for foxes, and I had every hope that before long the covert would become a sure find once more.

Soon after he had completed the replanting of his covert my friend became seriously ill. I went to visit him and it was obvious from his appearance that he had not got many days to live. But as usual he was full of interest in the latest doings of the hunt and made me give him a field by field account and the outcome of every run we had had that week.

At last, when I got up to go, he said, "How I should have loved to have seen a good fox go away from that covert of mine and give you all a good run, but I am afraid it is too late, I am only fit for the knacker now."

A few days later he died and I attended the funeral at the Parish Church of Quarndon, which is on the outskirts of Derby and from whence I gathered that his family originated.

One day during the following season, hounds met at Etwall. There was a tremendous scent and we had a great hunt of fifty minutes in the morning, killing our fox in the open. We finished not far from my friend's covert, but the replanting was little more than a year old and I did not think it would hold. I decided to give it a miss and indeed I had not bothered to draw it at all that season and moved off to draw another place. As I rode along, hounds clustering round my horse's legs, eager for their second fox, I began to think of my friend and for some reason (which I cannot explain), I felt a compelling urge to try the covert after all.

Calling to the Field-Master that I had changed my mind about the draw, I sent the Whippers-in on, and put hounds into the covert. Almost immediately a hound opened and, a few seconds later, a holloa from the west side told me that a fox was away. As in the morning, there was a screaming scent and hounds fairly flew, and I had all to do to keep in touch with them.

As I galloped along in their wake, it quickly struck me that the fox was taking a very unusual line. So far as I knew there was no earth he could be making for and certainly there was no covert in the direction we were going. Such was the pace that within a few miles only half a dozen members of the field, the first Whippers-in and I were in touch. Presently I saw that hounds had checked on the bank of the Mackworth Brook, which was then in full spate. One by one they slipped in, shook themselves on the opposite bank, and took up the line again. It seemed incredible that a beaten fox could have faced such a torrent. As luck would have it, a bridge was at hand and I and the remnants of my field pressed on after the fast-disappearing pack, though our horses by this time could scarcely raise a canter. After a further two or three miles (by this time, for the sake of our horses, we had decided to stick to the road), houses began to make their appearance and I realized we were in the outskirts of Derby. It was also clear that the fox was sinking, scarcely able to hold the line. Soon the road became a street with houses close set on either side and I began to worry how much further into the city hounds would take us. Suddenly there was a savage burst of music and clattering round the corner of the street I saw that hounds had at last run into their fox at the foot of a churchyard wall.

I soon had the brush and mask off, and after we had rested our horses for a few minutes, I looked round for some landmark which would indicate our nearest way home. Happening to glance up at the church tower, I suddenly realized it was Quarndon Church where my friend had been buried. Handing my horse to a bystander, I entered the church gate and soon found the grave.

I still had the fox's brush in my hand, and with a feeling of awe and reverence, not unmixed with fear, I laid it upon the headstone. As I stood with bowed head looking at the newly-inscribed lettering I was conscious of a figure beside me. It was my friend's son (one of the few who had survived the run).

"What a curious thing, "I said, "that this gallant fox should have been found in your father's covert and died within a few yards of his grave, after what must be one of the greatest runs in the history of the Meynell."

He smiled gently, "You will think it even more curious when I tell you that today is the first anniversary of Father's death."

1968-69

There were going to be a few changes as the season went on. Cliff Standing was going as huntsman to the Zetland. It was also going to be Richard Perkins's last season. He had been a very good Field-master. Dr Bowden was giving up the Chairmanship of the Supporters' Club. He certainly had done a very good job to get it up and running. The Supporters' Club again raised seventeen hundred pounds that year. It was to be taken over by Hugo McGhee.

In 1968, we took on another farm adjoining ours. Fred Wood had decided to retire so we added another fifty acres. However, our landlady was really getting impossible. We were always being told that this was wrong, or that was wrong. There were a lot of farmers emigrating at that time, so I sent for all the particulars of the farms around Perth in Australia. I was keen to go; I thought the children would have a better life and if Tim wanted to go into farming there would be a better future for him there than there would be here, but in the end Linda didn't fancy the move. I have kept the particulars of these farms and perhaps one day I shall go and have a look at them.

We turned some of the out-buildings into a few more loose-boxes for the horses we now stabled. I was hunting a bit more. One day, Richard Meade was out hunting and we were talking in Osmaston Park. I clearly remember what he said:

"You've got a good reputation for selling hunters. Why don't you do it a bit more seriously?"

"Well, I'm too busy farming," I replied.

"Perhaps you are, but think of it this way – You can get lots of people to sit on a tractor and drive it down a field, turn around and drive it back again."

HORSES SOLD TO PATRICK DRURY-LOWE

Richard was a big friend of Dermot Kelly, who was Huntsman as well as Joint-Master, and whether he had a word with him I don't know but at a wine and cheese evening at Uttoxeter Racecourse Dermot came over and said he would like me to meet Captain Patrick Drury-Lowe. After the introductions, Dermot said, "Patrick is going to be my Joint-Master next season and I would like you to buy all his horses." That was a bolt from the blue, to be followed with the news from Patrick that he wanted only grey horses. I had actually seen him when he had had a day with us (and had bought a big black horse of Dermot's called Socks) and to be quite honest considered he was not cut out to be a jockey. I knew it would be a tough order to fall on any horses, let alone grey ones. He evidently wanted all grey horses because of a picture he had seen painted by Lionel Edwards showing hounds going away from Hilton Gorse in 1928 with Sir Harold Nutting with them all mounted on grey horses. The Meynell have always been known for grey horses. I thought I had better ask Patrick what sort of money he was prepared to pay for a hunter, bearing in mind he was about fifteen stone. When he said he would give one thousand pounds for a hunter I could have dropped. At that time you could buy a decent hunter for two hundred and fifty pounds! I suppose in these days it would be about ten to twelve thousand pounds.

The first horse I bought was from Trevor Banks from Yorkshire. I had to say the horse was hardly up to Patrick's weight but as he would be having two horses a day the jump was more important and this horse did jump. I saw him jump about five foot nine in Trevor's indoor school. He was also a very good horse in front, which is what you need to hunt with the Meynell. As long as the front end is over, the back end does not matter so much. Trevor said, "Take him and have a day. Let me know what you think." We had a tremendous hunt from Wardley and I am afraid he got a few cuts and bruises but Trevor was very good. He told me to get him better and then have the vet. Anyway, we bought him. He was passed on to Dermot Kelly to hunt hounds off and when Patrick got John King to paint their picture, Dermot is riding him with his arm in a sling, having broken his collar-bone the week before.

I had asked how much he was paying for a Whip's horse and the price he gave was three hundred pounds. I bought one from Frank Salisbury of Aston on Trent. We called him Grey Lag; the one we had from Trevor Banks we called Nice Guy.

One of my classic stories about horse-dealing begins one day in May when Patrick rang and asked if we had heard of a grey horse in Scotland belonging to a Major Borthwick. He had bought the horse in Ireland from a fellow called Ned Cash for his sons, but they had both been killed in a car crash. Patrick said that the horse was on the market now. He had looked them up in *Who's Who* and they seemed to be all right.

"Steady on," I said, "there's a bit more to buying horses than *Who's Who*. Anyway I couldn't possibly buy a horse for you until I'd seen it hunt or had hunted it myself, or even cubbed. I'll be interested in September if they still have the horse."

One day in September he rang and reminded me about the horse, that they still had. He arranged a meeting, as I had suggested. We were to have a day with the Eglington. Baldwin, the chauffeur, would pick us up and we would catch the midnight sleeper from Derby.

That's what we did. It wasn't long before he was paddling into my compartment with a bottle of whisky saying, "I can't sleep, let's have a drink." I just had a small glass thinking I had got to keep my wits about me if I was cubbing, but he came into my compartment again about six-thirty, dressed up to go in his hunting gear saying, "Come on. It's time you had your breeches and boots on. We're due in Kilmarnock at seven-thirty."

I replied, "If you think I'm walking across Kilmarnock station, in hunting kit, you've got another think coming."

Their chauffeur met us at the station. He drove us up this very long drive and we came to a castle – and I mean a castle, a proper one with turrets and the lot. We went straight to have a quick look at the horse. What a lovely grey, about 16.2, with loads of dapples! My first imprsssion was: "Hardly big enough." Then it was into breakfast in this huge dining-room with everything set out on a very large sideboard. Anything you wanted – kippers, kidneys, every kind of egg. I really tucked in. Patrick could not eat a thing. They had arranged the meet for nine-thirty. I was really looking forward to riding him. George Orr (who later became our Kennel Huntsman), was Huntsman there.

The hounds hunted very well. I could not find a really good fence, although I had been told I had free range, but I was still looking after Patrick. He was riding a strong horse and was a bit nervous. I did manage to find a small hedge and put him over it. Then I said to Patrick, "Yes we'll have him. I think he'll jump the Meynell fences but I'm not exactly sure. We'll have to chance it." The upshot was that we bought him for eight hundred pounds.

Only then did I ask, "We came by train and we're staying the night, but how are we getting home?"

"We're flying from Glasgow to East Midland and Baldwin is picking us up there," said Patrick as if there was nothing special in it, but I had never been in a plane before.

"In that case," said I, "I've looked after you all day, now you'd better look after me."

We got above the clouds and the whole sky looked as though we were floating on cotton wool. So we called him Cotton Wool. In the picture painted by John King, Patrick is riding Cotton Wool and George is the Whip riding Grey Lag.

Cotton Wool, the third horse I sold to Patrick, arrived with us on the Wednesday. I rode him round the farm on Thursday and Friday and hunted him on Saturday at Radbourne. I did jump some big fences including a parallel of rails where they were putting gas-mains through. Pat Rohan, the racehorse trainer, was out that day. I told him the horse's history and later on he came to me and said, " That horse will do," in his Irish brogue, but we had used hunting-time to talk to each other, much to Dermot's annoyance. (I think Pat went to train in Dubai).

At first Carol Archer was his groom: then he had a stud-groom called Bill when Carol left to start her own livery yard. Kevin, who had been a Whip with the South Staffs, came to help Bill soon afterwards.

I could not go on finding grey horses so I was ready to look at anything. I bought a nice chestnut horse, a good jumper, up to his weight. Soon I was not only buying horses for him but for him to mount his friends on as well. I went to look at a very good horse called Facey from Mr Barker of Northallerton and stayed with the Barkers overnight before having a day with the Bedale. I did jump some useful things that day and as he had won the Grade B Championship at Peterborough I bought him. Prince Charles, who was a friend of Patrick's, started to hunt with us and he always asked if he could ride Facey. He was a favourite of the Prince's.

I was hunting on a horse I had got from Pennwood, half-brother to David Broome's Top of the Morning, (I was told he was the half-brother but

Patrick riding By Chance

one never really knew). Patrick came over to me and said, "I like that. Ought I to have a ride on him?" Although he was only five years old he knew plenty so that when Patrick got off him he asked how much I wanted for him. I said, "One thousand pounds." It was the most I had ever asked for a hunter but Patrick said he would have him. We decided to call him By Chance. He and Facey were with Patrick until they were twenty-seven and twenty-five respectively. They did him well.

Other horses I bought for him were Perky, a very high-class horse, from Ralph Raper at Doncaster: Marble Arch, a grey, a magnificent type of weight-carrier that was really for his friends; and another grey was from John Masserella, a lovely big horse, but he was a bit chicken for this country, so I sold him to Frank Gilman of Grittar fame, who hunted him with the Cottesmore for a number of seasons. Frank was a hard man to deal with. He sat in our kitchen for two hours arguing over fifty pounds – but he loved it.

I had bought a nice liver-chestnut mare from Fred Harthill and I was on my way home with it when I came across the hounds as they were drawing the Brick Yard. I stopped the lorry and Patrick came over and said, "I need a Whip's horse." I was able to tell him I had one on board and dropped the ramp. He just said, "I like that. I'll have it." I took it out to try it on the Saturday. It was all right, a bit blood for George, but he coped with it.

One day Patrick came out with a new idea: "I don't want to breed any horses but I would like to buy some young horses that would hunt for me in the future. If you see anything buy it."

At Leicester Sales one day and I happened to see just the sort Patrick was looking for – a big bright bay, 16.3, five years old. It had hunted on Exmoor and seemed to jump well enough in the paddock so I bought it. That night I rang Patrick to say I had started a stud of young horses for him. He was very excited and asked when I was taking it out. I said Thursday at Croxall. "I'll be out" he said. The horse behaved himself very well at the meet. Patrick called the horse Time Lag. After a few more hunts I said to Patrick, "This horse is all right, but not for you. I think we should stick to the tried and trusted way; they must have show-jumped." So we went off the idea of inexperienced young horses. Let someone else make them and we would buy the finished article.

THE HUNTSMAN'S HORSES

At the end of the season Dermot also said, "If you come across a horse for me buy it." It happened that I had been buying a few horses from Maurice Ellison because the jumping people around Liverpool had really no outlet for show-jumpers that did not make the grade. (I had bought one from Maurice for James Stanford, a big friend of Dermot's, who named him Sefton. Failed show-jumpers for hunting are not over-dear. To make him a bit cheaper, Sefton had only one eye but he was a good horse, about 17.1hh, and carried James very well for a few seasons). The reason I went to Maurice this time was that I had seen a horse at his place, a class horse, but I had no client for him until now when Dermot wanted one. We both drove up to see it. Because Dermot liked his horses to trot into a really big fence, they had to have ability to turn and that meant real athletic ability. I had seen this horse a few times at Maurice's and had always liked him and now he gave a faultless show in front of Dermot and me. Then I had a sit on him and jumped a very big hedge off the road on him. We bought him and Dermot turned him out through the summer.

When he got him back into work he rang me and said, "I have cubbed this horse today. He'll kill me. You have a ride on him." Hounds next met at Norbury. When I was queuing to jump a hedge – I would be about tenth – he saw the other horses jumping and suddenly set off, scattering everyone in front of me, just like a pack of cards, with me shouting, "Let me through please!" We got to the other side, just. The next hazard was to go over a sleeper bridge over a stream. The people in front of me were going through a gate. He thought they were jumping, we were off the bridge into the stream and back on the bridge before one could blink, he was so quick. So I went to Dermot and told him what was happening because I knew he didn't like being disturbed when hunting hounds (In fact when he was in scarlet, he was a difficult man, but more of that shortly). I took it home with me and between us we rode it for five hours on the Wednesday and then I hunted it on the Thursday. It was no better, just could not stand the sight of hounds. I had to ring Maurice and say, "This horse is no good as a hunter. Will you help me to sell him?" but he didn't want to know. He had sold the horse and that was the end of it. I suggested to Dermot that we should send him to Melton Sales and split the loss. You can't win them all, or so we thought..

Dermot was one for having an amateur Whip and one of them was Robin Smith-Ryland. One had to feel a bit sorry for him with Dermot giving him a hard time, but I believe he went on to be a very good Joint-Master of the Warwickshire and he also had a stint at the Quorn. Another Whip who had a good upbringing under Dermot was Ian Farquhar. I think he only had one season but he went to hunt the Bicester and then the Duke of Beaufort's and he certainly made a success of them.

As I suggested, Dermot and I didn't always see eye to eye. He sent me home three times one season, once for not doing anything amiss in my opinion. Once he said I was schooling while they were digging a fox out. In fact I was looking after Patrick, his Joint-Master, and went behind a hedge, having to walk over a small log in a gateway on the way. The second time I jumped a boundary hedge in front of him, but I was only competing with Pat Rohan. The third time Dermot shouted to us to spread out as we approached a newly cut-and-laid hedge. We did spread out and I thought I had jumped it particularly well. He came over and said, "Who told you to jump that hedge?" It was no good having an argument with him then, but as Linda and I were making our way home we happened to run into him.

"I think this time you have been a bit unfair, Dermot," I said.

What came back was, "One more word and you won't come out again this season."

That night I went to see Col. Farquhar and said I was not happy with the treatment I was getting from Mr Dermot Kelly. I told him what was happening and he promised to have a word.

The next morning who should drive into the yard but Mr Kelly. He wound down his window and said, "You think I have been a bit unfair to you."

"Whoops! I'd better be careful here or I might not hunt again," I said to myself, but blurted out, "Well, yes, I do."

"So do I. Let's go in and have a cup of tea," Off a horse or out of scarlet he was probably one of the nicest men I have met and he was a perfect gentleman to sell a horse to.

The very day Dermot and I were talking about sending the very awkward horse that had come from Maurice Ellison to the Melton Sales, Jane Whitfield (as she was then, later to become Mrs Ryman and then Mrs Michael Clayton) asked me if I had got a horse suitable for a friend of hers who was a good jockey but was living in London and wanted a nice horse to ride in Rotten Row. I told her about this horse that was a nice ride but too hot to hunt. The woman from London (I think she was called Mrs Packshaw but I can't be certain) was interested just the same: she rang and arranged to come and see him on the Sunday, and asked if she could bring her own tack. I told her she was welcome and could bring all that Moss Bros. had got as well. She came by car and we both went for a ride. I could see in a moment that she was a good jockey. You can always tell a good jockey by the hang of the leg: I learnt that years ago. He was a really nice horse and went well for her but he just could not get on with hounds. She liked him so much she said, "I'll find a bed and breakfast and be with you in the morning to try him in some really heavy traffic." I knew he was all right but she wanted to find out for herself. She duly arrived at eight prompt and he behaved himself beautifully; so she had a lorry sent for him.

A few days later she was on the phone and I thought, "Oh dear. What's gone wrong?" but she actually wanted to report that the horse had travelled down well. She had ridden on Rotten Row and he had behaved superbly. When she was riding him she felt like a queen. All's well that ends well.

Another one of Dermot's deals was a chestnut mare, called Satisfaction, that was surplus to his requirements. She was about 16.2 middleweight. While we were finding a client for her, we had her at our place and Linda hunted her. She rated her as one of the best five she had ridden. At length Dermot rang saying that a chap from the Quorn would be interested in buying her. So off I went for a day with the Quorn but the possible customer did not buy her. After that it seemed to get around that I had a mare of Dermot's to sell and that it offered a chance of a passport to have a day free of charge with the Meynell. We had a chap down from the Cheshire who had heard we had got one to sell and wanted to try this mare out. Ted Greenaway, the vet, rang me and said unless it came down the ramp nostrils flaring the customer would not buy it, but the chap had forgotten most of his hunting gear and we had to dress him. In the field, he was jumping here there and everywhere. What a nightmare! On top of that he didn't buy the horse. All he wanted was a free day with the Meynell.

So the way we worked when selling a hunter from then on was that anyone interested in it would come here to look at the horse and try it here. Customers could have all the trial they wanted but if they wanted to hunt it, they would first have to have it vetted locally and then they could hunt it for a day. If after that they thought it wasn't suitable or didn't like it, they could return it if it was in the same condition as when they took it out, meaning with no cuts or bruises and sound. We learnt to do that from the experience with Satisfaction. She was a tough mare and was eventually sold to a new Joint-Master of the Belvoir, Major-Gen. Wildbore Smith.

1969-70
THE MEYNELL JOINED BY THE SOUTH STAFFS

The season was memorable for the Meynell Hunt. We were going to amalgamate with the South Staffs. I didn't agree with it then and I still think we could have managed on our own. Any hunt thinking of amalgamating should think twice. They said there were only eighteen subscribers in the South Staffs but in the first season there were sixty-eight subscribers, and by the 1972-73 season we had one hundred and twenty-six. It was certainly them and us for a long time.

Patrick Drury-Lowe joined the Mastership. Major Gourlay gave up the Secretary's job and Miles Porter came in as Secretary; his proper title was Lt-Col. R M Macnish-Porter.

A lady who was a great help to me and the hunt in general was Mrs Ley. She bought a green horse from Ireland through Frank Allen (I think that was right), and his name was Romany. Our friendship went back many years. My first scarlet coat for competing at Harringay in 1950 was borrowed from the Leys. I did have some very good days with them. She was getting on in years but still went very well and she kept the field in order. She would have no barging or pushing. She would want to know the name of any new person who came out. She would say, "Linda, who is that man?" or "Who is that woman?" She was sister to Mrs Farquhar whose daughter Angie married Richard Meade. She and her husband were the proper old Meynell and everyone had tremendous respect for both of them. One night she rang up and said, "Would you like a day with the South Notts tomorrow? I'll pick you up in the car and George will take the horses." As we were going to the meet she said, "Don't tell the Secretary, (who happened to be Mr Wakefield), that the horse you ride is mine because then, as you are a farmer, it will only cost you a farmer's cap."

Another day when I was going out with the South Notts I said to Mr Wakefield, "I'll just pay for half a day; I don't want this horse to have too long a day." He said that was all right. However, I saw him at about 1.30. and he greeted me with, " You're still out I see!" I explained, "I'm enjoying myself so much you can have the other half of the day's subscription."

THE SEVENTIES

1970-71

In this season we had the same Joint-Masters and Kennel Huntsman. The only change was that Rob Hutchinson took over as Chairman of the Hunt Supporters from Hugo McGhee. The reputation of the Meynell seemed to be growing. Patrick Drury-Lowe was very popular and brought in a lot of people who had probably not heard of us.

Amongst those who hunted with the Meynell at that time were :

H.R.H. The Prince of Wales.

Maj-Gen D'Avigor Goldsmith who had some very good racehorses.

Nick Budgen who went on to be an M.P. and would always stand up and be counted when they were debating fox-hunting in the House of Commons;

Chris Collins who was a very well-known Point-to-Pointer and Hunter 'Chase jockey, had a very good horse called Credit Call, which he sold to Joey Newton. He had many good horses that W.A Stevenson trained for him. He went on to win the Pardebecha in Czechoslovakia. It was rumoured that he carried a pocket full of fivers in case he broke a gate or two. I sometimes followed him a bit but I never saw him break one;

Lord Manton who was a well known point-to-point jockey had a few days with us. He used to ride for Lance and Urky Newton who was now a subscriber;

John Stevens used to come from London to keep horses with Ronnie Marmont. He broke his neck,or rather a bone in it, that stopped him jumping and he became a Joint-Master a few years later.

Captain George Jeffreys was becoming a regular subscriber. He was married to Liz, one of the Meynell girls;

Ruggles Brise used to come from Essex. Linda jumped on him one day, poor man;

Reg Hollingshead, the trainer from Upper Longden;

Viscount Ingistre, the Earl of Shrewsbury, who had a few days with us;

Peter Lyster and his wife used to come up from Hertfordshire twice a week;

And Richard Meade also hunted with us twice a week.

Richard actually got me a livery (we had started to take a few liveries; they helped us pay for a groom). It was a lovely big horse called Budget, belonging to the Cootes from Devon, that had won everything when shown in hand and then won everything when ridden by David Tatlow, including the Supreme Hunter Championship at the White City. At the start, Richard did not know what a dog he had taken on. Budget would be cantering across a field and would suddenly stop dead. Nothing you could do would move him, so you just lit another cigarette and he moved off when he was ready. When the Cootes asked Richard if he would make an event-horse out of him, I thought he would never get past the first stage of dressage. He would be just the same – come to a halt and not move again. When Richard first hunted him, at Cubley, he must have had seven attempts to jump a small tiger trap. The next time was at Ednaston and he didn't fare any better there.

It was too much for Richard, winner of a Gold Medal at the Olympics: "You ride him." he told me. The Cootes were really disappointed. They had bred him and thought the world of the horse. So I started schooling him over show jumps, poles on the ground, anything that did not look too solid. Eventually we gained his confidence and he made a good hunter and enjoyed hunting. Richard had another day on him and on the strength of it said to the Cootes, "You had better send him down to my trainer Dick Stillwell." He had him a month but Dick said he couldn't get on with him, and so Budget came back. We took him to a few local show-jumping shows and then we asked Janet Hodgson if she would event him for the Cootes. We took him to Brigstock for his first event, still not knowing if he did his halt whether she could get him to move again. As a precaution, before he went in to do his dressage, Janet gave him a flat-out gallop round the park. He forgot his trick and went round. She actually took him through to Intermediate and then he was retired to the hunting-field in Devon.

Patrick was enjoying his second season and was occasionally being the Field-Master. He was also hunting with the Quorn on Mondays and he often took me with him. He said at the end of the season, "If you would like to go to Halls at Market Harborough and get yourself a new hunting coat, that will be my thank-you as I have really enjoyed myself this season." The following season my present was a pair of hand-made hunting boots.

Jim Thorneycroft was a first-season subscriber. His father was Master of the Vale of Clettwr and his sister helped us with the horses one season and hunted up here for a bit. I think she had had a tiff with a boy-friend. Jim was probably one of the first "D.I.Y.s" – he did the horse himself although it was stabled here. It was a big bay horse I had bought from Pennwood. It had got a dropped hip but David Campbell, who was our vet then, said it would stand up to hunting. Jim bought it, as it was only a cheapy, or, as Fred Harthill used to say, at bargain-basement price. Jim was working for John German. I think it was his first job but he used to go very well – a real enthusiast. He went on to work for the National Trust and then moved South.

Moonbeam was another horse who did his job very well – another case of the right horse for the right jockey. Sue Hawley was the buyer of Moonbeam. He was just the thing for a girl's horse, a chestnut gelding, 16.0hh, quite a blood type. Sue came into the yard one day and said she was looking for a hunter. She was an attractive girl; actually I think she was a model – and a better looker than a jockey. The family had the colour works in Duffield. She liked the look of Moonbeam but had nowhere to keep him in the winter, and asked if she could keep him at livery if she bought him. She rode him out and she hunted him quietly. The meet she really looked forward to was Boxing Day at Kedleston. It was only a few miles from her home and all her friends from Duffield would turn out on their feet. That was the highlight of her hunting year. She was a good owner and a good client at livery..

1971-72

Peter Lyster became Joint-Master and Field-Master for the Meynell. He did have one very good horse, Brandy, and you would have to say that he was probably Peter's best-ever horse and one of the best five that had ever crossed the Meynell country. We had some of the golden days of hunting then. Peter was a very good Field-Master, never too proud to ask for a lead, and I can honestly say I never heard him curse anyone. It is the Field-Master who suffers from nerves who shouts and gets very cross.

George Orr became Kennel Huntsman. I had met him when he was hunting with the Eglington and I was trying Cotton Wool for Patrick. He certainly was going to find this country very different. Derek Egdell, our Kennel Huntsman since '68, went as Huntsman to the York and Ainsty South where I believe he had a bad fall. He and Sid Williams used to come over and we would shoot rabbits. They stood in the back of the Land Rover while I drove. We got very good and it was great fun. I threatened to put ramps over the hedges, as the Land Rover was not a very good jumper.

That season the Hunt Club financed the building of the new whelping boxes, and they insured the hunt lorry.

VARIOUS DEALS

An important source of my horses was the Maguires, Jimmy and Tony. I first went there when Maurice Ellison had taken me and they were probably taking delivery of about a hundred horses from Ireland. Their place was just outside Wigan. Open coal mines surrounded it. Although they were crowded into every nook and cranny, the horses were certainly well looked after.

Another person who I bought from was Paul Goddard (who used to hunt with the High Peak but later started the Moorland Harriers and hunted them for a number of years).

I thought we would name the horses after well-known Meynell coverts so that a horse that I bought from John Masserella that year, 1972, was named Parson's Gorse – Joe Morley's covert, which always holds foxes. We show-jumped him and I even won a Foxhunter on him at a show in the hospital grounds at Mickleover. (That was run by the father of my very great friend, Miss Fay Fitch, later to become Mrs Doug Hibbert). Linda hunted him one day from Radbourne and came back furious. "This horse stopped and I've fallen off him." Despite that, he was a nice horse, about 16hh. After I had sold him to Judy Bradwell, who evented him, I was spectating at Chatsworth when I heard a great crash behind me. "There's only one horse who could make such a noise!" I thought. Sure enough it was him. He had hit the fence. The next time we saw him he was going round Badminton with Julian Seaman. (He went round Badminton and Burghley for years). Dorian Williams, the B.B.C commentator, said, "Here comes the Reverend by the Parson." He was no more by the Parson than the man in the moon.

Another one I sold that year was a grey mare that I had bought from Barry Pearson-Adam. I had gone to Hilton Park to watch the jumping and to look for a hunter. I saw this lovely grey mare, 16.1hh. and I asked Barry if the mare was for sale. Anyway she was, so I bought her there and then and could hardly believe my luck. I had hunted her a few times when I got a call from the Duchess of Devonshire asking me to get a horse for Lady Sophie, her daughter, to hunt. So I sold her the mare. It was just thirty-six years since we had sold them Nanette, my first good pony.

Another little story comes from Hilton Park. I was watching the jumping when in came a nice black horse ridden by Cathy Evans (later to become Mrs. Robin Simpson). It jumped all right but was not a champion. I went to her and asked if she would sell it.

"Yes," she said, "I want to make six of it."

"I won't bid you. I'll have to write you the cheque now," was my response. I wrote it out for six hundred pounds and gave it to her. She couldn't believe her luck – until she saw that I had taken her "six" for six hundred and not six thousand. It just shows how easy it is to be wrong, though I did buy it a few months later and sold it on to Cedric Stevenson from Mappleton.

I learnt a new lesson when John Masserella rang up and wanted something special. I was able to say, "I just happen to have the horse you are looking for." I couldn't believe it – a man who had bought hundreds of horses wanting to have a horse of mine. Anyway, he came down, looked it over, and said he would have it provided it went by the vet. He would send Gibson from Oakham. The horse was passed by the vet all right, but it got me thinking that if a man like him needed horses vetting before he would buy them, then I ought to as well. So, after that, if ever I bought one I always had it vetted. My instructions were: "Eyes, heart, and a quick look-over." I would already have ridden them, so I knew about their wind. I used to get the people who I was buying a horse from to call on their own vet. As I saw it, their own vet would know if there had been anything seriously wrong.

Zardie came from the Maguires. I took her on the ride with forty or fifty of the Pony Club members over Okeover. It was nearly as enjoyable as being out hunting. I sold her to Carol Dalton (later to become Mrs. Martin Price) and she carried on hunting for years.

I sold John Crooks a mare called Gerty, which I had bought from Fred Harthill, and John had actually bought for his wife, Sue. John had the mare for years; in fact I think she spent the rest of her days at Alkmonton. What good parties the Crooks had!

Although the vet said he had flat feet, I also bought Sceptre, a chestnut horse, from the Maguires, and sold him to Sheila Jones from Sutton Coldfield. He lasted her a long time.

Rob Hutchinson came with me to Pennwood where he bought a grey mare, just arrived from Ireland, with a rough tail that reached the floor and and a long mane to match. We saw her jump an enormous fence in the loose school. She was more like a gelding. Rob bought her for just two hundred pounds. He called her Ernie. (Benny Hill's famous song, "The fastest milkman in the West," was top of the charts at the time). Rob hunted her for a few seasons before selling her on to the kennels where George Orr used her for whipping-in, and after him the secretary, Phil Willmottt, had her.

In '72 I saw a grey mare out hunting ridden by Duco van Joolen. He and Gordon Berrisford were trying to get a horse-dealing partnership going. Anyway, I made a few enquiries about her as Linda was looking for an all-rounder at that time. We took her down to the indoor school at Hazelwood and popped her over a few show-jumps. That afternoon Linda jumped the biggest parallels she has ever jumped in her life. I bought her for Linda. Midnight Blue (We had been in negotiation over buying her until after midnight) turned out to be well worth it. Not very good at Autumn hunting, but once the opening meet had gone by she was superb, a real all-rounder. Linda represented the Meynell hunt in a few show-jumping teams and did loads of hunter trials on her. I too was actually placed a few times on her, including being second at Locko Horse Trials. But it was Linda who hunted her – besides many others – over the next thirteen seasons. I shall tell how her end came at the appropriate time.

BILL STRAWSON

Linda and I were hacking back to the lorry from a day with the South Notts (I think Bob Hoare, who had come from the Cottesmore, was the Huntsman then) when we came across this man riding a grey mare. He was Bill Strawson and had really enjoyed himself. He told me he would like to hunt more in Derbyshire, and asked if I knew anyone who would keep his horse, Shadow. He had come to the right chap. I said that I would but he would have to provide his own transport. I think we let him have a box for the night, and that was the start of a friendship that has lasted all these years. What fun we had.

The first horse I sold him was a horse called Jim, one I had got from from Gilbert Brown after he had bought one from me called Gilded Rock earlier in the year. (Gilbert had hunted for many years with the Wynnstay so knew all about good hunters. I was to buy several from him). Not only did Bill hunt Jim with the South Notts, he also hunted him with the High Peak where he had a farm. He also farmed in Lincolnshire and Derbyshire. Halfway through the season he said he wanted to ride him in the Members' Race at the High Peak. Jim was an intermediate eventer; one could not say he would be the fastest thing on four legs, but he would jump. The Members' Race at the High Peak was over small walls. As the races were always on Easter Tuesday, I thought he would be finishing hunting with him two months prior to the races, and I sold him Willie for him to finish the season on. We got Jim looking very well and I decided Bill ought to have a few lessons in jumping at speed. Amongst our show-jumps we had a grey wall nearly a replica of what he would have to jump. We went down to the jumping field – by now most of the farm was down to arable. I rode Jim because, as I said to Bill, "It will give you a bit of an idea what you have got to do." He was a very good ride. Then Bill clambered aboard. After he had jumped the wall a few times and was in mid-air he shouted across, "What's my style like?" I told him to forget the style and just try to cross the fence the quickest way.

He had no colours so I lent him mine and on the day, as he went into the jockeys' room, I handed him a back-protector. It was one of the old-fashioned sort – a piece of polystyrene with tape fasteners. All I said to him was, "You had better have this protector" and left him while I was fetching Jim into the Paddock.

When Bill joined us I thought he was walking very funny and said, "What's wrong? Why are you walking like that?"

"It's this protector. It isn't very comfortable," he said.

What he had done was to put it down the front of his breeches and I said to him, "It's not there that needs protection. It's supposed to go on your back." We both had a laugh about it.

I think he finished second but the race gave him lots of confidence so that he developed an ambition to ride in the Meynell Members' Race over fences. Off we go to the Sales at Doncaster to buy Corky, a nice little bay horse, for the occasion. He had been placed twenty-four times in thirty-eight races but he was crackers, I remember, when I took him cubbing at Okeover. What sort of hunting he had done before we had him I don't know but it was his only blip because he did become a very nice hunter. I had one particular good day, again from Okeover, when Corky and I jumped a particularly awkward place and were the only ones to see the fox go to ground in the middle of Waterhouses. It was nearly dark and I decided I had better ride home but I met Dermot and was able to tell him where the hounds were marking to ground.

The point-to-point was held at Lowsonford in the North Warwickshire Country. It was quite a high-class course and there was a valet there to help the jockeys get ready. Bill had his two lads there that day. When the valet was putting the silks round his neck, one of the boys said, "Why are they doing that to Daddy?"

"So he won't break his neck," the valet told them.

The boys were distraught. "Don't bother riding, Daddy. We don't want you to break your neck."

He didn't, he rode a particularly good race and finished second to a very good horse, being beaten by about a length. He also ran second over the walls at the High Peak. I think that was the particular highlight of Bill's point-to-pointing.

Next, he was saying, "I've asked to be a Joint-Master at the South Notts." To say I was astonished would be an under-statement, but when he was in charge I think they were the glory days of the South Notts – they were as far as I was concerned and I had hunted with them since 1952. When he took over he bought David Anker in as Huntsman and what a wonderful partnership they made! However, when David decided to go back to Hunt the Cleveland, Bill was devastated. Before that we had some fun. You just did not want the seasons to finish.

Being a Joint-Master, Bill wanted some horses not just for himself but for the hunt staff as well. Leicester Sales had become a bit of a dodge city; so I went to Ireland with John Goodwin (who had turned from motor-dealer to horse-dealer and very successful at it he was too. I bought quite a few horses from him). John seemed to know where we were going and what we were looking for. I bought a few nice horses, including a mare that I called Granard. She went for the Whip.

Another one was Kerry, a grey mare, 16.2hh. She came from Sarah Gell. Bill field-mastered on her and she lasted him for many years.

I can't remember all the horses I sold to Bill Strawson while he was with the South Notts, but ones I feel sure he remembers are a brave mare called Clare, as well as Willie, Harry, Watson, and Lawrence.

I think David Anker would say the best horse I ever sold to Bill was Rafferty. Linda and I had been to the Maguires on a Monday when they had just had a shipment of Irish horses over. I took immediately to a bright bay gelding that was five years old and a stocky sort, but with the most wonderful outlook on life. Anyway I bought him and took him out with the South Notts on the following Monday, when they met at the Bear at Belper. When I said to Bill, after about an hour, "Here is a horse for your Huntsman," he told David to have a ride on the horse that I had brought out, and let me take his. (A wonderful huntsman was David and, unusually for a man so good with hounds, he was a very good horseman as well). He had not been on five minutes before I knew that they had clicked, and after they had finished hunting he was telling me what a good horse he was and how he was just what he was looking for. " I'm going to get Mr Strawson to buy this horse for me." Suddenly, he went lame. It was a real shock to David, and to me. (If a horse goes lame and you can't see what's amiss, you ought to start at the foot, and that's what we did). David jumped off and picked his foot up, and, as luck would have it, discovered he had a four-inch nail in his foot which must have gone up the side of the frog. We were both relieved. I left it in till I got home and then pulled it out. After I had tubbed his foot with hot water and Dettol, he was sound straight away. I could be wrong about Rafferty, but I think he was David's favourite horse. When David left the South Notts to go back to the Cleveland, he had a deal with Bill and took Rafferty with him.

1972–1973

The hunt ball was held at the Perkins on March 3rd which was an outstanding success. Mrs. John Gibbs again ran the Fair, which made five hundred pounds. The Hunt Club had the Horse Show, Linda and I put out the show-jumps. There was a cheese-and-wine party at Shirley and two dinners, which were well supported. One was held in the Staffordshire side for the first time and the prints taken from the painting by John King, in which there were three grey horses, all of which I had sold, enabled the Hunt Club to place an order for a new combined horse and hound box costing in the region of three thousand pounds.

It was also in 1972 that Sutton Council, in whose area Springwood Farm was situated, visited us and told us they were putting a compulsion order on twenty acres of ground for building houses. After negotiations however, they withdrew that and we sold it to Wrights, the builders from Mansfield for potential building land. We did not make as much as we had wanted after getting permission to build, but we made enough to dissolve the partnership and be independent of each other. My brother Harold decided he would give up farming because of the pain his T.B hip was giving him. He went to Wigan to see about one of those replacement hips but he came away from the clinic very disappointed, saying they could do nothing for him. He decided to breed racehorses and bought a nice place, about thirty acres, from Richard Bowler at Shardlow. He was very successful and bred some very good horses, including Jack Fox who won about seven races for him when trained by Walter Wharton and ridden by young Wally. The best race he won was a good race at the July Meeting at Newmarket. As at that same meeting the Queen had a winner and Sangster had a winner, my brother thought he was in the top drawer of owners but, very sadly, he died in 1980. Mother was staying with Ann and Ces for a few days when a friend of ours called in to see Harold and found him dead on the floor. He had had a massive heart attack, at the age of 52.

In the year that we moved from Springwood and I bought his share, we had our first sunshine holiday. We went to Ibiza. When we got off the plane I thought we had landed on the moon – not a bit of green grass.

I remember selling a horse about that time to John Ryman, who was to become Labour M.P. for Blyth in Northumberland. Jane Whitfield who had hunted with us for quite a few seasons introduced me to him. I feel sure she had at one time been a Joint-Master at the South Staffs. He came over to have a sit on this horse, a bay gelding, a nice sort of horse with nice Irish bone. He bought the horse and asked if we would keep him at livery, which we did. He was quite a chubby fellow. He never seemed to have clothes to fit him. After hunting, he would stand in front of the Raeburn airing his knowledge and eating. I have never seen a man eat like him. What used to happen with his breeches too short and his shirt too short was a big gap appearing that showed a lot of hairy stomach. He ate a whole Christmas cake all by himself one night. The problem I ran into was I could not get any livery money from him. When I knew that he was standing for Parliament I said to him, "If you don't pay I'll tell the papers." That would scupper his plans to become an M.P. The day before the election I got paid. The Labour Party only got in by the narrowest of margins. He said that the horse had not been properly looked after. So before he left we had at our expense a full examination of his well-being by Mr. MacMurtry, the vet from Ashbourne, who gave him a clean bill of health. He married Jane Whitfield. On the first night of their honeymoon the phone went and it was Jane wanting to know how the horses were. I had some rare phone-calls in my time but no-one else rang me on their wedding night. I just told her to go back to bed.

One of the horses was a lovely big one I had bought for Jane from Mr. Thompson from Bally Walter in Northern Ireland. I am sure she would have said he was as nice a horse as she had ever had. He did go well for her. One day she lent him to her husband to hunt at Tissington. I did not think the horse looked safe for him to ride. Sure enough he fell off and the horse galloped loose through Tissington. On the road out there is a cattle grid. He galloped straight on to it and broke both front legs. I think that day the marriage started to dissolve and it was not too long before there was a divorce. After that she did not hunt for a few seasons.

Jumbo was sold to a vet in the Blackmore Vale country through being recommended by Hugh Davies, our vet, which I appreciated. In fact I appreciated anyone who recommended me to someone who then bought a horse from me. Sometimes I gave them a rug or if they were local I might take them out for a meal and if they lived a long way away I would probably send them a cheque. If you are a horse-dealer it is the only way to get more business. People like to be appreciated. One might as well play for nothing as work for nothing. I must add that, as a professional, Mr. Davies only got a thank-you.

HORSES SOLD TO JANE WALKER-OKEOVER.

My buying hunters for Jane had really begun one day in 1970 when Sir Ian Walker-Okeover drove into the yard. I invited him into the kitchen where he told me that Stokes (who was their stud groom) had had a stroke and asked if we would we have two of Jane's horses at livery. I said we would, provided Jane could provide her own transport. They had a horse-box for three so that was no problem, but her horses were now getting on a bit and that was a problem: Johnny suffered from a bad back and his jumping was getting very unreliable, while Peter was flat-footed and, with age, was losing his spring for jumping. Johnny went to Michael Stoute as a hack and Peter went to heaven and Sir Ian therefore asked me to look out for a horse for Jane. I bought her first horse through David Westwood, who had come to us when the South Staffs amalgamated with us. He told me where there was a grey horse that had never hunted but had been to Hickstead in some riding-club team. Sir Ian bought him but decided he was a bit green for Jane, and would send him up to Yorkshire to his own head nagsman, Bill Laing, to school and make a hunter out of him. In the meantime I was to find another horse for hunting that season. So I came up with Midas from Pennwood as a stop-gap. He had quite a big bursa on a hind fetlock but was a sensible horse. Afterwards, he was sold on to Jill Lyster, who adored him.

In the meantime we had got back the grey from Bill Laing that Jane decided she wanted to hunter-trial. So I rode him at the Meynell Hunter Trial when they were held at Stanton. From then on he was ridden by Jane, who also evented him, and gave him the name of Grey Arrow. She won at Corbridge. None of us knew much about dressage so we had a few lessons with Vere Holden, who was very good and so patient with me (I knew her when she was a pupil of Eddie Goldman). What we did know about was jumping. In those days if you could jump two clear rounds, one show-jumping and one cross-country. you would never be far away. When she qualified for the championship that year at Goodwood, Jane and Linda went down with her old Land-Rover and trailer, which travelled at about fifteen miles per hour. It took ages to get there. Grey Arrow went quite well and finished about in the middle. I remember when she was show-jumping at Hilton Park one day and was in the line-up behind Geoff Glazard and some other very good jockeys, Ken Beeston came over and said he was very impressed and thought she would make a good addition to the show-jumping circuit. She won quite a few working hunters with Grey Arrow as well, but he was outstanding as a hunter.

When Dermot was thinking of giving up his mastership of the Meynell, the Warwickshire were after him to hunt their hounds and a few of them, including John Thorne and about ten of the Warwickshire leading lights, came to see him hunt hounds. They found a fox in Radbourne Park and ran down to the railway line. Once across that they were running up towards Arthur Morley's Farm and turned right-handed to find a massive wide hedge in front. I don't think the visitors had ever seen anything like that to jump when out hunting. The only people to jump it were Jane on Grey Arrow and Pat Wint on Foston (I rate Pat Wint and Foston to be the best combination to cross the Meynell. He was a very big horse but she never looked worried, just turned him to practically anything – Magic! She was our top point-to-point jockey, on horses she had hunted properly. She trained for Spurrier, and Billy Foulkes rode most of them). I think Grey Arrow would have won a hunt race. He also could have turned his hand to anything, a very versatile horse.

Jane was by that time into making money from her hunters. She would buy a nice five-year-old, hunt it for two seasons and then sell it on.

Fair Enough, a five-year-old chestnut Irish horse, I bought from Owen Brennon who was bringing over a few hunters from Ireland. Jane sold him to Mrs Gibson, when she was Joint-Master of the Cottesmore. Kruger who came from Paul Goddard also went to Mrs Gibson. Paddy, from Jimmy Maguire, a bay horse, 16.1hh, was not really quite tall enough for her. He took a terrific hold going in to a fence, and so he did not last too long, being sold as a Whip horse, I think to the Zetland. The next horse I sold Jane was a lovely three-quarter bred horse, a bright bay, a very good-looking horse. About that time Dicky Stillwell was having a few days with us. He had started a pre-hunting course mostly for Joint-Masters. (Patrick used to go every year. He would stay in a London hotel, and Kevin would stay in the lorry, having taken the horses down for Patrick). The course Dicky was giving meant that he and his wife Joan were invited to have a day or two with quite a few hunts up and down the country. When he was with us the Meynell met at Okeover, and as Patrick had not got a horse for him Jane lent him the bay. The thing that worried me more than anything was that before Dicky got on he thought he would have to take off the martingale. The first fence he jumped was a good gate but on the topside of Okeover you are in the hills and into the stone walls. They can be unforgiving, and they were this day. The horse threw his head up going into a big wall. He didn't break his leg but he never did any more good. Eventually he was given away as a hack.

When Jane, being down to one horse, was wanting a new one, I found Jonathon in a jumping-yard. He was hardly Jane's type, just a stop-gap, and came through Tony. He gave her a bad fall at the bottom of the Old Gorse. (It was her friend who built this awful fence. He thought that as long as his dog cound jump it a horse could). Anyway, it broke her shoulder. We sold him to Derek Rickets and he sold him on to someone who seemed to be satisfied.

A horse called Christopher had been hunted hard by Sarah before he was given the summer off. Perhaps he was just a hunter but he was a nice horse. When they came up from grass we generally just fed bran mashes for the first three days and no hay. I used to give them a mild physic but that could knock them about. The old grooms used to say, "If a horse can stand one side of the box and hit the other side with its dung you had made a good job of getting the grass out of its system." Christopher had been in for about a week when at around twelve o'clock we noticed he wasn't very well. We called the vet out but by three o'clock he was dead – a twisted gut. Poor Jane wasn't having the best of luck with her horses.

The next horse I sold her was again a dark bay gelding that she called Bobby Brown. I bought him from Tony Maguire who was, I must say, probably the straightest dealer I dealt with. Jane went with me on this particular trip to Wigan. She took rather a fancy to this big horse with a tail that had been chewed by calves in Ireland. When he had been with me for a few days, Jane came over and wanted to know how he was going. I told her so far so good; I would be taking him to Calke on the following Thursday. "I'll come with you and watch him. I may wish to buy him if you think he's suitable for me." Calke isn't the best meet, but I jumped a few fences and he gave me a wonderful feeling. I said to her, "Yes, he'll do for you." He made a very good horse, not probably as good as Grey Arrow, but nearly. He show-jumped and evented for her and was a very fine hunter.

On a trip to Ireland with Norman Profitt, I bought six horses. One of them was a grey mare, about 16.2 hh, that was six years old and a real good stamp of a mare. Tim was hunting her one day when over came Jane. "I like that mare. Can I have a sit on it?" She tried her, liked her, bought her, and gave her the name of Mystery. That proved to be a mistake. After a while she went lame. We X-rayed her, tried everything, but could not find what was wrong, and the solution we chose was to send her to Jane Hall to breed with. Although she went to the stallion, it was getting quite late in the covering season, and she did not hold. As she was such a nice mare they thought they would keep her around to try another year, and so she was turned out on the hills. One day in December Jim Hall said he suspected Mystery was sound, and brought her on to the road, jogged her up and down and found that he had been right. Both Jim and Jane thought Jane Walker-Okeover must have her back to see if she would stay sound enough to hunt again, for she was still only a young mare after all. There was no return of the trouble during the years Jane had her. We did not know what had gone wrong with her. It's still a

Jane riding Mystery hunting with the Meynell at Tissington

mystery. Don't use the name.

Another horse she liked and bought was Jimmy from Peter Mellor in the Rockwood Country, a chestnut horse, seven years old. He wasn't quite big enough for her and another thing against him was he was very brave and jumped very big. I don't think she ever fell off, but she never really felt safe on him and so she sold him to an old school friend of hers, Fiona Shepherd-Cross from the Grafton country. When she came and tried him here she fell off him once, but still bought him.

Once, when I was in Ireland with John McAuley and had already bought two horses he persuaded me to look at just one more, that belonged to a dentist, but it was late at night, growing dark, and I had been up since four o'clock to catch the early plane from Liverpool. John suggested popping into a pub for a drink; he knew the landlord. John had his pint of Guinness and I had a hot whiskey, with some kind of seeds in it. It went down well. We had not had a lot to eat so when John said, "Have another," I did and then went on to see this horse, and to buy it, a lovely dark bay gelding, called Heritage, what I think of as an old-fashioned type of Irish thoroughbred. They had only one fence that he jumped a few times. I didn't ask, "Can he jump it backwards for a change?" and never found out if he could. He turned out to be a very good-looking horse that could buck you off out hunting at three-thirty in the afternoon. We were pleased enough with him and so was Jane. She bought him and had been riding him for some time, when David Tatlow was riding hunters for Mrs Jane Thornton and having a few days' hunting with us. He asked me if the horse Jane was riding was for sale; he had got a person who it would just suit. I told Jane to have a word with David because he had a client for Heritage. As Mrs Thornton's horse-box was going to Gloucestershire shortly afterwards, we arranged that he should be put on, but it was six months later before the deal was finalised.

When Linda was jump-judging at John Ward's One-Day Event she saw a grey horse belonging to Peter Mellor. She told Peter that I would probably like to buy that horse from him and suggested he should call at home and show him to me. Peter acted on the advice. I liked the grey's looks and jumped a fence or two round the farm. "What sort of money has it got to be for a poor man?" I asked – and nearly fell over when he told me. However, I had a horse called Kingswood that was a bit too hot to take out hunting but would make a marvellous eventer, and his grey, called Mac, was really a touch careless in the show-jumping. We agreed to a part-exchange and Peter was very successful with Kingswood, getting him to a Grade A show-jumper. I always knew he had a big jump. Mac took Jane's eye. He reminded her of Grey Arrow and was with her until she gave up.

One day Jane said, "I'm going on this trip to China – one of my risky holidays. I might not come back so I've altered my will and left you the horses."

"That's very kind of you," I said. "I hope you've left me something to keep them with."

1973-74

The only significant change was that Rob Hutchinson had done his three years as Chairman of the Hunt Supporters and was stepping down. Derek Dalton, probably one of the first Daltons to be interested in hunting, was taking over and was a good choice as he farmed in a big way around Brailsford. The family owned Lubrizol Refinery in Belper. A new horsebox that had cost £3,700 was handed over to the new Hunt Chairman, Col.Farquhar. The dinner that year was held at the Green Man in Ashbourne.

The tickets were sold out weeks before, especially when the people knew the B.B.C. Commentator, Mr. Dorian Williams M.F.H., was coming to speak on show-jumping and Mr. Michael Clayton, editor of *Horse and Hound* was to speak too. The best run of the season was from Hope Wood at Norbury to Snelston, and they killed their fox at Doveridge – what they called a six mile point, and eleven miles as hounds ran. Some ride over the cream of the Meynell country!

The season saw another addition to the ranks of the farmers on the hunting field in the one and only George Shaw who lived at Ludgate Street Farm, Tutbury, which is now all under bricks and mortar. He returned to hunting on Pluto who I had sold to Fay Hibbert in 1971. She had made a really good horse of him and as they were all friends let George have him to start on. He next bought a lovely big horse called Dungannon that John Crooks had bought from Tony Maguire. How I came to be involved was that John had not done a lot of hunting and thought Dungannon was a bit classy for him and asked me if I would hunt him. I did, and had a marvellous day and a some good half-days. Linda had a few days on him too. Then George bought him.

Another farmer in this part of the world who started hunting again around about then was John Ward, who had not hunted since he was a boy. I sold him Remington and I feel sure I sold him Midas as well.

We had a few ups and downs with a bay mare called Jemima, 16.1hh and threequarters bred, that I bought from Keith McGhee, who lived at Hulland Ward. She was a very good jumper. I remember Linda jumping some very stiff post-and-rails, not wooden ones but made out of concrete (they are still there, near Bentley Carr, and could be for the next hundred years) but she was not too good over walls. Linda went one day (what a life that woman's had!) with Rob Hutchinson to the High Peak, when I had gone to Ireland. When I got back she said, "I have a confession to make: Jemima is cut quite badly on every leg and is bruised with it too." We covered everything in Animalintex; the damage was only superficial. Then a client came out of Cheshire to see her. He liked her and said he would send the vet. We were going away and left the girl groom to see her vetted. It was Bobby O'Neal who came. After he had been in the stable he said to the girl, "You needn't bring her out. She's only three years old – not nearly experienced enough for the person who has sent me to vet her." He was right, of course. It can be difficult to tell a two-year-old from a four-year-old and I had never given it a thought. We eventually sold her to some people in Wales and a couple of years later she came back with them to compete at Locko Horse Trials and she stayed here overnight with us. When she walked out of her box it was too obvious that

Bobby O'Neal had been right about her age – She stood at least seventeen hands now. She had turned into a big mare. Fancy Linda hunting a two-year-old across this country!

Theresa Pearson, Lord Cowdray's daughter, rang me one night (She was a big friend of Patrick Drury-Lowe) and said she was looking for a hunter about 16.1hh. I was able to tell her I had actually got one. She asked if I would take it down for a day with the Heythrop as her guest and said I was to bring a friend. I rang Rob Hutchinson and asked if he wanted a free day with the Heythrop. Rob will always jump at a chance of a good day out, and so off we went early on the Wednesday morning. I think they met at Lower Slaughter but I can remember the day well enough, not for selling a horse to Theresa but for when Ronnie Wallace the Joint-Master and Huntsman came over to where Rob and I were standing at the meet, and said, "Welcome to the Heythrop. I can see by your outfit you are hunting farmers." We were both wearing velvet jockey camps and black coats. I was always very proud of my farmer's outfit. He talked to us for quite a time and when he heard we were from the Meynell he wanted to know all about Dermot. As I said, I did not sell the horse but we did have a good day out.

Selling David Nicholson a black mare was the start of a very good relationship as regards buying and selling. I am sure I sold him some good horses but I also bought some from him. He lived at Dalton Park at that time in the Holderness country.

During this season I bought Morse Code at Leicester, after Peter Lyster had given me an order for a horse for a Field Master. I hunted him and he was a bit special. He had actually evented or that was what it had said in the catalogue. Then Peter told me it would probably be his last season, and so he would not be buying any more horses. (It turned out that he did carry on for another season or two). That left me with Morse Code on my hands. To any future horse-dealer I would say: Always buy for yourself, never buy for anyone else.

We were all into hunting in a big way, but now it looked as if we would be going in for eventing too. Janet Hodgson, who rode Budget for us, had said she would ride for us any time. As Morse Code had evented before we bought him, we took the chance to have a go with him. We tried him out in Scotland because Janet loved the Scottish circuit and were placed at Fenton. Then we went to Windsor for the two-day event, hardly knowing what to do. We hired a caravan from Hulland Motors and went up the day before. Janet stayed with friends. I walked the show-jumping course with her and after I had had my say all she said was: "I have jumped a show-jumping course before, you know". I don't think we managed to get into the ribbons but it

Janet riding Morse Code around the Windsor Three Day Event (in the 70s the horse trial fences were a little different to today)

was very enjoyable except on the way back the liquid one uses for the toilet spilt over and we had an all-blue room to deal with when we got home.

Linda hunted him one day with the South Notts. As I was showing a client a horse at home I could not get out till later on in the day. Eventually I caught up with them.

"How's he going?" I asked Linda.

"Super jump," she said.

I looked at his knees. One was coming up right in front of my eyes.

"When you've finished, have a look at his knees," I suggested.

Actually, you often get big knees when you hunt over the walls on the top side of Ashbourne. The South Notts hunt over mostly sand walls with bigger stones; whereas the Meynell's are smaller and sharper. To deal with these injuries, we use Epsom Salts paste, especially if they have a cut as well. The salts clean out the wound. Or, if we think the horse might have a knee in the morning, we put on a fairly tight bandage.

Morse Code had been going very well so we thought we would advertise him in *Horse and Hound*. We had quite a few replies and sold him to Mrs

Clapham for Tiny to ride. They had quite a lot of success with him, but sold him to the Austrian Olympic team for, so they tell me, a lot of money. Good luck to them. As long as I get what I want it is always nice to leave a bit for some one else.

When I bought a horse called George from Ronnie Masserella, I bought a nice pony for Sarah too. It was described as a working hunter pony, but it was no hunter. As soon as it saw hounds it went berserk and ran away. That was that. On our way home, we happened to run into Tom Brown and I told him why I needed a hunting pony for Sarah. He knew that Frank Salt had just the pony. They had grown out of it and were looking to find it a new home. It was a brown and white pony called Prince. I thought every little girl should have a Prince, and so I bought him. He was brilliant – but he kept jumping Sarah off and then he would be up with the hounds and either Linda or I would have to go and catch him. When we both got fed up with him doing this we went to Hulland Saddlery and asked for the deepest-seated saddle that they had got for a child. They recommended I buy a Stubben. It cost a hundred and eight pounds, I remember, but it did the trick, and we all went hunting. In time he was passed on to Tim to make a hunter for him. Prince could certainly jump a big gate or post-and-rails; it was the wide hedges and ditches that found him out. He lasted us for years. We eventually sold him to Roy and Jean Simpson and he lasted them for years as well.

But to get back to George (or Maxwell, which was his jumping name) I bought him from Ronnie to give us something to do through the summer months. (Ronnie's son, Steve, had two or three seasons hunting here on a little grey horse he kept with us. I am sure he enjoyed the time). I show-jumped George and he was a lovely horse, with a beautiful temperament, and I won one or two decent classes. He went exceptionally well at Balsall Common and, I remember, Sarah who was only about 8 would ride him round the show-ground. Linda took him round a few Autumn Hunter Trials and loved him. She said she was really looking forward to hunting him. We never used to go to the Opening Meet; I always found that there were far too many fresh horses and nervous people, so we normally started on the first Saturday after the Opening Meet. That year the meet was at Tom White's at Boothhay and Linda chose to take George to it. When he saw the other horses and hounds about he started to sweat. After about half an hour Linda came over and said, "You can ride this one. He's crackers." We changed horses and had a tremendous run but he was still very hot and rushing his fences. I took him to Okeover on the Tuesday but he was worse than he had been on the Saturday. After we had drawn Cedric Stevenson's wood and come back into the park and he was still being a real handful. I let him have a gallop up the hill by the side of the Big Wood but it made no difference: I could not sell him as a hunter of any sort. Robin from Sheffield had asked if I had anything that would go eventing for a girl just coming off ponies so that was where he went. He was a nice horse, a good show-jumper and a good horse across country but he was one of the few horses that just cannot stand hunting.

Another one I sold that year was Rosie, a blue roan Irish mare, 16.0hh, a tough, stocky sort. Linda was hunting her one day. It was very boggy. We were running hard, having found in the Ash, and came to a tiger-trap. There was some-one in the bottom of the ditch. I was riding a young horse and said to Linda, "Go on, give me a lead. We'll jump the lot." She didn't, anyway. She fell in the ditch on top of whoever was already there. Everybody was all right, thank goodness. We do some stupid things out hunting. The mare went to the Buccleuch for a Mrs.Buchcannan-Jardine, who was recommended to buy one from me by Joan Wilkins (That was her maiden name. When she got married she and her husband had a hotel in Lockerbie).

When I was eventing in Northumberland I bought a horse which I saw in action there. Its stable name was Percy and I did not alter it. I hunted it a few times and sold it to John McDowell who then lived near Bangor racecourse.

I had known John from his show-jumping days when he rode for Mr Broad from Malpas. This is going back a bit. He had a good horse called Tip Toes which they sold to Janet Smith from Mottram near Manchester. He went well for her. I think she went to stay with Winkler in Germany and bought another grey horse called Romanus, a good horse but if any water was about he would not go into the ring let alone jump. He would only jump what they call a dry course, one with no water on it. Now they call it a dry *track*. I can't get used to these new names. Mr Broad's daughter Roma was a real good sort to us single lads. She would always help and advise on the food side. Mr Broad had some good horses. One Colonel Llewellyn rode for him was called Monty – a very good speed horse, especially indoors at Harringay.

Another two horses I sold that year were ones I had bought through Gilbert Brown who had hunted with the Wynnstay for many years and would know a nice horse when he saw one. One of them was a four-year-old bay gelding called Soldier that I bought for Linda. He was by Elf Arrow, quite a well-known sire at that particular time. She schooled him all summer and started with the Autumn hunting but it wasn't long before he put up a splint and had to have twenty-eight days off. (You can sometimes squeeze a lemon onto a splint. Sometimes it works; sometimes it doesn't. It's always well worth a try). He got better from that one so we put him back into work, and within a few days he had put up one on the other leg. That meant another twenty-eight days off. Towards the end of the season we did hunt him a few days and then sold him onto a dear friend of Patrick Drury-Lowe's. The other horse we bought from Gilbert Brown at the same time as Soldier was a real nice horse but more thoroughbred than we generally bought; only I always liked to buy two horses from the same place if it was at all possible because I felt that if I lost money on one I might get it back on the other. I turned him out with Soldier in late May. I don't think I actually rode him. When I was at the Doncaster Sales and talking to a few of the Scottish lads I knew from the Scottish show-jumping circuit, Mr MacMillan asked me if I knew where there was a point-to-pointer. I said that I had got one, a well-bred horse turned out at home, and he could have a look at him. When his party saw him they thought he was just what they were looking for and bought him. After they had been back to Doncaster they bought the box down, had a cup of tea and took him back to Scotland with them. He did very well. He turned out to be one of the best point-to-pointers in Scotland. MacMillan told me one day that when he bought him he had not realised what a marvellous engine the horse had got.

1974-75

The season was the last under the Joint-Mastership of Dermot Kelly, Patrick Drury-Lowe, and Peter Lyster.

From the report in the red book concerning hunting for the '74-'75 season written by Dermot Kelly, cub-hunting started late, owing to the late harvest. The hounds were out for thirty-two days and killed thirty-five brace. After the opening meet up until January sport was not outstanding. The ground was desperately wet. The scenting conditions were good but foxes would not make a point and got caught too easily. Hounds had a good hunt from the rubbish dump at Clifton with the fox finally being caught in the river below Alton Castle after an hour and fifteen minutes and a five-and-a-half mile point. After the opening meet the hounds were out for sixty days killing seventy-two-and-a-half brace. Dermot considered it was a disappointing season in which to finish his mastership. "In my thirteen years the hounds have been out on one thousand, one hundred, and fifty days and have killed fifteen hundred foxes. I have enjoyed myself enormously and I would like to take this opportunity to thank all the landowners and farmers who have made it all possible for me."

The Hunt Ball that year was held at Perkin's place, Nether Hall. A good do it was too. The Hunt Supporters' Club was going from strength to strength. Linda and I ran a show-jumping night at Hazelwood. Most of the hunts from the surrounding packs sent a team consisting of a Joint-Master, a subscriber, one subscriber under the age of twenty-one, and another subscriber over fifty. There was champagne for the winning team, whisky for the second and a bottle of wine for the third.

Round about then we heard that Mick Toulson from the Belvoir country wanted some good horses and I went on to deal with him quite often over the years. He was a very good chap with one that was perhaps a bit nappy or needed a horseman. One such horse was The Tyler. I had bought him at Leicester Sales. Hayden Lester who lived at Hazelwood brought him back for me. While I was backing the lorry I hit a low roof and knocked a lot of tiles off and that is how he got his name. He was a very good hunter. Down at Longford I jumped three iron gates and turned round and jumped them all back again. His trouble was that he would go nappy now and again, but if you gave him a moment he would be all right. Linda hunted him one day and he got in to one of his moods. He would go nowhere. He just planted himself and that was that. He moved when he was ready. With horses of that sort you do have to find the right kind of home for them, but, as I said, he was a good hunter.

I had another tremendous day on a horse called Quasimodo. They met at Kirk Ireton, but not a lot happened until we found in Pythe Wood. By then there was hardly any one left, but there had not been many out in the first place. I was nearly ready for making my way home when suddenly they found.The huntsman, blew Gone Away. They ran over Sunnyside by Rowlands, down through George Jones's and then they made to Ireton Rough. I jumped some very big post-and-rails in the middle of Idridgehay on to the road and then straight to Ireton Rough, over Eric Spencer's farm, through Garretts. When I got back on to the road by the Cock Inn I decided I had had enough. I was on my own and I get a bit frightened when I'm jumping by myself. As I rode home – it would be about three miles – it started to snow. My neighbour Jim Hall, who was a very keen hunting man, came past me in the car and told me they had gone straight through Breward Carr making for Kedleston. Soon it was snowing really hard. I was just like a snowman, but very happy. What a hunt! And what a great ride as far as jumping went! I suppose to some countries it would be the hunt of a lifetime.

I am a great believer in good scent before snow, but could write a chapter about the signs of scent. For instance, blue haze is no good, and black hedges look very good, but the best sign in my book is like when you take out a young lady and have a good idea what sort of evening you are going to have the first time you take her hand. When you put the hounds into a covert and they find a fox and push it out in to the open, you have a good idea what sort of scent there will be that day. That's what counts.

1975-76

The new Joint-Masters for the 1975-76 season were Marek Kwiatkowski, who had hunted hounds with the South Shropshire, and David Meynell, who already knew the country, which I always think is an advantage: it is better than outsiders coming in. We have always been very lucky in that respect. Peter Lyster was staying on as the Field Master.

Marek Kwiatkowski complained that the dry conditions did not help and there were no really good days until after Christmas. He thought it was a poor season for the start of his mastership, despite killing 55 brace of foxes

A horse we named Horoscope is the one we remember of those we sold in this season.. We heard about him when we went to see Sarah who had started school at Abbotts Bromley. He was a chestnut, four years old, and 16.2hh. I saw him jump on a line. It was enough to tell me he had a very big jump. We bought him in the summer and we played about a bit with him and did some Autumn hunting with him but I thought he would never make an event horse; he was too bad a mover for that. When you sat on him you could see these legs going like windmills on either side of you. I was on him when the hounds met at the Meynell Arms in Kirk Langley and found straight away. They ran over Doug Hibbert's, up to Vicarwood, through Ireton Rough, and on to Champion Farm, but, on the way to it, what fences! The hedges in that part of the Meynell are big and wide with scoops in front as well as behind. I remember saying to someone, "This is bigger than Bechers with a drop." We jumped a lot of post-and-rails, full of barbed wire. Going towards one, Billy Foulkes's horse broke a leg for no apparent reason. Apart from that, what a hunt! Afterwards, I said to Linda, "This has got to be one of the best four-year-olds I've ever ridden." That was a Saturday. Because he was tired I left him a week and took him out the following Saturday. Quite unexpectedly, I could not get him near a jump; he was frightened to death. I had dared him too often the previous Saturday and scared the life out of him. That week Duco van Joolen called in with some Dutch boys. They liked the look of him. I explained he had at the moment just lost his nerve a bit and suggested they might like to see him jump on the line. When they had watched him they could see what an athlete he was. They bought him and took him back to Holland, where, believe it or not, he went on to win a class at Boekelo the following year, even though he was such a bad mover. He was

Sarah on Prince with her proud Mother riding Brad

also first reserve for the Dutch team for the Olympic Games. He eventually came back to hunt and finish his days in England. Mike Seddon hunted him and field-mastered off him before he went back to Duco's girl-friend Louise Morten.

Another horse through our hands that year was Brad, bought from Mr Ralph Young from Bradwell just outside Sheffield. I knew him from show-jumping. He came to see me one day at home and said he had a four-year-old chestnut gelding, home-bred, and offered it to me. I said I would have him if he went by the vet. That was all right and I was soon hunting on him. He went quite well on the flat, and jumping too. There was one day to remember when they found in Atlow Rough. Instead of the fox running towards the Ashbourne-Belper road, it went straight over the tops. We had never been that route much before, a real rough old country, but I enjoyed it. Though the really memorable part of the day was being introduced to Dick Hern and the Cazlet family who were having a day out too. Linda rode him a lot that season, but Ralph came over in the Spring and told us how much his wife missed the horse and asked if they could have him back. He actually gave me twenty five pounds more than I had given him for the horse nine months before. I was not quite so pleased when he went on to sell him and I read in *Horse and Hound* that he had won the Puissance at some indoor show and jumped over six foot six.

Socks was bought through Gilbert Brown for Mrs Bill Strawson. He did not quite suit her so he was sold on to Mrs Pinney, whose husband was at that time I think Joint-Master of the Cattisock. I also sold Brian Fanshaw two horses through Dermot Kelly, one for Captain Fanshaw and one for his wife. He was at that time Joint-Master of the Cotswold and went on to be Joint-Master and Huntsman of the Cottesmore. He was the father of James Fanshaw, the Newmarket trainer.

1976-77

Hugo McGhee took over Peter Lyster's place in the Mastership. Phil Wilmott began her long service as Hunt Secretary.

I sold quite a few horses in 1976. I had sold Jemima, back with me from the people in Pwllheli, to Phil Wilmott. Kwiatowski kept falling off and Patrick asked me to find a safe conveyance for him, so I found a nice coloured mare that would suit. Winestead I bought at Leicester sales, where I met David Bartrum for the first time. He had been riding the horse for the chap I bought him from. Winestead could do a very good test and we had some fun with him, but he was always very hesitant on the take-off in the show-jumping side. He won a few rosettes all the same. When I sold him to go into Gloucestershire they sent up Mr Brain to vet him. He made out the horse was nine years old. I said he was six and had the papers to prove it. Vets!

Twink came from Hulland Motors. I sold him to Duncan Douglas, as good a horse as he has ever owned. Duncan was not very old, a slim young thing. Twink carried him safely round Badminton a few times and I am sure he had a lot of fun. Bronze Light I bought at Leicester Sales from Cyril Light because Cathy Evans recommended him to me.

Cathy went on to become Mrs Robin Simpson and mention of the Simpsons reminds me that when they used to farm in Brailsford they once asked me to go and have a look at a horse they had. It was standing in a cow-shed, a bay gelding, I should think about 15hh, blood type. They asked six hundred pounds for him but I didn't buy him because he was too light in the bone for us. Anyway, Ann Moore bought him, named him Psalm, and he went on to win a silver medal at the Olympics. That shows how much I know about horses!

But to get back to Bronze Light. I show-jumped him a bit. He was all right, but no champion, and looked more of an eventer. So we schooled him over natural fences and took him down to Jim Hall's water-complex. He was taking a bit of getting in but suddenly jumped in. It frightened him, and he jumped a barbed-wire fence on to the gravel pits and stood on the top of the settling lake. I was upside down with my foot fast in the stirrup. Luckily, he stood whilst I extradited myself. I showed him to Chris Collins, who didn't buy him, but Jim Bealby did. He was Joint-Master of the South Notts, and later became Joint-Master of the Quorn. His wife insisted I start up the clippers to see if he was good to clip. I have never been asked to do that, before or since. He was a very good horse to them. Ashley Bealby won the Melton Hunt Race on him and so did his brother. Not many horses win it twice. Ashley also rode him in the Foxhunters at Aintree.

Turnaway, bought at Leicester, was the next one. Sally Parrot evented her successfully and she was a favourite hunter of Linda, who did a lot of hunter trials with her. She was one of the few horses to have jumped Miles

Turnaway with Sally

Porter's open ditch at Hill Top Farm. We sold her to Judith Hassal who moved to Lincolnshire and hunted with the South Wold. She has bred a number of foals out of her and I will be hard pressed to find another one so genuine.

I sold a big bay horse, 17hh, one I had bought from Paul Goddard, to David Crooks, who lived at Scotland Farm in Ockbrook. I had known David since we went to school together. He must have hunted that horse for twenty-five years with the South Notts. The reason why I never made any money from horse-dealing was that the horses always lasted too long!

The Banker was another eventer that Sally rode. He went to Mr Snowdon who was at that time the Joint-Master of the Zetland, while Cliff Standing, who had been our kennel Huntsman in Dermot's day, was the Huntsman. He must have been a nice horse since Mr Snowdon only bought nice horses.

I sold Monty to Sue Moon, who was, or is, a real hunting fanatic and was always very interested in dressage. She was also a tremendous help with the Pony Club. It was quite a sad day when she moved to the Tynedale. She was sadly missed. Monty was quite a butty sort of horse, a bit green when she bought him, but she was a good jockey and she made him a good horse. Sue's husband was Clerk of the Course at a few of the Midland tracks and her daughter Belinda married Marek Kwiatkowski, our Huntsman. Belinda was quite a good artist. I asked her if she would paint Linda on Midnight Blue. The result was super – except that she had made Linda's face a lot older than it was. When we told her about it she said she would take the painting home again and repaint the face. I paid her the agreed price but I have not seen the painting since. Linda will about have caught up with the face now.

HORIZON

That year I sold to the Hon. Louise Astor a horse I had named Horizon because I thought he would be out of the reach of everybody. He was a quarter Cleveland and three quarters thoroughbred that I had bought from Foljambe of Osberton, who had started to breed a few of this type of horse. I made my mind up not to sell him, but I did. I had bought him in the summer and played about with him, jumped him a lot at home and hunted him quietly a few times. I did not make the mistake of working him too hard as I had done with Horoscope; I had learnt a lesson that day. When I took him to a meet at the Lesters at Hazelwood to hunt with the South Notts, they were very good hosts. I had a stirrup cup and then I had another one. Somehow, my sight seemed to have a wobble. We jumped the first fence all right, but at the second one I seemed a bit dizzy and we did not get it right at all. We really messed it up. The horse went very lame: he had cut his stifle quite badly. Luckily we had not gone too far and the horse-box wasn't far away. Linda was not out that day so that I could take the lorry back there and then. By the time I got him back to the lorry, blood was streaming from the cut. I got him home and had him stitched up, but he did look very sorry for himself and I felt so sorry for him too. After that I always restricted myself to one drink.

Still, we had a lot of fun eventing him. He was a lovely bay horse; he took after the Cleveland in colour, but that was the only bit of Cleveland about him. One never knew how he would do a test; he might decide to have a play in the middle, nothing vicious but he did like a play. He would cock his head from side to side and look as though he was so innocent. Sally Parrot rode him as well as Turnaway. When I advertised Morse Code in *Horse and Hound* in '73, Sally had come over to buy him and that was how we met her. Unfortunately for her I had already promised him to the Claphams and I couldn't go back on my word. I did tell her I had a horse that I did think might be better than him and offered her a ride on Horizon. She also rode Winestead and a very good jockey she was and we were very lucky to have found her.

To get back to Horizon, we took him to a few events. He would probably do a forty dressage one day and then maybe a thirty the following week, but nevertheless he was a lovely horse. We got him to intermediate level and decided we would enter him for the Bramham three-day event. Sally had no experience of three-day eventing and neither had we. My job was to get him fit, and he was fit. His coat gleamed. We read Sheila Wilcox's book and we did learn a lot from that. The whole event was a lot of fun. Linda and I had been very insistent that should he get tired on the cross-country she was to pull him up. When we were in the 'ten-minute' box with all our bits and pieces, he still looked quite fresh to me. Anyway off they went, but Ernie Fenwick on Scoobie Doo did not seem to be going fast enough. He kept getting in the way. Sally and Horizon kept going and finished very well. When I was leading him back to the stables he bucked and kicked – he had really enjoyed himself. He finished sixth, which was very good, considering he had been produced by novices.

At the time when Louise Astor was going to become a Joint-Master of the Meynell she took a shine to him and she was very persistent that I should sell him to her. After weeks of thinking about it, we did decide to sell him as he would have a home for life. After she said she would like to have him vetted and his feet x-rayed, I took him to Campbell of Burton-on-Trent.

Sally going around Bramham Three Day Event on Horizon

Everything was perfectly all right. However, after about three months she rang to say he had got a seedy toe and part of his foot had dropped off so she would not be able to hunt him for quite a while until his foot had grown again. It had not shown up on the x-rays; so it was bad luck. He came right again, thank goodness.

TWO MISHAPS

Another horse I sold that year was a horse called Stephen, a really nice liver-chestnut horse, good enough to win a show class. I had bought him out of *Horse and Hound* and hunted him a few times. One night I heard a lot of noise coming from his box. He must have got cast. It was very dark but I saw the door fly open and he came trotting out, broke into a gallop and ran straight into a barbed-wire fence. He cut his neck very badly, just missing a jugular vein. After that I made very sure no horse did the same thing: I took the fence down and put up a post-and-rail fence. It took him most of the summer to get right, but he did and I hunted him the next season and we got

122

very brave again. We were having a good hunt across Tom White's. (I can take you to the very hedge now – big, and very wide). We did not quite make it. He came down on top of me. It was a good job I had my leather hunting boots on because he lay on me, crushing my foot under him. I had a pair of nickel stirrups that day, but never again. I always use stainless steel now. Being nickel, they just bent around my foot and squashed it. The leather boot saved my foot. I could not blame the horse. I had ridden him a bit slow.

It was Karen Kelly who rang me to see if I had got a horse to suit her uncle Captain Loder. I said that this chestnut horse would suit him very well. They bought him but instead of saying they would send the vet, they took some hairs from his mane and tail, and said, "We'll put these in the black box, and let you know. We haven't a lot of faith in vets." They came for him a few days later. He must have been all right. Captain Loder's son, after being a very successful trainer in Newmarket, had just moved out to France to train the two-year-olds for Godolphin.

I bought a three-quarter-bred horse off John Fairclough that I had seen him hunting. No disrespect to John but the horse was never up to his weight. When Mr Samworth, the Joint-Master of the Cottesmore, rang up for a horse, I suggested this one. He came and tried him. He liked him. As it was in the summer, he had no shoes on. Mr Gibson came to vet him and he passed. A few days after Mr Samworth had picked him up, the phone rang, "This is Samworth. The horse I bought off you is lame. I've ridden him round the yard and he's gone lame." Of course I rang Mr Gibson and told him that the horse he had vetted for Mr Samworth had gone lame. I told him he was definitely a sound horse and they must have done something to him, but Mr Gibson advised, "Have him back; he could buy lots more off you." He never did. They never do. What had happened was that he had white feet, probably a bit shelly, and with having no shoes on had gone foot-sore. I sold him to a Meynell farmer, Adrian Grain from Ingleby, who had him for a number of seasons. (He also went on to own a good National Hunt mare called Shepherds Hymn). Although the horse – we called him Fair Comment – was a very good jumper, he was not as good as his jockey who could and would jump a good gate or a wide hedge on his own feet.

1977-78

There was a shortage of foxes, said to be caused by the poaching of foxes by pelt-dealers or by poor breeding since the '76 drought.

The Home Policy Committee of the Labour Party announced its

intention of getting their anti-field sports policy into the next Labour Manifesto.

Nothing daunted, a Cross-Country Team Championship was held, sponsored by J.C.Bamford Excavators Ltd, in which the Silver Jubilee Event was won by the Pytchley Alcoholics team with the Wynnstay Hedge Hogs second. In the afternoon the Championship was won by Lunatic Fringe, with the Tory Party second, and the sober Zetland Hunting Farmers in third.

The previous year had seen the introduction of the Cross-Country event, and this year the first Terrier Show and Dance was arranged by George Orr and Peter Clark, both to become regulars in the Hunt Calendar.

The weather was mild for our indoor jumping at Hazelwood and all the fur-coats and ear-muffs proved unnecessary. There was even a Fancy Dress Class that Pat Wint won.

1977 was a good year for selling horses. Sunset, a chestnut horse bought from Fred Harthill, I sold to Jennifer Pearson for her daughter, Jane. (Jennifer and I go back a long way, to when we were in the Pony Club together and she was Jennifer Penny). Jane (who was to become Mrs Craig Dalton) made a very good horse of Sunset. They had him for a number of years. The Abbott, another chestnut horse, 16.2hh, I bought from Tony Maguire and sold to George Rich. .Jane, a grey mare, was another Maguire model. Linda hunted her a lot and took her hunter trialing. She went especially well at the Pytchley. I sold her to Mrs Norton who lived at Findern. Jane's offspring are now hunting with the Meynell. Mrs Norton's daughter, Clare, is riding one of the few grey mares that she has bred.

Thomas, a Harthill chestnut horse, 16.1hh, was a very difficult ride, but a sound good hunter if a little hot. I sold him to Sir John Barlow, the Field Master of the Cheshire. Stephanie, a chestnut mare with a few white socks, a very good hunter, came from Paul Goddard and was sold to Tricia Sevier.

Magpie a black and white horse I also bought from Paul Goddard. Although black and white, a very well-bred horse, 16.1hh. I had some very good days hunting on him, but he suddenly went quite lame. We had a few vets to look at him. (When vets came into the yard I generally made a bit of use of them). After they had said their piece, we decided to take him to Newmarket, to the Research Hospital for x-rays to his feet, to get to the root of the trouble. The chap there said, "I've taken twenty-four photographs of his feet and I'm afraid he is not going to do any good. The blood is not going to his feet properly. It's very interesting. I would like his feet for my students to look at so when you put him down, which you will have to when you get home, would you send them to me?" It was a long journey home that night.

Linda was with me, and we decided, as we had about twenty acres of bogs, we would put him out down there and forget about him. After about nine months I just happened to see him trotting around. This was July so I fetched him and rode him for a few days and found he had become quite sound, which pleased me because he was a nice person. The problem was that we did not know how long he would stay sound. As we were going on holiday I asked Paul Goddard if he would take him to Melton Mowbray Sale for me, which he did – and sold him for six hundred and fifty pounds. The new owners then took him to sell at Wolverhampton the following week and made nine hundred and fifty pounds. A woman in Cheshire bought him and she show-jumped him for a number of years, even getting to Wembley. He was eventually put down, owing to old age. Quite a story.

After I had been away looking at some horses, Linda said, when I got home, "I hope you haven't bought too many because I've bought one. It was advertised in *Horse and Hound*. I saw it ridden and it was a bit nappy but I knew you could sort him out. I had to buy him. It was only two minutes away. Some new people have taken a farm and stables at Players. The phone never stopped ringing and they delivered him for me." It was a lovely horse, one of the sort you can't wait to get on – a bright bay gelding, 16.2hh, six years old. We put on a saddle and bridle and climbed aboard but he would not go out of the yard. Under no circumstances would he move. So I went round to these people and said, "I can't get this horse to move. If you can come and get him to walk round the fields I'll say you are better than me, but if you can't we'll have our money back." They came, and although they could no more make it move than I could, I was never going to get the money back. There was nothing for it but to persevere. I tried driving him round the yard in long reins; I tried leading him off another horse; but it was no good. I took him to Melton Mowbray Sales. He looked magnificent. An ex-mounted-police officer bought him, unwarranted. We lost six hundred pounds over that deal. It was the end of Linda's horse dealing, I'm afraid. She has never bought a horse since then.

Robert Lightwood, the blacksmith, told me he had seen a nice bay mare, called Happy, in a riding school in Tamworth. I went to see her and bought her from Mrs Hales (whose husband became the owner of the very good steeplechaser, One Man). I show-jumped her a bit. She was very useful. I sold her to Tony Maguire and bought in exchange Davy Lad, a bay gelding, 16.1hh, ex-show-jumper, which all Tony's horses were. I hunted him a few times. Mick Toulson rang up saying he was bringing a client over. It was my first meeting with one of my best customers, Graham Vere Nichol, who was at that time married to Jane Kidd, sister to Johnny Kidd, and an old friend. In the show-jumping days I had actually known his father, who had ridden for the army. Graham was a very good jockey and at one time assistant to Ryan Price the trainer. He could ride most things. He fancied himself as a horse-dealer and was a good outlet for something a little dodgy. On this occasion he sold Davy Lad on. Being as good a jockey as he was, he did not really have to buy first-class horses, but one day he rang me, wanting a cheapy. At the time, I had an Irish ex-show-jumper that I had bought from Tony Maguire, a lovely bright bay, 16.2hh. I had hunted him a few times with the South Notts. One could not describe him as a show horse but he was a good jumper, and cheap. His one fault was he was difficult to get on, but if you faced him to a wall or something he could not jump, he was not too bad. I told Graham about it, and how I coped with it. He came over, tried him, liked him, and wanted to have a day on him. We went through the usual routine: "If you can produce this horse back to me as it left here . . ." Graham, as nice a fellow as he is, never actually lets you know he is buying the horse until perhaps a week later. He took the horse and this time rang up after two days: "You've got to have this horse back," he said. He had hunted with the Quorn on the Monday, got dragged off in a gateway and could not get back on him. He had had to walk four miles back to the lorry. "I'd got a new pair of hunting boots and I've about worn them out. At the moment I've got my feet in a bowl of water." I had to have a laugh, but the horse had to come back, of course, and I sold him to the army – the best place for him. Graham said he knew every fence in the Quorn and Belvoir country, but started to hunt more and more with the Meynell, and became a full Hunt subscriber. His mishap did not stop us having a lot more deals. Often he would take two or three at a time. I shan't mention just now every horse I sold him. The sort he liked was the butty type. We all have our preferences.

Another person I was lucky enough to meet in 1977 was Mrs Watt, wife of Michael Watt, a director of Tattersalls. She just loved horse dealing, and riding different horses. She hunted with so many different packs she knew everybody. I think Mattie would be the first horse she bought – a nice, middleweight, chestnut horse, 16hh. After him there was Beringo, a 7/8th bred bay horse, which Michael Watt himself came to look at but only saw him in his box as it was dark. A biggish chestnut horse which Michael himself hunted for many years was Newborough. Linda herself hunted Bonny quite a lot and loved him, a liver-chestnut horse, square model. Stone Fox, a five-year-old, had not had all that much experience but was a nice-bred chestnut horse, a three-day event type. All these horses were bought in Ireland. Mrs Watt would not have anything that had not hunted in Ireland and she would ring up at least twice a week for a chat. One night when she rang she said, "John, I have some bad news for you. I'm in Switzerland, having treatment for cancer but there seems little hope; so would you and Linda come and stay a weekend with Michael and me. Bring your horses and have a day's hunting with the Grafton as our guests." On the day we went Colonel Foster was having his last day and anyone who was anyone was out. I was riding Billy (who was sold to Mrs Joan Gibson who was taking on the Cottesmore) and Linda was riding Murphy (who we sold the following year to Mrs Murry Smith for Michael Farrin to hunt the Quorn hounds off). Two very good horses. What a country after the Meynell! I got so frustrated walking round the edge of ploughed fields. I jumped more barbed wire that day than I have jumped in the whole of my life. Poor Mrs Watt did not last much longer – a wonderful person who loved life. Michael hunted a horse I had sold him for many years after that.

Sparkler I bought on the 5th November out of *Horse and Hound* – a dark bay gelding, five years old, 16.2hh,. He was a very poor jumper. As he would walk through a hedge when we got him, you could say he wasn't a jumper at all. He was stupid but very brave: if they are brave then they will learn to jump, but if they are chicken you stand no chance. As I have mentioned, Sally Parrott from Stafford, a very good jockey and very strong, was riding our eventers for us at the time; so I paid her subscription to hunt with the Meynell. She must have had twenty days on him and made a very good job of him. I was able to sell him on to George Rich.

Norman was the next horse we bought. He came from Davina Lee-Smith, a bright bay, 16.1hh, and six years old – a chunky fellow with a hogged mane. The problem with buying a horse in the winter with a hogged mane is that it has probably had sweet itch. Luckily, this horse had not got it, but if anyone was unlucky enough to buy one with sweet itch, I found our vet Hugh Davies would give it an injection at the end of April and another one after about six weeks. An old fashioned remedy I find very good is putting plenty of Neatsfoot oil on the mane and tail. We also have an eco-warrior type rug to cover all his neck, body and tail. If he is kept in the stable, two fans there are also a help. I believe the trouble all starts with the stallion.

I bought Thistle, a bay mare, 16.1hh, and five years old, out of *Horse and Hound* from a lady who had a livery yard below Bottesford. Linda and I hunted her and also took her to a few hunter trials. She went especially well at the South Notts Hunter Trial. I sold her to go hunting with the Atherstone. When we went to the Burghley Horse Trials I would often see the people and they would say, "Thistle is still going strong." That must have been twenty years after I sold her.

Captain, a very nice dark bay horse, 16.3hh, seven years old, and an Irishman, came from Tony. I remember him particularly well because I was out hunting one day, galloping quite fast, and I slipped up on the flat. They are some of the worst falls you can have. I badly wanted Sir Peter Walker Okeover, Sir Ian's son, to buy him. Jane and I thought it would be nice if we could get him hunting again. (He had hunted from Melton whilst he was in the army. One day out hunting he said to me, "I bet you would like to buy this horse." I did not like to tell him that I did not think it was sound behind). He came over and had a ride on Captain. He was quite a decent jockey, but he did not buy the horse, saying he would not be doing any more hunting: he preferred to shoot. Now he is the Meynell Hunt Chairman. It was Norman Proffit who bought him.

1978-79

The Hon. Louise Astor replaced Hugo McGhee in the Mastership.

We lost a lot of days because of one thing and another, mainly weather – thirty days in all. We had one or two good hunts though, especially from the Meynell Arms Hotel, Kirk Langley, and another from the Ostrich Inn, Longford. A scarcity of cubs was again followed by a scarcity of foxes resulting in a poor season when only twenty-five brace were killed in all.

The Point-to-Point this year, which should have been held at Mucklestone, was abandoned owing to the weather. Yet the generous sponsors did not withdraw their support. The Hunt Fair was still being held and was now being run by Mrs John Gibbs, and a sum of £800 was given to the funds. At the Cross-Country event, the car parks were full by mid-day and the crowds were enormous. There were some notable teams and the winning one, named the Tory Party, was led by Lord Oaksey. The profit was £3000. Thanks were again due to Tom White and Bob Sessions for the use of Booth Hay. To mark the twenty-fifth anniversary of the Hunt Supporters' Club there was another terrier show and dance; a clay pigeon shoot; the annual show at Longford Hall; the annual dance at the Cedar Tree; a Christmas draw; a cheese-and-wine at Houndhill given by Mike Seddon; show-jumping at Hazelwood, and annual dinner in March. The Abbey Life Hunter Trials were held at Jim and Jane Hall's farm. Fay Hibbert and Andy Adams were asked to go on the Hunt Supporters' Club Committee again.

Captain Player, a great friend of mine, who I had known a long time, passed away. He had held most of the offices during his life-time. He was sadly missed. One of his favourite stories was The Skail Pool Fox. The following copy of it was sent to me after Major Maurice Kingscote's death. (Major Kingscote was Master and Huntsman of the Cricklade from 1931 to 1936, of the South Atherstone during 1936-37 and of the Meynell from 1937 to 1952).

The Skail Pool Fox

"For many years I was closely associated with Maurice Kingscote with regard to hunting and as a young man I whipped-in to him for two seasons prior to taking on the Mastership of the Craven. This was before the war, and some time after the war I became the Joint-Master with him at the Meynell. Because of this I got to know Maurice very well indeed and despite the difference in our ages we became and remained great friends.

Many of the old generation will know that Maurice was somewhat of a character and there are a great many stories still circulating about him, some true, some untrue and many of them libellous! The story I have to tell now is absolutely true and I hope in no way libellous!

One of Maurice's foibles was that he was an ardent attendee at his friends' and acquaintances' funerals. It was an obsession. He gave me the impression that he enjoyed them. We were discussing this subject one evening – I believe it was over port after attending a mutual friend's burial – that he turned to me and said, "Old boy, you are a lot younger than I am and are pretty certain to outlive me, so I want you to promise that you will come to my funeral. You will do that, won't you?" I replied that after knowing him for so many years it was unlikely that I would not be there and I more or less promised him that of course I would attend, hoping that it would be a long time before that day dawned.

Every spring I go and fish the River Naver in the extreme North of Scotland. While I was there, my wife telephoned to say poor Maurice had been killed in a motor accident the day before and that the funeral was to take place"the day after tomorrow." Could I get down? Owing to the distance and lack of time it was just not possible. There was nothing for it but to get someone to represent me at the funeral.

Nevertheless, I had not forgotten my conversation and what amounted to a promise. It gave me a definite feeling of guilt. I fished the next day, which as far as I remember was uneventful. On the same day as the funeral I was fishing the No.3 beat and, as all who fish will appreciate, my mind was completely absorbed in fishing and the funeral was, I regret to say, quite out of my mind at that time. However, not for long! At about midday, an hour or so before the funeral service was due to take place in Gloucestershire, I started to fish Skail Pool which is rather an eerie and isolated place, the water being deep and dark and on the opposite side there is a steep rocky brae and birch trees. I started at the run-in at the top of the pool and after a few casts I was conscious that I was being watched. Looking up, I saw at the bottom end of the pool about seventy yards away, a large greyish-coloured fox sitting close to the water's edge looking directly at me. I stopped casting and froze and watched. My ghillie – who was sitting on the bank – had by this time also noticed the fox and he likewise kept quite still. To my amazement the fox got up and slowly walked towards me up the opposite bank and came and sat only about thirty yards away. He got up again and walked slowly up to stand and look at me from exactly opposite, not more than fifteen yards away from where I was standing on the edge of my side of the river. I think I said something to him but even that did not make him hurry away. After what seemed an age in time, but was probably only two or three minutes, he slowly turned and walked up through the birch trees and up the brae. When he reached the top, he turned back and gave me a last look before disappearing from sight over the skyline. My ghillie, Johnny Duncan, was a man of over seventy and he had spent most of his life on the river. He told me he had never seen a fox in that particular place before and never had he seen a fox behave in such a manner. I certainly had never seen anything like it either.

Anyone reading this story may well imagine my feelings and understand when I say I did not fish very well for the rest of the day!

1978 was a great year for selling horses.

Tony Maguire rang one day to tell me he had some Irish horses for me. He would particularly like me to look at one called Billy that had won four Foxhunters. He wanted me to hunt him and see if I could sweeten him up. The fact was he bucked, and one jockey he had thrown off had nearly hit his head on the roof of the indoor school.

I rode him round the farm for a day or two and decided he wasn't too bad. I would take the other two. I rang Phil Arthers to ask him if he would ride Billy. He did and had a good day's hunting on him – really enjoyed it.. After Linda and I had hunted him too, we agreed he was probably one of the best we had had. If there was an awkward place out hunting, people would be calling out, "Where's Billy? He'll give us a lead." One Sunday morning Gerald Deville came over, with a picture of the English Channel to be put in Billy's box, "because he would be expected to jump it one day".

Tony had him back but we had done no good as far as show-jumping was concerned and so he sold Billy to us as a hunter.

I was on him one day when hounds met at Ednaston, drew Peat Moss, and found straight away. The first fence was a hedge with a small ditch towards. The Prince was out and had to make two or three attempts at it. Sir John Miller, who was the Prince's advisor at the time, came over and asked if I had a horse that would suit His Royal Highness.

"I have probably the best horse I have ever owned," I told him.

"May he have a sit on him?" Sir John asked.

"Certainly. But I want to make £3,000 of him."

"I won't let him spend that sort of money for a hunter."

"There's no point then," I said, "in him riding this horse."

I sold Billy to Mrs Gibson when she took on the Cottesmore. No one else rode Billy the whole time she had him. I sold her other horses. She would come into the yard with her husband and say, "Which is the horse we have to look at?" and I would bring it out and show it. "Gibby," she would say, "are you looking at this horse?"

He would turn to her and say, "If John says it's all right, then it is all right."

Some horses did not stay with me very long. One, a lovely big bay horse, what I call a true Irish thoroughbred – stood square, with loads of bone – I bought from Tony. I was riding him one day when Dr Tom Connors was out having a day's hunting with us. He came over and told me he liked him and had a client for him. With that, I said he had better take the horse back with him. He did just that and met me later at Rempstone Church with the money.

Another one was a chestnut that I sold to Mr Hercock who was wanting a horse before becoming Joint-master of the Quorn. I had bought him after seeing Jenny Ellis on him out hunting. (Jenny used to live with her parents at the Yew Tree Pub at Ednaston and has turned out to be one of the best girl grooms in the country. She groomed for the Edgars, for Glazzard, and is now with Geoff Billington looking after It's Otto. She rode for the D.N.S. They were her sponsors). The chestnut turned out to be a good horse for him. His son still comes out for a day with us, and once, when George Shaw and I went to Ireland we stopped in a place and asked for dinner, bed and breakfast. Who should the landlady be but his daughter, Sally Hercock? She had married an Irish eventing fellow.

John Sheddon, who had won Badminton on Golden Willow, rang one Saturday night. (That weekend was a record in our business: I had sixty-three orders for horses). John said he wanted a horse to go eventing. I had just bought a grey gelding from a girl who lived in the village – if you can call Mercaston a village when it has only ten houses. He was a nice horse, five years old, 16.1hh, and 7/8 bred. John wanted to know all about him so I painted as good a picture as I could. I must have done a good job because he said, "I'll send my man for him, with the cheque." Afterwards, he rang more than once to say how pleased he was with him.

A very good horse I sold that year went to Rosemary Shields. (She was Rosemary Lavender when I first knew her and we were showing ponies and apppearing in gymkhanas against one another). He was a nice middleweight chestnut gelding, 16.1hh, not a Quorn-type horse like those she was used to but very suitable. He was a bit difficult to clip but that is not such a problem as it used to be, now that the better types of drug are available. Before they appeared we used to do difficult horses in the lorry. They would probably knock their heads on the roof a couple of times and after that they settled down.

I sold Mrs Murray Smith, when she was Joint-Master of the Quorn, several horses for herself and Michael Farrin. About one of them she wrote in her book "Magic of the Quorn": *"John Betteridge sold me in 1978 a beautiful big horse, but just when I had solved the slight problem we had with the brakes and was delighted with him we had a very nasty accident when his hind legs went through a concealed and very deep drain at Prestwold. I have not been able to ride him since so I hope when he has recovered next year he will prove to be as brilliant as I think he is."*

The Quorn huntsman, Michael Farrin, was probably the best horseman who came to try the horses here. Murphy was one horse Linda wanted to keep for herself. He was only four years old when she rode him but I could see as he developed into a five-year-old he would get bigger and stronger and then he would probably be too much for her. So we let Michael have him and he said, "Good, he'll be able to keep in front of two hundred jockeys trying to get past me."

Another horse he had was one I had bought from John Masserella. He was one of the best moving horses I have ever had. He could gallop just as fast on a ploughed field as he could on grass, and I jumped the biggest ditch by the Dizzy Beds at Sutton on him.

The horses mentioned here that went to the Quorn are only three out of many. I think both Mrs Murray Smith and Michael Farrin would agree it was the way the horses were produced for them to ride that was so important and they would have to thank their stud-groom, Peter Houghton, and his wife, Liz, for that. Peter often came over to see what had arrived and he was the one who would probably first recommend to Mrs Murray Smith what she ought to buy.

I sold a horse through Shirley Edwards to another Quorn Joint-Master, James Teacher. In fact Shirley was a very good agent for me. She was the amateur whip for the Meynell and knew most of the people who hunted with the Meynell. Through her I sold to General D'Avigor Goldsmith a very tall horse that came from George Coombs (who has probably hunted on more days than anyone else in the country).

We did not have Remington long. He was a big horse, 16.2hh, and had been John Ward's second mount. He went to carry the Whip of the South Notts and was sold on to Yvonne Statham who lived in Hulland Village. He had not moved far in his life.

John had got very keen. With Remington he had moved up from Midas and was now moving up again, going more towards the blood-type animals. His eldest daughter, Gillian, was also very keen and was to be followed into the hunting-field by Katherine and Sarah. As well as the Wards, there was a strong contingent of families who were hunting together: Phil and Jenny Arthers with Richard and Mandy; George Shaw with Alistair and Stewart; Tom Brown with Graham, Valerie and Caroline; Linda and I with Sarah and Tim; Mike Norton with Carl and Clare; Nick Budgen and his son, who was dressed as well as his father with holes in his jodhpurs, not like the rest; Mrs Moon with Belinda, Mandy, and Pippa; Diana Foulkes with Joanna and Helen; Doug and Fay Hibbert with Julian and Charles; Rob Hutchinson with Nick and Chris; Joe Morley and Rachel; Roy Prince with sons David, Charles, and Michael; George Startin with Caroline; Mrs Chadfield and her family; Denham Smith and his son; John Crooks and his family; and Richard Frogatt and his family, Patti Guest with Maria and Emma. These were great days for parents and children hunting together.

Smurf was the next one to be sold. A grey horse, Irish-bred, bought from Tony Maguire. What I particularly remember about him was that at the top of Okeover, when Linda went to open a gate, he jumped it from a standstill. Since then, she has always been wary of opening gates.

Also in that year I sold a nice grey four-year-old mare There is little call for four-year-olds today, because very few people wish to make them. They need a finished horse <u>now</u>, but I loved a good four-year-old. After Christmas they all become five.

I remember buying a nice chestnut horse in Leicester, where John Craven was the vet The thing about that was I would tell him to make a thorough job of vetting each one because he might have to come and vet it again for a new buyer next week. If he passed it at Leicester, I should expect him to pass it at home.

Dan was another horse I sold that year. He went to Alan Edmunds who was at this time selling a lot of horses. I would meet him on his side of Kegworth with the horses. He would have them for a few days, hunt them and nine out of ten times he would find a customer – a very good outlet. It was a pity he could not have kept on being a horse-dealer. He was very good at it, but his trouble was what I have always said: a dealer needs a second income. In Mother's words, "Feathers one day and fowl the next." And liveries are not to be relied on for income: the owners used to think you lived on fresh air from April until August, but now it is often until just a few days before the opening meet when the horses come in that they remember their horses, and their debts.

Another horse that year to be sold was Bucklow Hill. We were doing the horses up one night about four o'clock when a car pulled in to the yard without warning and out stepped Bill Tellwright, "I called in to see if you've got a horse good enough so that I can go out hunting on my own and cock a snook at everyone out hunting." I told him I had got just the horse, a dark bay gelding, 16.2hh, and thoroughbred – more so than I generally bought – but he was a very good hunter, and I liked him. He asked if he could have a ride. It was just about going dusk by then and we had to go down the road to our jumping field because all the other fields roundabout were ploughed up. There were some big hedges down there. The fellow went jumping here there and everywhere. He cut Bucklow Hill to ribbons and then said it was not quite what he was looking for. After that, people that tried horses jumped what I told them to jump. I had learnt a lesson. Bill was a very good jockey, rode all Spurrier's and Pat Winter's point-to-pointers and rode a lot of winners for them. The poor fellow got killed by a horse. His son, Will, is a very nice fellow and has been a full subscriber to the hunt for a number of years.

Tony Maguire sent down two horses for me to try, a chestnut and a bay. They came on the Thursday and we tried them on the Friday. I said to Linda, "The hounds are at Muggington tomorrow. You ride the chestnut and I'll ride the bay." She thought for a moment and decided against it: "We've not had them long. You'd better ride them." I rode the chestnut first, a good horse that had won £210 show-jumping. He behaved like a Christian going to the meet, a mere three miles away. The first draw was the Old Gorse, where they found, and most of us went through the hunting-gate at the bottom of the wood. He walked through there all right and then – Whoosh! He took off down the hill. Luckily by the next gate there is a bog, and I steered him into that. He went right up to his belly. That stopped him. We got out of that, through the gate and to the bottom of a very steep hill. I said to him privately, "Now, you bugger, get to the top of this as quick as you can." He did just that, but I still could not stop him at the top, so down the other side we went and that was just as steep. Eventually, when I did manage to stop, I was only two fields from home and was able to walk him back, get the bay horse ready, and take him out. He was no better; he was crackers as well. I decided I would take the chestnut out again to the Tuesday Meet at Snelston. I had only had a snaffle on him so now I got the severest bit I could find, a three-in-one. The first draw was Johnny Roe, and they found in a ploughed field behind it. The chestnut and I set off across this plough, at a hundred miles an hour, and knocked poor Henry Jefferies off his horse. It was ages before I got him stopped. He went back with the other horse to Tony's.

The following season I was at Hilton Gorse, which was always the first Autumn Meet (I could get up early then, better than I can now). David Meynell, our Field Master then, was riding a new horse, a chestnut. I thought to myself that I knew that horse but I could not quite bring it to mind. Anyway, the hounds found and we got into the big grass field opposite Mick Bale's. David was at the front and we all went round this field, and then we went round again, and when we were all on the third circuit, I said to myself, "Hold hard! I know that horse." It had come to me it was the one we had sent back to Tony the year before. John Crooks had taken him and David was trying him.

1979-80

Douglas Hinckley joined the Mastership.

There was an improvement in the fox population but after Christmas they became hard to find again, although the sport and the scent improved. Hunting ended on March 23rd with the best run of the season after an enterprising fox that ran a four-and-a-half-mile point from Beryl's Gorse to the outskirts of Rocester over some of the best of the Meynell country.

The Hunt Ball that year was held at Houndhill by kind permission of Mike Seddon. 500 people paid for tickets (as usual, not too many hunting people turned up) and a donation of £1600 was made to Hunt funds. £750 was given to Hunt funds from the Fair in Derby, all thanks to Mrs. Gibbs. The Cross-Country was growing in popularity. The Tory Party led by Lord Oaksey won again. Donations were made to St John's Ambulance, Save the

Children, and the Animal Health Trust and £2,000 was given to Hunt funds. The day's events took place on the land of those great contributors, Tom White and Ken Bradshaw.

The Point-to-Point had to rely on sponsors and Mucklestone was not going to be available again because of change of ownership, leaving John Fairclough to look for a new course in our country.

The Hunt Club arranged for the old Transit and Mazda to be replaced by a 4 x 4 as the Knackerwagon.

Although I had bought plenty of Irish horses, 1980 saw me going to Ireland to try to do my own buying there for the first time. Doug Hibbert and I decided to go to the fair in Kilrush. We had flown into Dublin, hired a car, and then taken it in turns to drive fifty miles at a stretch. We got down to Kilrush at about five in the evening, booked into a hotel, and had a look round. I recognised a few people I had met around the shows over the years. There were a few horses about but none that would suit us. We found a nice place to have a meal and retired to bed. Next morning very early we could hear the horses arriving; they were tied to anything they could find down the the high street, the side streets, – anywhere. Although there was every type of horse or pony you could think of, there were only one or two you could have gone hunting on, and they seemed to have been sold. Most of the others were two- or three-year-olds. We soon learnt that the big buyers such as Ned Cash, Frank Kernon and the others had men stationed on every street leading into Kilrush so that we stood no chance of buying anything. In the circumstances we decided to make our way back to Dublin, but when we got to within about fifty miles thought we would stay overnight, found ourselves dinner, bed and breakfast, and put the car in one of the local car parks. When we were ready to leave next morning, at about eight o'clock, and went to get the car, the gates were locked, with a really big chain, and a notice saying, "Open at nine." Well, we had not allowed ourselves that extra hour to catch the plane so we went to the local ironmongers, bought a very large chain-cutter, cut through the chain, made haste to get the car out and were on our way. We were not quite in the clear yet. The airport was checking everything. As I had given a lot of money for this implement I did not feel like leaving it behind. I put it at the bottom of my overnight case and hoped that it wasn't questioned. I just kept my head down and walked through Customs. I had those chain-cutters for years.

The second time I went to Ireland was with John Goodwin who had a dealing yard just outside Alrewas and had suggested I went with him. He seemed to know his way around. We flew from Birmingham, picked up a hire-car in Dublin, and toured round. He seemed to know a lot of people but, believe me, it is a totally different thing buying horses in Ireland. You literally have no trial. You probably see one in a field and if you believe what the seller says and like the horse, you have to buy it on that. The first horse I bought like that was Frankie, a very big tall horse, a bright bay. I never rode him or saw him ridden. John could not believe I could buy a horse like that. He said, "When you buy one from me, you want to take it home, hunt it, have it vetted. I wonder why."

It was Wimbledon week when we were over there and was it hot! We had to wait a few months before we could hunt Frankie. The first time I was able to take him out was to Radbourne and who should be out that day but Michael Clayton. It was about the time that he married Jane Whitfield, a great friend of mine. The first time I met Michael was a number of years ago when he was writing an article on the South Notts and I like to think we have been friends ever since. We gave Shandy to him for his daughter when Sarah had outgrown the pony that Urky Newton had given us. Michael gave us a free subscription to *Horse and Hound* for a year – very handy. It came as a shock when we had to start paying for it again. Anyway he had a ride on Frankie, liked him, bought him and wrote how pleased he was with him. He certainly made a good horse for Michael but I always think Josephine was his favourite hunter. The Claytons were full subscribers for a number of years.

Another one I bought in Ireland that day was Granard, a bay mare about 16.1hh, which they said had been really well hunted. After I had hunted her she sold to Bill Strawson for a Whip's horse and fitted the bill very well. I also bought a pony to make up the load, as John had also bought a few. It was a 13.2hh pony that Sarah jumped a few times and then sold it on. It was just a nice pony, that was all.

Back at home, during 1979, Linda and I had ridden Gibbon a few times – she got on better than I with him – before we sold him to Margaret Oxby who bought him for Tim Brown to show-jump. He did win one or two good classes on him. I had known Margaret for more years than I can remember. She always said she would marry someone horsey and her husband, Denzil, who is one of the leading course-builders in the country, certainly was that. They ran some very successful shows at Kinoulton, a good ground.

I started buying a few horses from Gillian Milner. I had known her father for a number of years and her mother, Valma Craig. who, sadly, died quite young Gillian had some very good show-jumpers. One called Luke came to us. He was a very nice four-year-old, 16.2hh, bay. But what a poor season we were having! When I sold him to Alan Robertson, I said to him, "Alan, this horse has beautiful manners but I can't tell you how he jumps because, out hunting, I haven't jumped a fence on him." George Shaw had a good grey horse and I think he too only jumped two fences on him all season. You would not think it possible in the Meynell not to jump a fence, but I am afraid it was true. Politics were starting to come into the equation, which every hunt goes through one time or another.

I sold Juno for Annie Chandos-Pole, who was giving up hunting for a while. I think she was helping in some exhibition in America. It was to be a season or two before she hunted again. Goostrey was the name of another horse I sold. I bought Swain from Tony, a very good looking horse that Tim rode around the Meynell Hunter Trials when they were at Sevier's, before he went to Mick Toulson. I bought Copper at the Stoneleigh Sale from two sisters who show-jumped, and lived near Wigan. One of them was a trained masseur and looked after the players at Wigan Rugby Club – a nice job for a girl. Copper was a middle-weight chestnut, 16.2hh, one of the first horses Sarah rode. I have a lovely photograph of her jumping a hunter trial fence. He went to John McDowell who lived at Bangor-on-Dee.

I bought a very good chestnut mare, even though chestnut mares have a reputation for being hot and kicking other horses, but so do chestnut geldings and bay mares. Some of the best hunters I have owned have been chestnut mares and Linda will always say one of the best she has ever ridden was Satisfaction. (We had her to sell for Dermot Kelly, and she went to Wildbore-Smith when he became Joint-Master of the Belvoir). This chestnut mare came from the Zetland Kennels, had carried the Whip. I have always been dubious about buying hunt-staff horses because very few settle in the middle of the field, and I am also a bit wary of buying proven event horses – they like to cross country in front of everybody. Show-jumpers are in my opinion the best to buy, but there was nothing wrong with this hunt-staff mare. Mike Power, who had been a Joint-Master of the South Staffs, bought her. When he came over to look at her Mike was not in his first flush of youth, but he jumped the biggest of our hedges to try out the jump she had in her. It was a brave ride he gave her before sending Hugh Davies to vet her. She carried him well for many seasons. If I am to enjoy my hunting, the horses I sell have to go well.

I bought a nice mare, about 16.1hh, from John Goodwin. She could have been Dutch but when they have no brand they are always difficult to sell. However, Sarah hunted her and let it be known she was a very good mare, and I was able to sell her to Roy Sevier. That would have been the third I had sold to him and Tricia.

Phinees and another came from Ireland; Shirley Edwards bought them. They were both chestnut geldings. (It is funny the way you seem to buy runs of chestnuts, or greys, or bays just by chance. You don't mean to). Brocksford was a lovely big chestnut horse. We named him after Tim's prep-school so he had to be a good horse. I used to sell Tub Ivens a few horses but he would only buy a really nice one. He bought Brocksford. We would stay with him, a real nice fellow, when we were show-jumping for a couple of nights. He used to ring up and say, "I need a horse. Have you got one that can jump your big holly hedge?" We have a lot of big holly hedges on the farm; they are particularly good for schooling over. (A relation of Tub's has been a subscriber for a number of years).

Now around this time I bought the most lovely grey horse we called Ivan, at the same time as Chips. George Coombes rang and wanted a horse for Lord Belper so I told him about Ivan. He asked if I would like to take him over to a meet at the Belvoir and he would try him out. The day would cost me nothing. Once we were there, George seemed to like the looks of Ivan, but I hunted him for about an hour before he said he would like a sit on him. I rode his horse – a bit stuffy but he could jump a good ditch towards. He would place his front feet on the edge of the ditch and heave himself over. We did have a very good hunt. When I kept asking him what he thought, George would say, "Yes. He's all right." At about 4.30, not being able to get him off the horse, I had to say," It's make your mind up time!" It was a bit of a surprise when he came out with it: "He's not just what I'm looking for." At least I had enjoyed a day with the Belvoir, the first for quite a long time. A few days later Shirley Edwards rang wanting a horse for a great friend of ours, Theresa Woolley. I had known the family for many years. Theresa has, as long as I could remember, been associated with the Pony Club. Anyway, I was able to bring out a good horse and they bought him. Theresa had Ivan for many years and went very well on him. (I don't think she would mind me saying she is not in the first flush of youth). The only fault she said she could find in him was he used to get so dirty on the morning she was going hunting that she had some pyjamas made for him.

THE EIGHTIES

1980-81

The Joint-Masters were down to two, Marek Kwiatowski and the Hon. Louise Astor having resigned.

The Opening Meet was at Longford Hall; a brace was found in Reeves Moor and they hunted hard until they blew for home at 3 o'clock. The best hunt of the season (What a ride that was!) ran from Bentley with a five-mile-point, eleven miles as hounds ran, and the fox given best. Another very good day was from Cyril Goodall's at Trusley. Around Sutton is some of our biggest country. It was a difficult season – very wet, affecting theDerbyshire ground particularly.

The Hunt Fair was as usual held at the King's Hall but it was thought to be the last as the King's Hall was going to be converted into a permanent swimming-baths. Mrs Gibbs, who had done such a marvellous job running the Hunt Fair and raising so much money for the Meynell, stepped down. The major project for the season was the painting by Rodney Lovesey for Marek Kwiatkowski on his retirement. The prints were sold on behalf of the Hunt.

The first Cross-Country Ride (not to be confused with the Team Event) was organised – a bit like the Melton Cross-Country Ride from point to point – and set up in the space of six weeks. The effort deserved better than the awful weather on the day – torrential rain and a howling gale. 42 riders from an entry of 70 set off. The winner was John Crowther from West Yorkshire who beat Bill Tellright by a neck.

The Point-to-Point was run at Mucklestone after all.

BEGINNER'S LUCK

The story around one of the horses I sold in 1980 stands out in my memory forever. Fay Hibbert rang saying a friend of hers needed a horse to ride and probably to hunt, so one Sunday morning into the yard came Michael Hall, Fay's friend. He is a jeweller from Derby. The mare I was going to show him was Sadie, a chestnut mare, 16.2 hh, middleweight, and six years old. I had hunted her a few times. She was a bit special. I said to him, "This is the one I have in mind for you," but looking at him and looking at the mare I wondered if she would carry him. Although it was snowing it had not settled too much. I put a saddle and bridle on as it was no good putting a head collar on her and giving her a jog – he would not have known what he was looking for. He climbed on board and I told him to walk, only because he did not look too safe. "Walk down the drive and back and I'll see how you suit one another." Afterwards, we put her back in the stable and he stroked her neck and he stroked her nose and then he said:

"I'll have her."

I was a bit taken aback. "That was a bit sudden," I said. "What has made up your mind so quickly?"

"Oh, I know we're going to get on fine. She likes my smell."

I had heard plenty of reasons for buying a horse, but never that one. All I said was, "You'll have to wait a bit and then as soon as we can go on a field for a canter I'll give you a ring."

After about three weeks the field was clear so he came over for a ride, bought her, and left her with us to keep for him. He would come over and ride every day.

One day he told me that one of his clients had asked him to be her guest with the High Peak and asked if I would take Sadie there on the lorry for him. When he said he had never been hunting before we fitted him out with some hunting clothes and I advised him to stay in the middle of the field and keep a low profile. I would pick him up at 3.30 p.m., and warned him not to be late! So off we went to his friend's place where the meet was being held.

At 3.30 I was back at the starting-point and he was waiting with a beam on his face. He greeted me with, "What a marvellous day I've had!" and told me all about it when I asked him. For most of the day he had kept a pretty low profile and had jumped a few walls until they came to a big one and the chap with the bugle's horse kept refusing. He'd asked if anyone would give him a lead. "I can!" shouted Michael – and he did. Sadie cleared it so well that the huntsman asked Michael to ride with him for the rest of the day. He'd had a marvellous time.

After that he hunted for a number of years and kept the horse at livery with Shirley Edwards. He was certainly very generous to the Meynell Hunt with his sponsorships and gifts of jewellery. He had a friend who was a nice jockey, a chap called Andrew Macara, who had the Caravan Centre at Spondon until he gave the business up to be an artist. He painted some very good pictures too. When the Meynell were short of money and held an Auction and Supper at J.C.B. at Rocester, a painting by him called *Gone*

Fishing made £530. At the same do, Michael Hall gave a pillbox in the form of a snail-shell, mounted in silver-gilt, I think, a piece set with ruby and decorated with engine turning that made £205. Not bad from two people I introduced to hunting!

I saw Trotsky jumping at Solihul show, a grey horse, 16.2hh. I would say he was three-quarter bred – Tom would probably say thoroughbred just to be different. He had a few pounds on his card as a jumper and also two points on his card for dressage. We brought him back with us on the Sunday and Tom – that is Tom Brown – rang that night wanting a horse for his son, Graham. They came on the Monday, liked what they saw and bought him; he would be as good a buy as they ever had. He made a Grade A show-jumper and he was probably one of the best horses to cross the country, not just with Graham but with his sisters, Valerie and Caroline, too.

Look Again was a mare I had seen hunting and noticed she had the most enormous jump in her. She was a black mare, about 16.1hh, but she had not done the world. I hunted her one day with the South Notts and she was going so high over those stone walls that they all, not just the ones with drops on them, seemed like Bechers. I had a feeling we should hurt ourselves if we stayed out much longer. A bit later I was talking to Geoff Mallaber at a show when he mentioned he was looking for a novice jumper for Jane, his daughter, and I told him that I rather fancied his Onedin for my daughter. (Onedin had been leading pony jumper in England). Anyway, we did a swop: Look Again went well for Jane and Onedin went well for Sarah. He was probably not the most careful pony but was always a good pathfinder.

We bought Forever Diamond out of *Horse and Hound* from Joe Raines, a dairy-farmer who lived near Baslow. He turned out to have been a wonderful buy. We can't recollect how many classes Sarah won on him, but I remember the English Grand Prix at Lincoln and when she jumped with Willian Funnell in Belgium for Great Britain, and then won the Belgian Pony Grand Prix. They brought tears to my eyes.

After seeing him jumping at Southport Show, I bought Happy Roy. He looked a girl's sort of horse and proved to be one. Sarah was a Foxhunter finalist at Wembley and a qualifier for the Olympia in the Vauxhall Young Riders. When I bought him, Roy had a big knee, so I rubbed it with goose grease – just smeared it on every Monday through the winter – and it went away.

When Sarah had finished on ponies, Tim took over. The two big shows I particularly remember are Bakewell, when I thought Tim had jumped the best two rounds I had ever seen a pony jump; and Stoneleigh in a qualifier for the Horse of the Year Show. He jumped two superb rounds and finished fourth

Sarah jumping Happy Roy at the Horse of the Year Show

Sarah and Forever Diamond at Hickstead in the Meynell Pony Club Team

Tim winning the Vauxhall Young Riders at Wrexham on Ben

when it was the first three that would go through to Wembley. The pony that beat us was Solway Lord. I told Tim that I reckoned the pony was big and asked him if he thought I should make an objection. He said he wouldn't bother, and so I didn't. A few months later I noticed Solway Lord was jumping in Horse Classes. Tim had missed out.

When it was time to look for a horse for him it was no use buying a very expensive one while he was still at school. At a show in Cheshire we saw Ben, owned and ridden by Edward Evans. We bought him after Tim had ridden him and liked him. At Ashbourne, at the first show we took him to, Tim was having a good round when Ben suddenly took off and ran two circuits of the ring before Tim could pull him up. After that he became a good horse and Tim did well on him. He won the first round in the Vauxhall Young Rider at Wrexham, although he had been celebrating the night before with friends on degree courses at Harper Adams. He probably rode better in the second round up in Scotland. He went well, but not well enough. Norman Proffit had offered to take him up for us, but would take nothing for it, not even expenses, but accepted when I offered him a day's hunting with us, with me

144

paying his cap. He thoroughly enjoyed himself and it started him on a new career.

It was Derek Dalton who introduced me to Tessa Hibbert from Hazelwood. She only wanted a quiet hack. Her father had hunted with the South Notts, but she did not want to hunt. She just wanted to start riding again. As I did not have that sort of animal I made enquiries locally and especially at Riding Schools. I must admit we had to look at quite a few before eventually we came up with a white cob, about 15.1hh, from a Riding School in Matlock. She enjoyed her so much and called her Marble. Tessa lived about six miles from us so I had quite a shock when she rode into the yard one day. We had a coffee and then I offered to take her back in the horse-box, but no, she had enjoyed riding over and would enjoy riding back. No-one in their right minds seeing her ride down the drive would have thought that one day (1993) she would be a Joint-Master of the Meynell. As I have said before you need two horses in your life – the first to get you going and the last to take care of you. Marble was a classic example of the one that gets you going. It was a disappointment that she never asked me to find her another horse. She would not be the first to do that.

It happened with Dallas, a brown and white gelding, seven years old, with Irish bone. The first time I hunted him was at Kedleston and he took a fierce hold down the Park when I had only a snaffle on him. The next time I took him out I had a bit more in his mouth and found he could jump. I had a wonderful day on him from Cubley when we had a lot of visitors out. He could out-jump most of them and we could easily take our own line. At that time a Miss Ferranti was hunting with us, as well as her father Sebastian Ferranti who had subscribed for a number of years. They saw him going. She had a ride on him and bought him on condition that I took an old grey in part exchange. I rarely took horses in part exchange but this one I did. What a good horse Dallas turned out to be for her; she hunted him with so many different packs. One day she came as a visitor and was riding a different horse. I was finding out all about it and asked her why she hadn't asked me for another horse. She said she never gave it a thought,

Rossal was a grey I bought from Pennwood and hunted him a few times. The South Notts rang up, wanting a horse for the Huntsman, so I arranged to go on the Nottinghamshire side of the country. I rode him for a while; then the Huntsman took over. At the end of the day he said, "This will do for me." I asked if he was really sure. "Oh yes, very sure." He fetched him a few days later but a few days after that he rang up saying that they could not do a thing with him. He was berserk, had broken out of the stable and was found halfway up a tree. So fast was he in the tree that they had had to cut it down to free him. I had him back here and got the vet to examine him. He came to the conclusion that what with hounds barking and the smell of blood and dead carcasses it had made him go crazy. When he had come back he was dreadful, always breaking out in sweat; so we had to put him down. The vet thought the trauma of being in hunt kennels had affected his brain.

Jerry was bought at Malvern Sales, a bay gelding, 16.1hh, a very good horse with the longest pasterns behind that I have ever seen on a horse by Elf Arrow. Linda and I hunted him a few times. Other horses sold that year were Carat, George, Milly, Dan, Hugo and a few others. Sometime we only had them for a few hours or days. It is often said that if a horse has more than one set of shoes there is no profit left in it.

1981-82

David Meynell and Douglas Hinckley were joined in the Mastership by Mike Seddon and John Stevens. Both had hunted with the Meynell for a number of years. Mike Seddon had been living at Houndhill (where the Hunt Ball had been held, and some very good wine-and-cheese parties). My sister bought it from him and he moved to Somersal Herbert. John Stevens had a cottage in Foston but really lived in London, where I believe he was in publishing. He was a very brave man to take on the Mastership as he had a bad fall by Tom White's farm, and, as I have already said, had actually broken a bone in his neck. I have a photograph of him riding a horse called Ted that he had bought from me. The photo was taken at the top of Callow by Jim Meads, the running photographer, from in front of me. Of course, after breaking his neck, John was not allowed to jump and as hounds started running he had to make straight for the road. The horse's name was changed to Tarmac Ted but he was a super horse for the way he never looked back, never shied, and was always very good in traffic once he had turned away from the field. John was a very knowledgeable hound man.

The Huntsman was Graham Roberts; and the whip Trevor Adams, both of them newcomers.

In September '81, I had been at the Leicester Sales and the class horse of the sales was a lovely bay horse, 16.2hh, 6 years old, middleweight, but full of quality. While I was looking him over, Douglas came to me and asked if I was interested in the horse. If so, would I buy him, and if he was all right Douglas would give me a profit. When the horse was being sold, I dropped out of the bidding, telling Douglas that I had had enough, but he went on and bought him. Then he asked me if I would have him to hunt and give him my opinion of the horse. After having him at livery for a while and hunting him a few times I reported to Douglas: "You have bought yourself a very nice horse, but he is not a front runner – the sort that likes to be given a lead." I knew that Douglas liked to take his own line Just before Hollington, which is a very big country, there is a hedge with the most enormous drop and a strand of barbed wire about six inches down. When I saw him setting sail for this hedge and drop, I thought, "Bloody hell." I always jumped the hedge at the top of the field where there was a much easier place and so did everyone else. As I cantered back down the field he was sitting on the ground not looking too bad. I asked if he was all right and he seemed to say he was. Jim Hall went down the field in his Landrover, and took him to the road where the ambulance came and picked him up. By ten o'clock that night he was dead. A burst aorta was the cause.

The Hunt Ball was held at Hollybush Park but only 200 tickets were sold and, regrettably, not many to subscribers. The Point-to-Point was held at Sandon for the first time and it was the best attended for many years. The expenses were shared between the Meynell and the North Staffs. Not too many runners due to the ground being too firm for lack of rain, but the move was declared to have been a success. The Cross Country Team-Event took place in November, at Booth Hay, with thanks again to Tom White and Adrian Bradshaw. Rumenco and Bass Worthington were the Sponsors. Four teams took part. The Cumbrian Ratcatchers took first place, and second place went to the Hunting Farmers.

In this year Sir Ian Walker-Okeover passed away. What a marvellous man, exceptionally generous to the Meynell Hunt and to me also! He would come and sit in our kitchen and want to talk about the Meynell Hunt. We would pull no punches and spent many happy hours just talking hunting.

Lord Oaksey was the guest speaker at the Annual Dinner at Hilton House. Joe Morley had lent his ground for the very successful Horse Show. Neil Seaton was given a new Landrover that was presented to him at the Opening Meet. John Crooks deserved full credit for getting it at such a competitive price. The Cross-Country Ride, sponsored again by Michael Hall, was held at the Hollybush, with 72 starters. A spectacular ride produced a thrilling finish. Bill Foulkes just got up to beat Kate Cooper.

Autumn hunting started early and we killed 29 brace. We had a good hunt from Longford which hosted the Opening Meet. The hunting was going all right but not sparkling. The meet on the 8th December was cancelled owing to snow and ice and we only had one day for the next seven weeks. There were only two real hunts that season – one from Sudbury Coppice and the other from Radbourne Rough.

In 1981 I sold Timmy to George Shaw who, I am sure, would rank him as one of the best horses he owned. I had actually had a hand in the first two horses he owned after he returned to hunting when Alistair and Stewart were starting off. They were Pluto and Dungannon that he got from Fay Hibbert and John Crooks as I have already described. Now that George was hunting a lot I bought Timmy for him from Brent Iddles of Wolverhampton (who I had met a few times at Pennwood and seen him show-jumping). Brent told me that he had a very good horse to sell that he had hunted with the Albrighton. I bought him and the first time I hunted him was when they met at John Ward's and that day I jumped the biggest ditch towards I have ever jumped. The problem was that it was right into a field of seeds – and it was very wet. I went and apologised to John but he did not seem to mind and said it was worth the mess to see him jump that. George came straight over and bought him. He enjoyed some wonderful days on him.

Hilton was a chestnut with four white legs that Sue Perkins tried out at Hulland. I thought him very suitable, but she didn't. In fact, Sue tried a few but never actually bought anything from me. He finished up in the Wynnstay country for a client of Gilbert Brown's.

I sold a chestnut gelding called Tanner, that I had bought in Ireland, to Lesley Price, who lived between Solihull and Stoneleigh. I sold quite a few horses to her but this one, named Shilty, she wanted for John Curry, the Olympic ice-skater's brother. Other horses sold that year were John's Mum, Eve, Niki and Resolution.

HORSES SOLD TO ANNIE CHANDOS-POLE

I had wanted a hunter for Sarah and bought Manekin from Tony Maguire. He was probably a bit older than I normally bought but he was an ex-showjumper, had been to Wembley a few times, but loved his hunting. However, Annie Chandos-Pole was wanting to start hunting again, and as her mother was our landlord and Annie wanted him, I thought it was best to let her have him. He proved a great success. Annie said up till then she had met only two gentlemen in her life: one was her father, and the other was Manekin. She took him hunting one day with a Leicestershire pack, had a bang on the head, but was all right. As we had him at livery, it was only right that we should fetch him back here about 8 o'clock at night. The next horse I sold her was Mavis. When I was wanting a horse for Tim for the Christmas holidays, I had seen Mavis hunting at Mercaston with Jennie Arthers riding her. She was not a big mare, about 15.3hh, but moved like a pony. Linda had a day on her and we bought her. It was about the middle of November. When Tim came home we sat him on her and his feet came just to the end of the saddle flaps, but what fun he had on her!

This is taken from Tim's hunting diary, which he has written up every hunting day since 1980.

27th December, '82. 15 couple. Kedleston Hall, 4 miles. On Mavis. Good weather. Scent not good. We drew Kedleston Park, Vicarwood, Brewards Carr, Salts. Pilot went to ground. It was a poor day, no foxes. Mavis jumped a very big hedge, third, followed Auntie Fay over it. Mum was in good form with the throttle wide open. All of the family were mounted on horses for the first time. 60 people were out.

We did not do second horses; it is quite hard work at the end of the day and there is no money in it, but one day when they were round Shuckton I said to Annie, "If you take Manekin first and you are near, Mavis will be ready for you." I remember the hounds came through our farmyard and she swapped horses. We then crossed the road to Jim's, where they found and ran to Kedleston. I can see her now. Lots of people came back for tea and she sat on top of the washing-machine as we do not have a very big kitchen. Her face was still flushed with excitement. She did feel she had arrived.

Mavis, the mare we had first bought for Tim at Christmas, went lame and as it was very difficult to know what was wrong with her, we decided to send her to the kennels to be put down. We waited for the lorry to come and pick her up, but when it never came we turned her out. When I saw her moving in the open I thought she was looking a bit better so we put off sending her away. Again, like Mystery, she came right and not only hunted again but had a few foals as well.

Another horse I sold her was Bud, a lovely lady's horse. Norman Proffit rang me to say that he had got this nice horse, 16.1hh, 7 years old, that had won a lot of money show-jumping. Tim hunted him and thought he was very special – took a grip but was easily manageable. Annie took a shine to him and bought him. One day hounds went away from Johnnie Roe and Bud jumped her off by the side of a gate, quite an awkward place. When I caught him and took him back to her, she said to me, "I can't understand why you sold me this effing horse." I told her if she ever spoke to me like that again her horses would move from Shuckton. She apologised but she was always a fiery little character. Bud was a very good horse to her and gave her many good seasons. She eventually gave him away to Cedric Stevenson as a hack. There was Huggy, too, a stocky chestnut gelding who had also been show-jumping Another horse I sold her was Mayo who I bought in Ireland. The first time I hunted him at Hoar Cross I jumped a few fences on my own and was very pleased with him. A lot of these Irish horses have never seen a hedge but he was all right. Annie bought him and hunted him for a few seasons. When she gave up she sold him to the Field Master of the Blackmore Vale, and she also sold Clover Nook, the last horse I had sold her (who had come from Ann Hunter and won about £500 show-jumping).

1982-83

After Douglas Hinckley's tragic death, the Joint Masters were reduced to three.

The hunting that season was quite good. The hounds killed 34 brace, 5 brace more than the year before. Autumn hunting started on the 7th September, with some very good hunts especially from the Waterings on the 26th November and again in December, and, as I have already described, when they met at Biggin on the 18th January and ran from Sunnybank by Rowlands to Breward Carr and finally had to be stopped in the gathering gloom and snow. Another good hunt was from Reeves Moor to Brailsford Gorse.

Phil Willmott retired after 13 years as Hunt Secretary. She was Assistant Secretary to Miles Porter for six years before that, and was the last owner of Jemima, the mare that started her hunting career as a two-year-old, in '73. She had Jemima for many years and had a few foals from her.

Talking about foals reminds me how Henry Jefferies asked me once when we were out hunting, "Will you find me a good sort of mare, one I can hunt for a few years then breed from. I should like to hunt one I'd bred myself."

"I've just bought a very good sort of mare from Bill Toye; an ideal sort to breed from and also a very good hunter. She's six now, Henry, so you'll be able to hunt her for say eight years, and then you'll put her to the stallion. You should be able to hunt any foal that she has as a five-year-old. As you're seventy now, do you really want to be riding a five-year-old across the Meynell when you are 85?"

He bought her anyway and after he had had her for a few years he asked me to find another like her. About three months later he rang and told me to cancel that order. He had been diagnosed as having cancer. Poor Henry! He had not started riding until he was forty but he did enjoy it – he entered all the hunter trials, and any cross-country race, and had his successes. All his rosettes, and lots of his horsey memorabilia were buried with him.

Joint-Master John Stevens gave public thanks to the Puppy Walkers who take bitches to whelp, or walk hound puppies, or do both. It is a particularly important service to the Hunt and is usually performed by people who do not themselves ride to hounds.

At the Cross-Country event, held at Booth Hay again, 32 teams took part in the Novice section and 15 teams in the Open. £2000 was made for the Hunt. Bass again sponsored the event. The Chairman's ride which Sue and Richard Perkins organised was a great success and took place at Nether Hall on the 22nd March. They gave lunch as well. I have known Richard for many years; Mother gave him some of his first riding lessons but she used to become exasperated with him. She used to say he is more interested in turning the church into a hangar for an aeroplane than concentrating on his riding.

In the Cross-Country Ride at Snelston Park, the third to be held, fifty competitors out of an entry of eighty faced 30 fences on a course of nearly 4 miles. There was an exciting finish with three riders neck and neck over the last fence. Not far from neck and neck at the finish, Gill Fleming-Williams was first, Mike Roberts second, and Fred French third.

Anthony Bamford and his wife ran a very successful auction and supper. Hunt Funds benefited to the tune of £8000, all raised in one evening. John Ward gave half a ton of oats that made £50. A ton of hay that T.Brown, G.Shaw and P.Wint gave made £45. A chamber-pot given by Jeremy Allen made £32. We gave a week's livery for a hunter and that raised £35. Highest price of the night came from Richard Perkins – a week in a villa for four people in the South of France made £550. Phil Arthers took over as Chairman of the Hunt Supporters. I remember him giving his first speech at the Annual Dinner when it was held at the Green Man. Linda and I were on the top table with him. We knew how nervous he was, but he came through all right and he never looked back. The Wine and Cheese was given by Mr. and Mrs. Jeremy Allen in their lovely old house at Chartley Manor. I know I enjoyed it.

John Fairclough arranged some mouse-racing.

As usual, more horses passed through my hands than I can readily remember. A very nice bay horse, four white socks, 16.3hh, came from Norman Proffit. He was named Ed after Norman's girl-friend at the time. He had a big jump over a straight-up but a ditch found him out. Luckily, we found a home for him in the High Peak where ditches would have to be looked for.

Olivia was a black mare bought through Gilbert Brown, who lived below Shrewsbury. We were spending a day looking at horses in Shropshire and North Wales. Gilbert took us to a farm – I have no idea where it was, apart from being on a mountain – where a school had been bulldozed into the mountainside. He put this mare around the school loose and told us she could jump six feet – and she did! I sold her to a girl moving up from ponies who lived in Sheffield and went to work for Brady at Worksop. The mare got to Grade A. but I lost touch with her after that.

Kingswood, a big fine chestnut horse, came from a friend of Sally Parrott near Stafford. I sold him to Ian Crawford, who sold him on to hunt in Leicestershire. He was a typical Leicestershire type.

Barry and Sandra Pearson-Adams bought a very nice mare from me, blue and white, 15.2hh. When they had had her for about three weeks, Barry rang to say the horse had produced a thoroughpin in her hock and he was not too happy. I suggested they should leave her where she was for another week and we would talk it over again. I thought it was just a change of diet and so it proved to be. They were soon able to sell her on to Lady Boyne.

When we were nearing the end of our few days' holiday in the Lake District with Frank and Joy Salt, and had been to John Peel's grave, we were meaning to stay in York and have a look around the city but we saw the notice in *Horse and Hound* for a horse-sale at Rufford Park and gave York a miss. I bought the most lovely half-bred Cleveland Bay. Why I bought him I don't know. He was not a marvellous mover, and besides he was unbroken. I reckon never to buy unbroken horses; you have to keep them far too long. Young Walter Wharton (who had ridden Jack Fox, six times a winner, for my brother), had moved into the stables at Church Broughton and he made a good job of breaking him. I had hunted him a few times when John Wrathal came to see him. He had been married to Margaret Lockart (owner of the pony Jean that Norman Swinnerton had ridden to win the National Championship at Blackpool) but he was now with Judy. They bought him and sold him on to an Event Team. I know only that they got him to Intermediate, nothing more.

I sold a few horses to Eric Wright, who I knew well from the show-jumping days, a hunter-dealer from Leicestershire who was the starter for the Melton Cross-Country race. Joey was a Leicestershire-type horse, mostly blood. He actually came from Alan Edmunds. He also had Trudy, a dark bay mare, quite a tall sort, with a bit more bone. Eric would also bring clients here, on commission, and was always very straight. He knew his clients well and their capabilities. Today there are very few people like him – a proper horseman.

Halloween and Tango, both came from Ireland. Tom, my cousin, was farming down in Buckinghamshire and sent this customer who was a Joint-Master at the time and he bought both of them. They must have been all right as I never heard that they weren't.

THE CRAFT OF SELLING HUNTERS

Dominic and Trooper both came from Tony Maguire. I did not have them very long; in fact I only had one day's hunting on them. Not taking them out two or three times makes selling them too much of a gamble because the first day is all such a shock to horses that they don't take in what is actually going on. They seem to be numb, but during the second and third days out they begin to realise what is happening. In fact, John Sheddon would say they need to have seen hounds at least twelve times before you really know if they have settled.

Phillip Payne-Galway of the British Bloodstock Agency came to buy horses and went back with Jerry. He was trying to get the British Bloodstock Agency interested in selling hunters as well as the bloodstock in which they are experts. The scheme did not take off. Selling hunters is entirely different from selling race-horses or potential race-horses such as yearlings. With a racehorse you are sure of the breeding and absolutely sure of the age. Those certainties are basically what they are bought on. It does not make buying yearlings and potential racehorses easy, but it is a different matter buying hunters, to ride or sell. That should be obvious by now. There are so many things to consider and so many things that can only be found out after quite a long trial. Can the person who wants it manage it? Is it good to clip, good in traffic, and good to load into a trailer on your own, etc., etc.? Where is it going? To the High Peak country with those walls to jump? To the Quorn with their ditches towards? Or to the Meynell with those and all the other types of jump? Who would be a hunter-dealer except someone who really liked hunting? Even then, I'm afraid we can't always get it right.

There were many more horses that went through these stables but I really can't write about every one. I would be writing until doomsday. I pick out the ones that had something special in their history that makes me remember them, but there was something special about them all. I should not have bought them otherwise.

1983-84

We still had the same Joint-Masters, David Meynell, Mike Seddon and John Stevens, and the same huntsman, Graham Roberts, but David Gaylord was the new Whipper-in instead of Trevor Adams (who had got married and gone as Joint-Master and Huntsman to the Romney Marsh and later went to the Buccleuch). Robert Howarth came as Kennelman. He was Meynell born and bred.. His father is farm manager to the Clark Maxwells. Robert went on a few years later to become Huntsman to the Holderness where he does a very good job: Trevor Stockill tells me they do more jumping now than they have ever done.

We started cubbing on the 1st September. I didn't because I am not too good at getting up in the mornings unless I have a new horse to try. Besides, we had three evening meets which suited me a lot better. The Boxing Day Meet, held at Kedleston Hall, was always the place to turn up to. They said Lord Scarsdale would be up all night making the stirrup cup. Hundreds of people used to attend – so did a few "antis." This year we had a really good run from one of the coverts in the park to Dalbury. Hounds were running for over an hour, making a four-mile point and seven as hounds ran. That went down well on top of the Christmas pud. We had a good hunt from Tom White's, but then we usually do, and another from Snelston. There was a good ride round the Hollybush to finish the season. During it they had killed 41 brace.

Kevin Gilmore built the course for the Cross Country Team Event, held at Booth Hay again. It made a profit of just over £2000. The fourth Meynell cross-country ride, 32 starters from 53 entries, was held at Roy and Paddy Prince's farm, thanks to their generosity and the other farmers whose land was used. What a stalwart Paddy Prince has been to the Meynell. She must have supplied and served more meals that anyone else in the history of the Meynell. The event raised £1,048 for the hunt. The Point-to-Point was again a great success, attracting 257 entries, about 100 more than the usual number. Again we have to thank John Fairclough for all his hard work. £2,500 was given over to the Hunt Funds. £600 was made from the Hunt Ball which was again hosted by the Robinsons at Alkmonton. The Hunt Club donated £2000 towards a container for the horse-box. Fiona King joined the Hunt Supporters Committee and Gillian Ward was co-opted on to look after the younger generation. Mr and Mrs. Pratt gave a cheese and wine at Church Broughton and the annual dinner was held at Hilton House. The Majors had a disco and barbecue. It was a very good year for entertainments.

Hunting was under a greater political pressure than it had been since 1948. The Hunt Committee insisted that everyone who hunted should be a member of the B.F.S.S. It was not a good year for selling horses. We were all suffering the dreadful uncertainty – would we hunt again or wouldn't we? Luckily, we did.

Tony Maguire rang and said, "I am sending you a horse. He is the nappiest creature you have ever come across. Won't go anywhere on his own but he's all right with other horses." He turned out to be a fine chestnut horse, 16.1hh. Well, we tried him going down the drive on his own and that didn't work. We could have given him a good hiding but Mr. Powell used to say you can knock the devil into them but you can never knock the devil out of them – Very true. He would go anywhere with another horse and it was not much trouble to provide him with the company he wanted. He was a wonderful hunter. Out hunting he had no nap of any sort. We called him Kennedy. I saw Sarah jump some very big post-and-rails at the top of Okeover on him. No-one followed her.

HUNTING BY MOONLIGHT

Sarah was on Kennedy and I was on Esso in one of the great hunts of that or any season. They found in Chairman's Thorns, ran over Ilam, the Thorpe road, over the shooting-range, and out into country I had never been in before. Up there in the hills it was hard work for the horses. At last the only people left in the hunt were Graham Roberts, Sarah, and I. We kept on even when dusk was making it hard to see and we had to look twice before we jumped anything. We could see the lights of a town. The moon was full but more scary than helpful. The hounds were screaming along. They had found about half-past three and it was now seven o'clock. Graham could not stop them, and they ran to a kill ahead of us. We could tell by the change in their voices. We did our best to help Graham collect his hounds and then we thought we had better make our way home, but we were completely lost, and tired and hungry too. There were lights not too far off that we thought must come from a farm. Once there, the only way forward was to jump quite a big wall into the farmyard. I said to Sarah, "Close your eyes and follow me." We made it to the road and luckily a car-follower gave me a lift to the lorry while Sarah waited with the horses. In Ilam, Linda was about hairless. What a hunt! – I have never been that way before or since.

Mick Toulson rang wanting a horse for a girl. I told him I would send him Kennedy. I knew Kennedy would be all right with him because he had a big livery yard and the horse would not have to go out on his own. He rang me a few days later to tell me he had sold him to the Duke of Rutland's daughter, the Hon. Teresa Manners. A few months later I asked him how she was getting on with him, and learnt that everything was fine. In fact, when she went swimming in the lake Kennedy went with her. (I've never tried that but wish I had)..

Another horse I sold that year was Esso, the one I had been riding on the great hunt just described. June Nuttall had bought him but sent him back, saying he had got sweet itch. I had not noticed it as I had bought him in the winter. He was hogged, which is a tell-tale sign, but there are quite a few horses about with no mane. He was a patent-safety thoroughbred bay gelding, 16.3hh. I bought him from a chap at Hulland Ward after being told his wife had left him and he needed the money. It turned out that his wife hadn't left him but the horse had sweet itch! I sold him to go into Lincolnshire, after explaining his history. As long as you tell people, you can't go far wrong. I never heard any more from the chap; so he must have been satisfied.

BUYING AT SHOWS

That season I went to lots of shows trying to buy show-jumping horses. I made enquiries about sixty-three, but I actually bought only three. I always went into the collecting ring to find them. That was my scene of operations. My approach would be: "I like your horse. Would you be interested in selling it to me as a hunter? I am looking for a horse for myself." (If it looked like a lady's horse I would say I was looking for a horse for my wife). I got used to being rebuffed. The owner would say, "I'm not going to sell this horse. He's going to be a champion." The horse would probably go into the ring and refuse three times at the first fence, but they would never come round to say, "I will sell you the horse. I feel sure he would make a good hunter." They would sooner struggle on, believing they will win, but they don't – the horse always wins. In my searches in the collecting rings over the years I tried to buy Tees Haneur as a four-year-old at Solihull. I tried to buy Welham when he was in the Novice Class at Derby County. I tried to buy a bay horse from Liz Edgar at Cosford that year, but can't remember its name. There were several others like that. My memory goes blank sometimes.

One horse seen in the collecting-ring I do remember very well. I was at Markfield Show looking for hunters and I saw this dark grey horse belonging to Di Lampard. He was called Private Treaty, otherwise known as Tiger. He jumped quite well. I bought him from Di, took him home, and had him passed by the vet. Tim hunted him first and wrote in his diary that the horse pulled a bit but was generally all right. One day at Tissington he jumped onto a boulder and was lame for quite a long time until eventually we had to turn him out. Now Di had said he had only one fault and that was walking through any hedge when he was turned out and so I put up an electric fence. That stopped him. We never had another problem with him, and when the lameness had quite disappeared we sold him to Alan Edmunds.

At the Southwell Ploughing Match Show I saw a horse jump especially well over a gate. He was a big chestnut horse, home bred, 16.3hh, five years old, a bit back at the knee but a sound horse and that is the first essential in buying a hunter. They can have all the looks, ability – everything – but if they have to stop in the stable because they are not sound you had better forget them. This one was said to have won £15 as a show-jumper. I thought that was quite good. I knew his owner, Mr Clarke, whose son was actually riding him. I found it handy to name horses with the surname of the person I bought it from so that, later, if the name rang a bell I could put two and two together and place the horse in my memory. Tim got on with Clarke all right but I did not enjoy him although he had won that £15 for show-jumping. He missed too many fences out for me and held his head far too high for my liking. When Sarah show-jumped him she won a class or two, but nothing to write home about. I sold him to hunt with the Vine and Craven. A few years later I was surprised to hear that he had gone eventing, and had been round Burghley once and Badminton twice I couldn't believe my ears. – It just shows!

Another nice horse to arrive that summer was Bertie. He came from Northern Ireland, from a Mr. Thompson. I had not dealt much with him before but he sent me over the horse, a chestnut gelding, 16.2hh, five years old, an Irish blood type. Both Linda and I hunted him and I remember jumping a particular big hedge and ditch by the side of Booth Hay. He was a good horse. I sold him to Stewart Campbell, a Leicestershire dealer. One day a few weeks later, I was exercising when I saw Penny Sevier riding by on a nice chestnut horse. "Hello," thought I to myself, "I know that horse. It's the one I sold to Stewart Campbell. She needn't have gone to buy one in Leicestershire when there was one on her doorstep." He made her a good horse though. He was nice-natured. She would hunt him side-saddle. She had him a long time. We did sell a few more than I have written about but I feel these are the interesting ones.

1984-85

David Meynell was joined in the Mastership by Gerald Deville, a farmer from Doveridge, Ken Beeston, a cattle-dealer from Sudbury, and David Pennell. Helena Cholerton was now Secretary and in came Dick Chapman as Huntsman and Nick Jones as First Whip. We were sorry to see Mike Seddon go. He had done a good job but being Joint-Master in this day and age is very difficult. They say that being an M.F.H. years ago used to open a few bedroom doors. Nowadays you can hardly get into the kitchen. John Stevens, very knowledgeable on hounds, had also done a good job. Graham Roberts had gone to hunt the Linlithgow and Stirlingshire.

During that first season when Dick Chapman was Huntsman it was as though we had been playing at going hunting until then. He was unlucky this season – the kennel cough, bad weather, snow and ice, the "antis", no scent before Christmas, but when we were able to hunt – did we hunt!

The Hunt Ball was held at Orgreave Hall, £1200 was made selling 540 tickets. The Coldstream Guards played the music. A calf scheme started. I think we got the idea from the Wynnstay. A farmer was given a calf, he reared it, and when it was ready to sell took it to a special sale at Lichfield. Subscribers were able to help towards the cost of the calf. The scheme made £2000 profit to go into hunt funds. For the Cross Country Ride it was a dry day but the ground was very wet after the heavy snow in February. Facing the 27 starters there were thirty-four fences in just about four miles. A very good supper and disco was held at the Kennels, Lady Ley made a presentation to Neil Seaton for his thirty years as fence-repairs man. Dermot Kelly was Guest Speaker. The Hunt Supporters' Club was going from strength to strength under the chairmanship of Phil Arthers. New events were the sponsored ride, which raised £1000, and the Farmer's Ball, or Party. Another development was the making of a function-room at the kennels by knocking a few stables down in the yard. It proved very useful for committee meetings and other gatherings.

The saddest part of '84 was the putting down of Midnight Blue. I have already told how I came by her but must remind myself of what she meant to all the family. I bought her from Helen Evans from Weston-on-Trent. Duko Van Joulen was cubbing at Hulland when I first noticed her. A really dark grey mare about 16.0hh, and four years old then. I had a ride on her, bought her, told Linda I had a present for her, and gave her Midnight Blue. Although Linda would ride lots of different horses during each season, I liked to keep one special one for her own enjoyment. Blue was always a bit of a handful and far too hot to go cubbing – but then lots of good hunters won't settle to cubbing. Not only did she hunt her but Linda also hunter-trialled and show-jumped her, although the mare was not careful enough to be anything more than a fun ride. Her highlight would probably be representing the Meynell in a team-jumping competition at Stoneleigh. As Sarah was growing up we thought she would probably be more of an event jockey than a show-jumping one. So to have an idea what to do if she wished to go eventing we thought it would be a good idea if I did some to get a feel of what we would have to look out for, and Blue was the obvious choice for my mount.. I had some dressage lessons from Vera Holden. (I had known Vera from the days when she was with Eddie Goldman). She was very sweet with me, saying I was beyond helping really but she would do her best. Sometimes I went into Cheshire where she lived or quite often she came into Derbyshire but the main thing was for me to memorise the test. I was to walk the test on my feet in the dining room and remember it. At Locko Trials I forgot it and I was docked two points but I was only those two points behind Janet Hodgson who was in the European Event Team. I finished fifth that day. I went up to get my rosette along with those other nice little girls. In January Linda had two falls off Blue. She wasn't jumping so I asked Tim to have a ride on the mare. His diary says: *I fell off Blue. Something had gone wrong with her back. It was her last day.* Very, very sad as she had been a wonderful fun horse. Animals of that sort never do live long enough, do they?

DODGY CUSTOMERS

As one door closes another one opens. Tony Maguire rang up wanting to know if we would buy a couple of hunters – from a chap who was going to prison. Linda and I went to Tony's and he took us on to see them where they were stabled on the outskirts of Wigan on some waste ground. They were two

Linda hunter trialling Midnight Blue

159

lovely horses: a chestnut, by Snuff Box, 16.2hh, that Tony had bought in Ireland, and a big grey. The chestnut had been competing on the Abbey Life Hunter Trial Circuit but also show-jumped. This chap got on him, went straight into a gallop, and jumped the cross-country fences that were spread about on this waste ground. I had a ride on him too, and liked him. I had a ride on the grey. He was a very classy horse but I thought he made a squeak of a noise. I don't like that; they never improve. So I bought the chestnut horse and arranged to meet the owner just off the M.6 on that side of Congleton.

I had one or two telephone calls along these lines: "I believe you've bought a chestnut horse from this person just outside Wigan. He owes me money. Would you let me know where you are meeting him?" I said that was all right and said the meeting was arranged for 2.30 p.m. the following Wednesday. That was put off to Thursday, and that was put off too. I had to keep ringing the callers to say the meeting had been cancelled. And then it was it was a case of: "I'm afraid that if he owes you money you'll have to get it yourself. I think this man knows you're after something." We next arranged to meet on the Saturday at 1.30.p.m. and kept it to ourselves. Sarah went with me in the lorry. We waited two hours. It was a January day and freezing. Just as I was thinking he was not going to turn up and started the lorry up, a car pulled up in front of us. It was the chap himself – "Just thought I'd pop along to see if anyone else was here. Don't worry, the horse will be here inside half an hour." I was quite angry but I liked the horse so much I thought I had better be careful what I said. He had just got someone else (I think he was the look-out) to bring him and now he said the horse was in this pub yard by the lights on the M6-Congleton road. He was a big horse that they squeezed into the smallest single trailer imaginable but he survived. When we get horses home I generally leave them a day to settle, but as he had not travelled far I took him down to the jumping field on the Sunday morning, popped him over a few little fences, then jumped the big holly hedge on him. He sailed over it.

A few days later this chap rang me and asked if I would buy his grey as he was "going abroad for a few months". I agreed a price with him but I was not going to wait around up there for him again and bought him on condition he brought the horse to me at home. He arrived with him about 10.30 one night, in the same little trailer. I did not have that horse long. I sold him to Shirley Edwards, who was finding Richard Sumner a few horses around that time, and I think she sent him to Richard. (I knew Richard from the show-jumping days. He used to have a few days with the Meynell and his wife used to show-jump when she lived in Norfolk).

For his first outing with the hounds I took the chestnut to the meet at

Sarah riding Oliver and Tim riding Heritage across our farm to meet Prince Charles

Mackies, Church Broughton. He bucked all the way up their drive. Hounds soon found in the Spath. When we were running, the first fence was a big post-and-rails, and he really jumped that superbly. I did not have a long day but after it, when I got home, I said to Linda, "I'm going to give you this horse as your very own." That was Oliver. She had some fun on him – she field-mastered off him, child-minded off him. What a horse he turned out to be! Hardly ever sick or sorry, his only fault was that he could buck and he

161

bucked Linda off one day on the farm. It was three years before she rode him round the farm again. I used to have to give him a canter and pull; he would just about run away with me. She hunted him for sixteen seasons. Always a difficult client, my wife. Wonderful, wonderful horse. I could go on and on singing his praises but I have to come to the end of his story some time. It came fifteen years later when I held him while he went to his happy hunting-grounds. He was a horse of a life-time!

It was a bad year for selling horses. A lot of politicians were against hunting. The Co-op banned hunting on their land – and they owned thousands of acres especially in Leicestershire.

Herbie, about 16hh, came from a girl in Essex and had done quite a bit of show-jumping, but he was still only five years old. I bought him in Leicester. The first time I hunted him was round Kirk Ireton. While we were going across the first field, Sue Wilson, used to be Darcy-Clarke, probably one of the oldest hunting families in the Meynell, came over and said her horse had probably come to the end of the road and she would be looking for another. (She must have had him over twenty years; he certainly did not owe her anything). Anyway she sat on Herbie, liked him, and bought him, and at time of writing still has him. Joan, a bay mare, bought from John Drew, was an awkward thing; Tim hunted her plenty, but found her very slow. She went to the Grove and Rufford, which was ideal; they mostly have hunt jumps.

1985-86

Ken Beeston gave up the mastership after one season which surprised a lot of people as we all thought it had been a life-long ambition. He had hunted the South Notts and the Atherstone, two adjacent packs. David Pennell's wife took Ken's place. Richard Chapman was still Huntsman but Nick Jones had moved on to be Huntsman to the Vale of Aylesbury. Downing was the new Whip.

The Hunter Trials for the first time were held at Hulland Hall, making a profit of £125. The Supporters' Club bought a new flesh-wagon for the Kennels. Linda, after fifteen years on the Supporters' Club Committee along with Jim Boden, Gay Sowerby, and Martin Cholerton, decided to make room for younger people. There was a lamb roast at the Kennels, and a good dinner at Hilton House. The Show was cancelled owing to the bad weather. The Hunt Ball, held again at Orgreave Hall, was a complete sell-out, showing a profit of £3,250. The third sale, at Lichfield, of the Hunt Supporters' calves was a little down on the year before but still put £2500 into Hunt funds. The

Cross-Country Ride, held at Osmaston, saw 37 starters. Jeremy Allen had put on a lot of weight especially to win the Heavyweight prize. They say he backed himself and won a small fortune. Phil Arthers won the Farmers' prize. Thorntons Chocolates sponsored the prizes and £596 was made. Di and John Monier-Williams held a Young Thrusters Surprise Night out at Muggington. Linda and I did not go. We didn't think we qualified!

Until mid-November, there was such an abundance of grass about that farmers were reluctant to bring the cattle in and the opening meet had to be put back. We only had one day from the 23rd January to 11th March, with snow making the ground unfit for horses. One had to feel sorry for Dick Chapman, after the difficulties of the previous season. We always knew we had the finest country in the world to go fox-hunting over, but in the preceding few years we certainly had not made the most of it. Dick was by far the finest huntsman I have been behind but the two years he had here were awful for him. There are incidents that are still vivid in my mind because of him:

Cubbing one day I said, "You've an awful lot of hounds out today, Dick."

"Yes, sir," he said. "Forty-four and a half couple." And a blanket would have covered the lot!

On another day when to say there was a gale blowing would be an understatement – it was nearly blowing us off our horses – two foxes went away from Booth Hay. George Startin, who was on point, said there was a strong fox going towards Alkmonton Bottom and the other was going towards the Stydd. Dick said to George, "Mr. Startin, we will leave it to the bitches." What a ride we had! The experts say it was a four-mile-point on past the Stydd, but it must have been seven or eight with hounds running over some of the best Meynell country. Never tell me that hounds can't run into a gale.

When hounds again found two foxes – they were drawing Longford Carr this time – one went out towards Mammerton and the other towards Shirley. Gerald Deville was jumping up and down in his saddle: "We can't go towards Mammerton! I haven't cleared that part of the country." Longford Carr is a narrow covert. Dick jumped on to the Rodsley Road and just got to the other side of the covert as hounds were streaming away towards Mammerton. Within minutes he had stopped them and put them on to the fox going towards Shirley, giving us another marvellous run. We finished within half a mile from home, but it took us thirty minutes to go back and pick up the lorry and that was just one way.

They sacked him that night. He came over next morning, put his arms round Linda and said, "What have I done wrong, Mother" What he had done wrong was having one woman too many. Hounds certainly loved him and so did some women. I am saying no more as to that, but we all tried to keep him. There was meeting after meeting but the Joint-Masters had made up their mind, and we, the paying supporters, were the sufferers. He certainly divided this country. It was a waste of a talented man, just like George Best, and David Meynell's departure was an equal loss. We have probably not had the best Huntsmen in the Meynell but we certainly have had the best Field-Masters and David would rank amongst the best and bravest. "Come on, men. Follow me. We'll think tomorrow of what we're doing today." I never heard him say a cross word to anyone.

I hoped to be able to sell more horses but they seemed to be getting more and more difficult to find, and sales were becoming more of a lottery. Leicester was at one time a meeting-place for M.F.H's, especially in the Spring when the big hunter sales were on. It was becoming a place for gypsies to meet and its reputation was going downhill, especially now it was so easy to dope horses. A little trick I always tried if I was interested in buying a horse was to keep a sharpened matchstick in my pocket and gently touch it on the coronet band. If there was any feeling it showed. If there wasn't any you knew it had been doped.

Stoneleigh was up and running but I was always a bit nervous of going there. The people were so smart and talked a different lingo. They might tell you to "Change the rein" instead of "Would you go round the other way for a bit?" and they talked of show-jumping "tracks" that I only knew as "courses", and so on and so on.

One horse we sold that year went to a chap called Jervis Percy. She was a good strong sort, nearly black, but with a lot of white on her legs. She had come, via Tony, from Dawn Cartwright (who had competed against Sarah on ponies). I hunted her once or twice and then someone who had hunted a couple of season with us came along, looking for a new horse. It was Jervis. He must have had quite a few on trial and had just about given up hope of finding the right one. He said he had toured England looking for a good hunting country and had come into Derbyshire and stayed. He considered this part of the world to be the best, where a man must ride straight if he is not be too late to see Reynard rolled over by the Meynell. He had taken a cottage in Shirley for the winter months and went back to Ireland in the summer. He tried her, and bought her, but would not pay me until I paid for a new set of shoes. He said he always thought that was part of the deal. It was a new one on me but he absolutely adored her – could not bear to leave her in this country when he went back to Ireland for the summer. I think he had a boat over there, and took her back with him in a very small single trailer although she was quite a big mare. They made the journey a few times until one year they did not come back, but he wrote sometimes, and that was nice.

TO IRELAND WITH TIM

What with one thing and another it was getting to be hard work to find good horses. I had been buying a lot from Tony Maguire, quite a lot from Jimmy and Paul Goddard, and a few from other people. When I had been happy with the dealers I always gave them a chance to sell me another but in spite of that I was not doing much good at the time. A visit to Ireland was indicated and so I rang Norman Proffit, who had been to Ireland plenty of times with the Maguires, and suggested I would pay all the expenses if he would go with me and he would be on a commission for every horse I bought. Tim went with me. It was something of a round trip. We picked up Norman, who was operating from somewhere in Wales at that time, went on the ferry from Holyhead to Dun Laoghaire and on the way home we sailed from Belfast to Liverpool, where Norman had some business. On this trip I bought six horses, having probably looked at thirty.

The first two I bought were from Mr. Thompson who lived in Ballywalter. They were chestnut geldings, both seven-eighths bred, and 16.2hh. We named the one horse Daley and the other Thompson. Tim and I liked them both. I saw Tim jump some big post-and-rails behind Neil Seaton's one day. He was always a spooky horse, was Daley, but he was only five years old. Thompson was six and knew a bit more. One day the phone rang and a woman's voice said, "I'm looking for two horses – for a friend of mine and for me – but they must be friendly." I explained that I had bought these two horses from the same place in Ireland and they were the best of friends. She said she lived in Shardlow, and would like to come over later that day and have a look at them. When she and her friend arrived, she introduced herself as Freda Cunningham, wife of an airline pilot. I told her I was a bit curious to know who recommended me to her and learnt that she had found me in the Yellow Pages. I put bridles on both of them and brought them out. "Oh yes," she said. "I like the look of them" (They did look well, too). When I asked if she would like to see them ridden, she was all for it, but after I had done that, when I asked if she would like to have a sit on one, she admitted that she couldn't ride herself and was going to have lessons but she wanted a horse of her own as well as one for her friend Donna, who was her son's girl-friend. The only stipulation she would make was that she would like to see

165

them ridden down our busy road. With Donna riding Daley, and me riding Thompson, we were able to reassure her how steady they were in traffic. I had a stipulation to make too: I wanted to go over and see if she had the proper facilities to be able to keep two such high-class horses. She said she must have them both, and paid me for them right away. I often went over to see if they were all right. They had a very good home. I am afraid Freda served a bit of time for sharp practice but she kept the horses until they were quite old. They had a very easy life. Freda went on enjoying having them and that's what it's all about.

Other people we called on in Ireland were Carolyn Smith and her friend James. (I never did find out his surname). From them we bought a lovely chestnut horse by Teaspoon. Vere Phillips had rung me up to buy Irish horses so when I brought these six back I called him over, but he did not like one of them, and that felt like a waste of time to me. I hunted this Teaspoon horse and he was very special. I remember one particular big fence behind the Queen Adelaide that he jumped superbly. You always get a special buzz the first time you hunt a new horse and ride it down to a big fence. You just test your nerve against its nerve. There's hardly another feeling in this world to match jumping such a fence in good style. Relief possibly has something to do with it. Judy Bradwell, who was also out that day, had a client for a potential Event horse. She came over, liked him, and asked if she could have him for a few days. Anyway, I delivered him halfway, and a few days later she told me she had sold him to Sally Bateson, who in due course took him on to Advanced level.

We found Arnold at a lovely farm where he had been bred. He was a chestnut, four years old, 16.3hh, and a promising-looking horse, but I left him, thinking he was too young. However, I had to go back and have another look. Tim insisted, "I do like him, Dad!" so we bought him. What a card he was! He was always standing on tip-toe looking over the hedge – must see what was going on all around him. I hunted him at Alkmonton and had a good day. Tim was right. It was a good job we had gone back and bought him. I sold him to John Howle who was Joint-Master and Field Master for the North Staffs. (I had known John from his show-jumping days when he had Doug Hibbert's black and white pony and I was riding for Mr. Powell. We sold him a bay horse that I had jumped (Tudor something, he was called). I told John that Arnold was a bit of a card, but with no nasty thoughts. I delivered him into Cheshire and we went in for a cup of tea. When we came out he had wrecked his stable. He was just being playful. The pipes carrying the water were littered everywhere. I took a horse in part exchange, a thing I rarely did but I knew John well enough. I always prefer to sell, draw the money and go and buy my own choice. The horse I took was Dixie, a bay, 16.2hh. He was a "warm blood", only the second I had had. A good-looking horse but to me these horses never seem to enjoy hunting like the Irish or English and I have found them a bit chicken. After we had hunted him a few times we could see why John had wanted to get rid of him. When I was over at John Goodwin's one day and he asked if I had a nice-looking horse about, I was very soon delivering Dixie to him. A few days later John rang to say he had sold the horse – to go to America. I could not believe it! Crossing the Trent was far enough, let alone crossing the Atlantic.

The next I bought that trip was Summer Cove, a grey mare, 16.3hh, and six years old. It was very dark when we saw her but she had a lovely kind eye – something you do not see every day. We had her out, saw lots of photos of her novice-eventing, hunter-trialling. I gave a lot of money for her but could not have left her. Tim was the first to hunt her when she came over. I have already told her story, how Jane Walker-Okeover bought her and made the mistake of calling her Mystery.

1986-87

David Meynell had been forced to retire following a fall during the Autumn hunting and so the Pennells and Gerald Deville carried on, with Gerald doing Field Master as well. He had got himself two good horses: a grey horse he had bought from Phil Arthers and a little bay horse called Bobby, a horse I had tried to buy from Ken Beeston as a four-year-old for Tim to jump. I had seen him as a novice at one of Pat Guest's little evening shows but Ken wanted to jump the horse himself. Bobby actually went on to win the Grade B Championship at Peterborough. The new Huntsman was David Barker, with Roderick Duncan as First Whipper-In. Roy Sevier was the Chairman.

There were many money-raising events: the Calf Scheme put £2,500 into the Hunt funds, but the Promise Auction at Croxall Hall raised a staggering £5,726. The Cross-Country Ride, held at Cubley and sponsored by Thornton Chocolates again, saw Phil Arthers moving up to the Heavyweight Division and winning it. I don't know whether Jenny had been feeding him better or whether he just wanted to beat Jeremy Allen, who was too full of himself since winning last year. The Cross-Country Team Event, again held at Booth Hay, made only just over £600 profit. Gone were the days when Princess Anne and Lord Oaksey were competing and the takings were over £2000. Nevertheless, it is still a very good day out. The Hunter Trials were again held at Hulland. The course was a big improvement on the previous year and a profit of £250 was made. The Point-to-Point was postponed from the 28th March until the 4th April due to bad weather. It was not a very nice day but £2000 was given to Hunt funds. The Hunt Ball was held at Orgreave Hall on the 26th March and an overall profit of £3,200 was made. The new Farmers Ball at the Town Hall was a great success. I really enjoyed that. There were two hundred people there, mostly farmers. Linda had a lot to do with getting it off the ground.

Phil Arthers retired as Chairman of the Supporters' Club. He had done a wonderful job, tremendous hard work and dedication, with enthusiasm probably the most important ingredient. In his last year there was an event nearly every week through the summer. He had improved in his speech-making in the four years since Linda and I were on the top table with him. Andrew Adams and Jane Hall retired from the Committee. The Earl of Shrewsbury and Nick Hutchinson took their places.

When I had been in Ireland I had met what is called a "guinea hunter"; in other words, John McAuley, a very well known horse-finder who lived near Kells. He gave me his telephone number so that when I wanted to buy I could let him know, fly to Dublin from Liverpool, and he would pick me up at the airport. I took the flight which arrived between eight and nine in Dublin, and usually about three-quarters of an hour later we would be looking at horses at a place where he had already been in touch with the sellers. It is very easy to buy horses like that. You pay his expenses and he finds the horses and after you have been a few times he has a very good idea what sort of horse you like. I should have liked to go with Norman, but decided to do my buying in Southern Ireland because travelling with Norman, who did his business in Northern Ireland, sometimes near Crossmaglen, felt risky all the time. We were going over the border once when Norman said, "Keep your head down; they are looking at you from the top of those mountains." When you went into a town the soldiers would stop you. You wound down the window and a rifle would be pointing in your face. I was frightened the gun might go off. One of the first horses I bought through John was Adrian, a lovely big bay, four years old but knew plenty. He came from Adrian Murray, who brought him over to John's place. He had been hunted a bit with the staghounds. We tried him in John's paddock and I bought him. I sold him to Graham Nichol, although he had not been hunted from here. Graham had actually bought him for himself and when he said he was all right, you knew he was perfection. In the autumn he rang me to say the horse was now seventeen hands and very handsome.

Tim was with me again on that trip. After Adrian, we bought Lawrence, a chestnut horse, 16.2 hands, and five years old. I don't know the name of the chap we bought him from. We never actually saw the horse ridden but we did see him jump. The owner, who said he had been hunted, pulled out a few poles from the hedge down in this grassy lane and sent him down loose. We were in such a hurry, and Tim was keen, so we took him at his word. Besides, John knew the horse and said he was all right. We thought Lawrence might make a jumper, so we took him down to an indoor school. Tim was riding, trotting over some cross poles, when he stumbled. Tim landed on his feet – but he broke a leg in doing so.

The next horse we bought over there came from Meynell Watson. He was a nice horse, a bay gelding, 16.2hh, that had done quite a bit of show-jumping. As usual, we hunted him here, and called him Watson. When Bill Strawson came over, wanting a horse, he had a ride on Lawrence and thought he was fine. Although he liked him he still asked us what else we had got. I brought out Watson, and he had a ride on him too. That left Bill in a bit of a quandary: he didn't know which one to have. "Why don't you take them both?" said I, not too seriously. "Good idea," he said. "I will," and they were both despatched to Lincolnshire.

I may have said this before but my advice would always be that you should never buy a horse unless you have seen the owner ride it first. Giving advice is one thing. Following it is another. I had a week of nasty experiences. I was at Leicester one day when Bill Winter said he had a horse to sell, but told me he was a bit crocked at the moment. It was a very nice liver chestnut, one of my favourite colours. I got on him, went on to the Ashby-Burton Road, and – *buck*! His tail was hitting me in the back. Traffic was stopped. I was pleased to get off him. A day or two later I went to look at a horse near Chesterfield – and fell for the same sort of story: "My husband has been called away but this is the horse I am to show you. I don't ride myself." I tacked it up and got on but no sooner had I put my feet in the irons than it started to buck and plunge through this orchard. I got off as soon as I could, let it go, and said to the woman, "You catch it." Ever after that I always had the car turned round ready to make a quick exit.

The first horse I bought from John Whittaker was a big grey horse called Winston. He had bred this horse but he had not been cut properly, was still dribbling a bit so we had to have him operated on again. He came right and made a superb hunter and jumped some very big fences. An entry in Tim's diary: *We jumped some big fences around the Rough, – through Parson's Gorse and finished at Culland.* I remember one of them, a very big boundary wall at the top of Okeover. Derek Rickets bought him, as well as Jonathan; he must have been happy with him as he kept coming back for more.

169

1987-88

Jim Cunningham joined the Mastership. He had bought Western Lodge at Kedleston. He had previously hunted with the Whaddon Chase. David Barker was huntsman. (I had known him from the pony-jumping days and was also at the White City when he won the European Show-jumping Championship on Mister Softee). Although a Yorkshireman, he went to live in Buckinghamshire where he sold hunters and farmed.

Peter King took on the Hon Sec's job. (He and Fiona first subscribed in the season of 1984-85. I believe that Peter took up hunting because he seemed to be at a loss to know what to do with himself between the other two loves of his life, shooting and fishing).

The Cross-Country Team Event, again held at Booth Hay made £1865. Instead of the Cross-Country Ride, a Fun Ride was held at the Foulkes' because it was so wet. 65 people enjoyed themselves galloping and jumping over Billy's farm and Di did a lunch for about 90. The Hunt Ball was held at Okeover Hall. It was a sell-out and made over £3000. A Barn Dance was held at Corner Farm; about 500 people crammed in to that to raise £1490. Record crowds thronged to the Point-to-Point, held again at Sandon, on a lovely April day. A first hedgecutting competition was held at Bradley and had so many entrants they found Ted Fox's hedge wasn't long enough. The new Sheep Scheme provided the money for a Farmers' Party at Corner Farm, Radbourne. The Farmer's Ball was held again at Burton Town Hall and was a sell-out, producing £1000 to give to Hunt funds.

At this time Dick Chapman was hunting with the Heythrop, unable to get a job in Hunt Service. As he was selling some horses he had hunted, Linda and I went to have a look but did not buy anything. On the way home we decided to call on Liz, David Meynell's sister, who was married to George Jefferies. I had sold them a few horses in the past but now it was my turn. I bought Todhunter, a chestnut gelding, 16.2hh, and five years old. He was named after the Huntsman of one of the Fell packs who was in the news a lot at that particular time. He was a bit of a lad, but Tim hunted the backsides off him and I had some good days on him too. At the top of Tissington he splattered Tim by stopping at a hunt jump, right in front of everybody. Tim's ego took a fall as well. On another day, down at Rodsley, Tim and I jumped the biggest hedge either of us had ever jumped. He was riding Todhunter and I was riding another five-year-old, a grey gelding, 16.3hh, and three-quarter bred. We were in quite a narrow field. One or two people were attempting the jump. Billy Foulkes's horse got stuck in the middle: some horses stopped and the jockey got stuck in the middle. I told Tim I was going. The grey jumped it to perfection. I looked back when I had landed, just in time to see Tim coming over. He had a lovely big smile on his face. It is the only fence I have gone back and measured. Next morning, a Sunday, Geoffrey Fox was down, looking for horses as he was going to be the Joint-Master of the Hurworth. I said to him, "Come with me. I would like you to be a witness to a fence Tim and I jumped yesterday." We discovered it was 6ft 10ins high and 9 ft wide with a typical Meynell scoop in front.

(The grey I was riding I sold to Margaret Sherrington. I can't say much about him as we did not have him very long, other than when I was having a very good day with him at Sutton, he jumped some big post-and-rails, Margaret saw him and bought him).

Tim was away at college and although he show-jumped Todhunter he could not really get to enough shows. At Ashby Show John Lanni came over and asked if I would sell him a half share as long as he could travel with the horse and his son, Matthew, rode him. As I rated Matthew very highly I felt I would be lucky to get a jockey of that calibre riding for me. I was there when he won the B & C at Bakewell but I only saw him jump twice more – my fault as we were always made very welcome. The arrangement lasted two years, but when John told me he was being given very good offers for Todhunter I thought he ought to sell him and gave him the go-ahead.

TO IRELAND AGAIN, IN THE SADDEST CIRCUMSTANCES

Sarah's boy-friend at that time was Viv Kennedy. He was a professional jockey attached to Fred Winter. He loved schooling the hunters when he was visiting us and we were able to give him hints about horses jumping at speed – What to do with his body, legs and style in general. We went to Uttoxeter and saw him ride two winners. Linda and I went to stay with them over the August Bank Holiday. We left for home on the Monday when they were going racing at Huntingdon, where Viv had a ride for James Bennett. It is terrible for us to remember that as we left I said, "Hope you have as good a day as I had the last time I was at Huntingdon."

About four o'clock that afternoon Sarah rang: "Daddy, Viv has had a bad fall. They have taken him to Addenbrookes. Could you and Mum come down? I think it's serious." In the hospital ward he was on a life-support machine. He looked so peaceful; you just thought he was going to wake up at any moment. The Kennedys came over from Ireland.

After a few days his life-support machine was switched off. It was all very peaceful.

We went over for the funeral and stayed in a hotel not far from the Kennedys. The churches in Ireland are lovely. The night before the actual funeral there was a memorial service. The gathering seemed to start at one end of the town and by the time we got to the church there were thousands of people thronging the main street. I thought everyone in Ireland had come to pay their respects but on the day of the funeral more people than ever came; the church was packed and people were standing in their hundreds outside. A lot of people had flown over that day, including Charlie Brooks and Jo Winter, whose mother was Tom Pearson's daughter, born-and-bred Meynell. A great crowd of us went back to the Kennedys for tea.

It was not long before we were talking horses. Tom Cox, who owns most of the sheep you can see as you cross the Curragh asked, "Are you John Betteridge who John McAuley buys hunters for?" When I said I probably was, he said he could show me a few. I did not think it at all right to go and buy horses when we were in mourning, but after asking questions it seemed the ideal thing to do. I bought three. First there was Spike, a grey horse, 15.3hh, a very nice six-year-old. Tim loved to ride these horses. He rode this one round the front field first, and then asked to jump a small part of the hedge into the back field. Spike had no idea – He just walked through. It had been a very nice hedge separating a 6-acre from a 5-acre field but I am afraid before long it was no more than where a hedge used to be. But he did get better. Next, we went to see a bay horse, 16.1hh, but it was where he was stabled that made the big inpression, a mansion of a place. I asked who lived there, and was told it was the musician Bono. He was playing in America just then and wished to sell him. We were glad to oblige and called him Bono. The last was Happy, a bay gelding 16.2hh. I never tried him properly, and should have known better. A golden rule is to take them on to the road and jog them past the entrance to where they live – or try to. I didn't and bought myself a nappy horse. Still, we got him home, kidded him along, hunted him hard, and he became quite good. He was sold into the Belvoir country.

The first time we hunted the first two, the hounds met at the Jinglers. I was riding Bono; Tim was on Spike. The fencing man had built one of his traps again, a double this time, going into Archers pit. I went arse ove tip over this fence, and he stood by the fence laughing. I broke some teeth and had to have seven stitches in my neck. Next time I see him by a fence I shall jump on him. I took Spike home while Tim continued on Bono. In his diary he says that after we swapped horses he gave a flash on Bono over a big hedge onto Peter Hall's. That was the only time we hunted them, for Graham Nichol bought them both – the grey horse Spike for his son and Bono for himself.

When John Whittaker rang to say he had some horses I ought to have a look at, Sarah and I went up there. We looked at quite a few but they were mostly home-bred, and really too young for us. John thought a friend of his might have one or two that might suit us and that was how we first met Peter Mellor (He sold Jimmy to Jane Walkover-Okeover) I bought a few off Peter Mellor and sold him a few. I must say he was a straight fellow to deal with and I had some very good deals with John too. In fact I have been very lucky over the years to meet and deal with such very nice people.

1988-89

There was certainly a change in the Mastership for this season: Annie Chandos-Pole came in. (I have told how we had had her liveries for about seven years but now, when she became Joint-Master and needed to use a second horse, she kept her horses in a yard of her own, with Brian Birch as groom). Jane Walker-Okeover came in as well (We had had her liveries since about 1972 so she was part of the furniture. She didn't want second horses.

Our new Joint Masters: Jane riding Mystery, David Meynell riding Chuckles and Annie riding Mayo

She would come home when either she or the horse was tired). Their arrival on the scene was the best news of the season. They were both from old Meynell families. Annie's ancestors had been Masters many years ago, and Jane's father had been a Joint-Master when I hunted behind him as a boy. Coming back for a second term was David Meynell. The Pennells, after five years, were not going to stay on and Jim Cunningham had dropped out after all his falls, lucky to survive as long as he did. He did not leave empty handed, as he sold Western Lodge to Claire Evans-Schreiber. Fiona King became Hon. Sec, joining her husband in the post.

It was a very open season, only five days lost to fog and frost and we gave up at the end of February. Good hunts were had from the usual places: Booth Hay, Snelston and Radbourne.

For the Point-to-Point, held on a lovely day, with record crowds, Richard Froggatt was the new Clerk of the Course and Jeremy Allen was the new organiser for the sponsorship. I am told he was good value for money. Brian Goodall won the hedgelaying competition at the Scaddows Farm, Ticknell, my old home just after the war. The Hunt Ball moved back to Hoar Cross, again a sell-out with £4000 going to Hunt Funds. The Fun Ride took place at the Foulkes, not quite as many people as last year took part but those who did enjoyed themselves. Di again provided the lunch; she did a good job. The Calf Scheme auction took place at Lichfield, nine calves making £3,781, average £420 per head. The Summer Ball, held at the Pennells, made £4000. Richard Pitman was the guest speaker at the Annual Dinner, held at the Stanhope Arms. The Lamb Roast and Country Sports was a real good do for the Young Farmers and their friends.

David Meynell said that now he was Field Master again he would need at least two horses. I was going to Ireland anyway and would have David in mind although I would never buy one especially for him – or anyone else for that matter. I bought five that time. (Even when buying at Leicester Sales or anywhere I always tried to buy a minimum of two. One could make up for the other should it not turn out as you hoped).

The first horse I bought came from a farm opposite to the racing yard where Arkle was trained. We went over to see his box. It was in what looked more like a farm-yard than a racing yard, being surrounded by hay barns, implement-sheds and stores. The horse I bought was a chestnut gelding, 16.2hh, 6 years old, and three-quarters bred. I had a ride on him and the first impression I got was that he was a goer. The next one was on a mushroom farm, a bay gelding, 16.3hh, 5 years old, with a hogged mane but a grand temperament. We called him Mushroom. After that, too late in the evening, we bought Heritage, who went to Jane and served her well, as I have already told.

The fourth horse I bought on that trip was Mayo. With Annie being a Joint-Master for the first time, I thought he would make her a good horse. The fifth and last was Clinton a chestnut gelding, 16.1hh, 6 years old, with plenty of bone. I bought him from Mr. Derwin, who lives in the middle of Athlone and is probably the biggest dealer in Ireland. He had plenty for us to pick from and a very good place for showing them, plenty of cross-country fences and a sand arena, with two good lads to show them off. You would do well not to be fooled by the way they jump where there is only one fence and that at just the right stride coming off the wall even though it is set at a fair height. It serves well enough for hunters as it does show they have ability, but be wary of buying a show-jumper only jumping one fence.

It normally took about a week to ten days for the horses to arrive here and of course I wondered what they were going to be like, and how many mistakes I might have made. There were good reasons why it could take that long for the horses to arrive: the haulier had to pick them up from various places around Ireland; if the seas were rough the people at the docks would not let them travel; and the vet had to look them over. (I never once had a horse fail the vet. Whether they were all seen I don't know. All you got was: "This horse is sound enough to do what you have bought him for and that is to go hunting." To be fair only a few would not get past the vet here, first time). When the five arrived, the one I bought that should suit David Meynell was so tired that when we put him in the box he lay down and did not get up for a week. He took the travelling badly. He was as sick as I have ever seen a horse. When he was looking brighter I rang David and asked if he could come in on the Sunday. David wouldn't have anyone else ride the horse he was going to buy; he preferred to be the first. On he gets and goes into the front field, trots around, and jumps the hedge very fast. That was the way David rode. The horse was getting stronger and stronger and I was thinking to myself, "It's a good job it's David riding him," and David, with a big smile on his face, said, "It's a poor man who can't hold a horse." He wanted a day's hunting on him. When the day came I saw him take on a big fixed iron gate on him. He was flying – cleared it by two feet. He came over: "I'll have this horse." We called him Chuckles because of the smile on David's face.

I sold him another one that week that I got from Norman Proffit. Norman had the stables near Crewe at the time and I had seen this big fine chestnut horse there and bought it. Norman was meeting me with him at a café just before you get on the A500 by Blythe Bridge. We went into the café and Norman introduced me to the man who was with him as the horse's owner. We sat down and had a cup of tea. During our talk he said, "I've no reason to sell this horse. I am a millionaire." I said I was sorry; I didn't know, but I got the horse just the same and he suited David, who had him a long time. I enjoyed selling horses to David. He was a true gentleman to sell horses to.

Mushroom was the next horse to go. I hunted him a few times and Susan Raynes, a girl who used to ride out a few times a week but had never hunted before, also hunted him twice. He was a real patent safety, a good horse, and went into the Quorn country. Mayo and Heritage went respectively to the new Joint-Masters, Annie Chandos-Pole and Jane Walker-Okeover.

I was a while finding a buyer for Puzzle, a grey gelding, 16.3hh, four years old, that had come from Tony. Tim recorded in his diary that he had a really good day on him at Tissington and was very pleased. We found he was difficult to shoe – he was Irish and had not been shod many times. I rang Alan Edmunds to find out if he might be interested. He said, from the sound of it, that he might have a client and suggested we meet where we generally did, in a lay-by about two miles on his side of Kegworth. Alan took him back with him and he must have been all right as he met me with the money a week or two later. It is always best to be on good terms with your neighbouring dealers. You never quite know when you may need them or they may need you. Quite often they can sell something you have had for a while, or vice versa. But when a dealer, or anyone else for that matter, sells you a horse or brings a client and you have a deal, you must arrange their fee or commission (I used normally to pay 5%) and, as soon as you know the horse you have sold has settled down, the money must be paid. If it isn't, you will probably not get another order through them. I know. I have had to whistle for a commission, and then that was that. They didn't get another chance. You might as well play for nothing as work for nothing.

1989-90

Phil Arthers became alternative Field Master. I think it meant that when David could not do it Phil was going to fill the breach. Sue Perkins joined the Mastership, just twenty years after her husband, Richard, had given it up. He had shared with Dermot Kelly. Martin Bluck was the new Whip, replacing Roderick Duncan, who was leaving and going as Huntsman to the Grove and Rufford. Roderick was a good Whip and a nice fellow with it – a real enthusiast and very good with the children. Linda was Ass. District Commissioner to the Pony Club at that time and could always call on Roderick for help. She started a scheme to get more children hunting: if a child was capable of jumping a hunt jump (which is about three feet) and the parents were not horsey, then either Linda or a responsible person would look after them for three rides and then they would be assessed to see if they were capable of going on their own. The important arrangement was that the parent or guardian would have to travel in the car in case anything happened to the child. It worked very well and the children's subscription list shot up. Roderick had a lot to do with it.

It was a very open season, only three days were lost to fog and frost. Again we had some good hunts, especially from Tom White's, Corner Farm, and another classic meet at Radbourne. In fact with the good going we had a very enjoyable season. Thirty-nine-and-a-half brace were killed.

The afternoon of the best day of all gave us a circular run of eight miles, after we had given our best wishes to Senior Joint-Master Annie Chandos-Pole on her marriage to James Chicester.

The Hunt Supporters were again very busy with such events as the Terrier, Lurcher and Family Dog show; a Lamb Roast and Country Sports Evening; Open Evening; Summer Ball; Hunt Supper; and Annual Dinner. The sponsored ride at Roger Hough's made a profit of £600. Jenny Arthers and Pam Haines ran a Promise Auction at Abbots Bromley and that made £6,500. The Hunt Supper was held at the Hollybush and the Supporters' Dinner was held at the Stanhope Arms. Jim Bealby, Master of the Quorn, was the main speaker. (I had sold him Bronze Light a few years earlier – a horse I had bought from Cyril Light at Leicester Horse Sales after he was recommended by Cathy Simpson. Not only did he win the Melton Cross-Country twice, ridden by Jim's sons, but he also went round the Foxhunter at Aintree). The Cross-Country Team Event was held again at Booth Hay. The ground was rock hard so the entries were down. After a three-year lay-off, John Fairclough was back as Secretary of the Point-to-Point. John has been one of the stalwarts of the Meynell Hunt for many years and was always good for a laugh.

The Beefeaters Steakhouses Inter-Hunt Relay was the fun day of the year for us. The Meynell Team consisted of Phil Arthers, Sarah Betteridge, Valerie Brown, and Sarah Ward. (The girls had come up through Pony Club). Sarah was riding Jessica, the Dublin airport mare. The competition was two identical show-jumping courses, one on either side of the ring. There were ten other Hunt Teams and they were all flying but our team won and that qualified them for the Royal Show where the winners were promised a trip to the Royal Dublin. I was really looking forward to going to the Dublin Show as I had never been. (I normally went a couple of weeks later when you could not buy anything there that would just go hunting. The owners all thought their geese were swans). Before we got to the Royal at Stoneleigh our team had been practising the whip change-over with great determination. When the day came, we were first in the preliminary Turnout Competition. In the big event the three girls had pushed themselves well into the lead when Phil started. He had a run-out. We could not believe it. The grey he was riding was Mighty Blue, which went on to represent Britain in many show-jumping Internationals with Robert Smith, but the team did win £480 for their second place and it went to Hunt funds.

The first of the three horses to come out of Ireland that year was Matthew, a big bay gelding. I bought him from a Mr. Matthews, who was a Joint-Master of the East Down. When we went to see him, although the children at the nearby school were having their playtime, they just brought this horse into the paddock and he was a real handful, very strong. They put up a fence and he jumped it, as well as I have ever seen, but we left him and said we would go back later in the day if we had time. Between 1 o'clock and 2 o'clock we had to see Jessica, who belonged to a baggage-handler at Dublin Airport. She was a liver chestnut mare, 16hh and 5 years old. I saw her in a very small paddock in a row of houses. A pole on a 5-gallon drum was all they had for a jump but she jumped it in such fine style that she was one who was on her way to England. The next one to view was Tarragon. He came from a butcher in a small town but it was at a livery yard with a very nice indoor school that we saw him. He was a lovely big horse, 16.3hh, a horse of real quality. He had been going round the school for a while before the girl groom told us the horse had been hobdayed. I was very disappointed, as I had never bought a hobdayed horse. (I am always very wary about anything to do with a horse's wind because it is a thing that never improves). Anyway, I left him, but horses I wanted were so scarce on this trip that I had to go back and buy him. And I went back and bought Matthew as well.

When Tarragon came over in May, I had a client waiting for him. Claire Evans-Schreiber had bought Weston Lodge and was wanting to go hunting. She made no difficulties about buying him; she did not mind him being hobdayed and the only thing she insisted on was that I should put him in the lorry, take him down to Weston Lodge, and let her ride him on the very busy road that goes in front of her house. He passed that test and she bought him and enjoyed the partnership. One day I saw her leading the field on him round Ireton Rough. She still owns him but he is lent out.

We thought Matthew might make a jumper. To give him a try, Tim rode him at Markfield and had sixteen faults. It was no surprise when Tim said Matthew was not the horse for him. With Linda being as involved as ever in the Pony Club, she had as a sidekick Annabel Startin, who lived and breathed it. These two happened to be together talking horses one day when Annabel

Sarah hunter trialing Jessica

said she could do with a horse for herself to ride quietly and for Tom to do a bit more with. Following the usual course of events, she and Tom came over. I must say Matthew had turned into a real nice horse, a good-coloured bay that must have stood about 16.3hh. (When you are selling horses you never say 17 hands. It gives the buyer the idea that it is common). They bought him on condition that I should deliver him and see him safely in his new home. When I arrived I expected to see Annabel in her jodhpurs, ready to ride, so you can imagine my disappointment when I saw her more ready for a bit of mucking out. She had gone to some trouble though. To make sure I found where he was going to live she had put up a big notice by the road: "Matthew's New Home". Tom certainly made a good job of producing him; he got within a few points of being an Advanced Eventer before they sold him. He certainly owed them nothing. They made a few bob and had a lot of fun while they were at it.

James Stanford, one-time owner of the one-eyed Sefton, moved into the Pytchley. He rang one night: "Now John," in his military voice (He was a Captain in the Army), "I want you to find a horse for a very dear friend of mine. It's for a Mrs. McCall and it has got to be right." Shortly afterwards, as arranged, Mrs. McCall rang and gave me a good idea of what she wanted – one for her to hunt herself but to do other things as well. We had Donny, a 16hh bay gelding who came from Tony Maguire. We had taken him show-jumping at Ling Farm and Tim's diary for the last day of the season on him says, *Fun day. Jumped about 35 fences – Seemed to be a lot of empty saddles.* After they had been to try him, and vet him, I was to deliver him – to a lovely home as I found out. They turned him out while I was there and he galloped about, but the ground by that time of the year was rock hard. The next day Mrs. McCall rang to say he was lame, almost hinting he might have been doped. I was relieved two days later when she rang to say he was all right, but I did learn a lesson from it all. After that every horse that went from here had blood taken from it, the vet keeping one sample and I keeping another. We never had an occasion to use any of those samples but we were ready should it have been necessary.

Sometimes Mrs McCall rang, saying how pleased they were with him, and then she rang to say she needed another. I had just had a load come from Ireland and among them was a likely horse called Quin. (It is so easy when you name them after the person you buy them from). Mr Quin was always the first call after landing at Dublin Airport. He lived about sixteen miles away. His lads used to hunt as well. He always had a nice horse but if he had not got just what you wanted he always knew someone who had. Quin gave a very good performance in the paddock, so he was another one on the way to England. Mrs. McCall liked him and he proved to be one of her favourite horses of all time. She used to ring up to tell me about "Dear Quin".

The next horse I sold her was a very big chestnut horse that I bought from one of Mr. Quin's friends about a mile down the road. He must have been a good 16.3hh and was a superb mover with a wonderful step to him. I never had any papers with him and it was always in the back of my mind he could have foreign blood in him, which I never liked, but things were changing and it was getting more and more difficult to tell since they just called them "Sport horses" and there was nothing more you could do about it. (Long gone are the days when they had a nice mare on the farm who could do everything from chain-harrowing to pulling the cart. They were called Draught mares and they were put to a thoroughbred horse). Mrs. McCall had hinted that she would like to do some dressage so I rang and told her about this horse. I thought he would be an ideal horse for her. She bought him and then rang me to say she had had the most marvellous day's hunting; she had jumped the most enormous gate on him – so the dressage had gone by the board. The next horse she bought from me was Clinton, the chestnut horse that was one of the five I had bought in Ireland.

180

I was in Ireland a little while ago and visited a dealer known as the Fat Man, who has some very nice horses from Kells. During a chat he said:

"Do you remember when John McAuley had lost his licence and the punt was level with the pound, and he asked me to drive you and him over the border into Northern Ireland? He knew where there were some horses. He always did. We called on some people called Turkington – I think that was the name. Anyway, they pulled out this horse, a good sort, and you asked to see it jump. They started him off at about three foot. That was enough for you but John wanted to see it put higher and it turned into a really big fence. John was thinking he might have a good client for him as a jumper. You still wanted a ride on it and while you were going down the village the phone rang. It was the absent husband:

'Have they arrived? What do they think?'

'Well,' she said, 'he has jumped really well. He must have jumped over five feet.'

'Oh you silly woman! You're showing them the wrong horse! That's the Grade A jumper. He's worth a mint of money.'

'How on earth do I get out of it?'

The Fat Man smiled and told me the rest of the story: "You didn't know how you were letting her off the hook when you slid off the horse and said, 'No, it's not for me', did you?"

THE NINETIES AND BEYOND

1990-91

When Phil Arthers stepped up to be Full instead of Acting Field-Master it was not going to change things very much.

Shirley Edwards gave up being the Amateur Whip. She had been whip to six huntsmen in over thirty-five years of continuous service to the Meynell Hunt and knew every yard of the country. She was much missed, but she continued to indulge in her second love, which is golf.

When Lady (Vidi) Ley and Ken Beeston died, the Meynell lost two of its greatest supporters, both having been Joint-Masters, and I lost two of my owners. I had ridden some wonderful horses for them; we went back many years. Lady Vidi lent me my first scarlet coat for Harringay in 1950.

The season's hunting was not helped by frost and snow. We hunted on foot in the snow in coverts where the keepers invited us. On either side of the cold spell we had some excellent runs. There were more foxes than usual and sixty-one and a half brace were killed.

Of all the fund-raising and fun-making events I particularly remember the re-introduced Lamb Roast and Country Sports Evening at the Kennels. Seventeen teams, mostly Young Farmers, took part. Plenty of water was splashed about and they all got wet on the outside. When it was all over they got very wet on the inside. The Hunt Supper was held at Shirley House by invitation of Michael and Jane Thornton, as good a do as ever. I happened to be standing next to Hugh Davies, our Vet, when a woman I didn't know came up to me.

"I'm sure I know you," she said.

I sensed Hugh was pricking up his ears and thought I would make the most of it: "Perhaps you've seen me on the T.V. I'm a bit-part actor. Just now we are making an ad., promoting this new scent called, 'It for Men.' The words go something like this, 'If you have it flaunt it'."

"Ooh, really! You've made my evening." She was pleased. "I told my boyfriend I knew you."

What she didn't know was that the nearest I had been to a T.V. was the remote control. Poor Hugh didn't know what to do with himself. He still reminds me of it sometimes.

Mark, here on Arthur, bought from Phil Arthurs who had field-mastered off him

The Cross-Country Team Event took place again at Tom White's. (Incidentally, he once told me that he had never had a sheep abort or a cow cast a calf in all the years he had horses galloping over his farm). David and Sue Meynell hosted the Hunt Ball at Hollybush Park. The Point-to-Point was not the greatest success, a lot was going on that day. It made £3500 but the Members' Race was a disaster, only one entry. This is not really the country for Point-to-Pointers; it is far too big unless you get the likes of Pat Wint. Hunter Trials were held for the first time at Nick Hutchinson's, where Nick and Martin Speed built a very good course. The Cheese and Wine Party took place at Burton Town Hall which, with just the right atmosphere, always lends itself to events like this.

In the Inter-Hunt Team Relay we got to the Royal Show again for the finals. There were two or three bus-loads of supporters who were very vocal and excited. It was nearly the same team: Phil Arthers, Sarah, and Sarah Ward but Caroline Brown took the place of her sister Valerie who had had an accident. They finished third in the Best Turnout but second, to the Oakley, in the Relay. They won another £420 for Hunt Funds.

Another event that was just as important in its own way was meeting Sarah's new boyfriend, Mark Whitney, who was looking for a hunter. We had a nice horse recently come over from Ireland so Mark's presence gave us the idea of calling him Blanket. He was a five years old, 16.2hh, bay gelding and a very good hunter. I sold him to the Richmond-Watsons who had an estate just outside Towcester. They bought him down and had a day with the Meynell. They were very pleased with him but they never bought another horse from me.

At the time, we had nothing suitable for Mark so he turned the pages of *Horse and Hound* and came across a grey mare that looked promising. He went into Gloucestershire to see for himself but found she was not really big enough. Afterwards he rang me to say the mare's owners had a lot of horses and wanted to sell. He thought I ought to go and have a look. When Linda and I went down they showed us six lovely horses – and I bought them all! Here is a tally of them:

There was George, a very big horse, a superb looking bright bay, six years old. We hunted him a few times and Commander Ford, a retired naval man from the Grafton Hunt bought him. He was Clerk of the Course at Stratford, a very nice chap, who often invited us to see him but we never quite got round to it. When he hunted a day or two with the Meynell, George looked so well it was plain we had found him a good home.

Barnaby was one of our favourites. Everybody hunted him; Mark loved him. He was a liver chestnut, 6 years old, but slightly parrot-mouthed. (That means the upper teeth are more prominent that the bottom set. A lot of racehorses are like that). He was bought by Sorrel Woods to hunt in the Grafton Country, where I was selling a lot of horses. Like the Commander, she brought him to hunt with the Meynell, and was going so well she decided to subscribe to the Meynell.

Aero, a grey mare, 16.1hh, six years old, was the one Mark had originally gone to look at. She had a touch of Irish Draught. Mark bought her. She carried him very well across the Meynell, but, as we all knew, was not quite big enough, and, at the end of the season, was sold on to Robert Bell, a dealer in the Midlands.

Teabag, also, went to Robert Bell. He was more of a lady's horse, a bay gelding by Teaspoon. We did not have him many days.

Another fine horse that we did not have long enough to find a name for was a most superb heavyweight, dark bay gelding, five years old, with a hogged mane. Norman Proffit had him and often said what a good sort he turned out to be. I bet he was up to eighteen stone.

I have saved the best till last, another Winston, the jewel in the Crown, an Irish 7/8 thoroughbred chestnut gelding, five years old. What a lovely horse, a superb mover, probably one of the best horses we have ever owned! Sarah show-jumped him a few times, and won one or two classes on him but I could see he was too much horse for her. When Tim had hunted him a few times he said what a wonderful horse he was across country. I happened to be talking to John McAuley one night on the phone and told him I had probably got one of the best horses I had ever owned; he would make the most marvellous eventer. John immediately said, "Don't sell him until I've seen him. I'll fly over on the first plane I can get and will bring a jockey over with me who has the order for a potential Olympic horse. Two days later they arrived and he introduced me to David Foster, probably the best jockey who has been here, such a gifted jockey, and such a nice fellow. He could have made the horse talk but they never asked him to do too much – jump 3 ft 6 inches, trot a few circles. They bought him at that; I don't know who for but I got the impression it was a syndicate. I kept in touch with David and his wife, often calling in when I was in Ireland. He was going very well with Winston (Of course they had changed his name then) until he rang one night to say the horse had broken down very badly and would not event again. David was heart-broken, but that's horses and eventing is a high risk sport as David was to find out. He was killed when a horse turned over with him in an event in Ireland. What a dreadful loss! He died doing what he loved best but it's still a very sad tale. He left behind a lovely wife and family. Life must go on.

Another good horse I bought that year was Jack. John Whittaker rang.

He would like me to hunt a horse for him; it might do him good as a show-jumper. I met him on the Mansfield Road by Junction 28 of the M 1. Again I saw a horse of my favourite colour, liver chestnut, 16.2hh, a truly lovely horse. I could not wait to get him home and have a ride on him. His jumping was as good as his looks, but John had got him in close and he needed to stand off in our country where we don't get too many ditches toward. Instead, we get a scoop in front of a hedge and if you get into the scoop it can be disaster. That's what we had to watch with Jack and is probably why, when John came to our place and tried him over a few show-jumps that we had, he judged the horse had not improved as he had expected. He offered him to me to buy, and I accepted. It was a rewarding deal; I had what I think was one of my finest hunts on him, on a day when we met at Claire Evans-Schrieber's. Trotting down to the first draw – Salts I think it was – when he slipped badly on the road and went all his length. We picked ourselves up. It had all happened quite quickly and not many people noticed we had been down. Jack had just scraped his knee and I had done the same. Anyway, we found and ran to Brewards Carr, not probably that far but the fences were big. I saw Doug Hibbert calling a cab over one fence. It had got the most enormous drop but we were in full cry and weren't bothering to stop and take a look at what we were jumping. I know I jumped some chestnut paling fencing. I would not like to say how big it was but that jump made even Jack grunt (Smyth-Osborne, who is a racehorse trainer now, was out that day. I don't think he came again). Jane Walker-Okeover came over and said she would like to buy him. She had been Joint-Master for three years and needed a new horse or two. She kept Jack until her Mastership ended and then sold him to go into the Cottesmore country.

There is quite a tale to tell about Pierrot, a bay gelding, 16.3hh, and seven-eighths bred. Although he was bought in Ireland, he came from a Frenchman who lived there. Tim was the first to hunt him; he loved to be the first to try them out, but Pierrot was proving to be very hot. He was giving Tim a rough ride and then the nose-band broke when they were going across Longford Park. Although he was wearing a standing martingale he had already hit Tim on the nose and made it bleed so there was no way he could go on without a martingale. Reg Clarke, helpful as ever, said Tim could have his horse's nose-band and so Tim was able to continue. After we had hunted him a few more times he still wasn't settling any better. Some horses take up to a dozen outings to settle but we did not give Pierrot that chance. John Lanni, who had had the half-share in Todhunter, was having an auction for jumping horses at his new place, Arena U.K.. We thought Pierrot was good enough to put through the sale; if there was one thing he could do it was jump. I took him down for a trial and Matthew rode him. On the day, with Matthew riding again, he went very well. We did not make a fortune but came out of it all right.

Our Vice-Chairman since 1986 had been Di Monier-Williams. She owned a fine horse, Bobby, that I had tried to buy as a four-year-old at one of Patti Guest's jumping shows. I bid a lot of money for him too. Ken Beeston owned him and would not sell him then. He won a good class at Peterborough; I think it was the Grade B Championships. When Di had him she either gave or lent him to David Barker to hunt hounds off. I remember Mike Tucker also having a day on him.

One day in November, hounds found their fox in Peat Moss, ran over the Longford-Hollington Road by the Red Lion Pub, and straight down that field with a hedge and a ditch towards at the bottom. That day it was blind with lots of nettles and long grass in it. Oliver made one of his few mistakes and put his front feet in it and went arse over tip. By the time I had caught him and got Linda back on, she was quite dazed so, with the lorry being parked at Longford, we thought we would make our way home. We were going the same way the Hunt had gone and when we got to Foots Farm on the edge of the Longford Estate there were lots of people about who started to tell us that Di Monier-Williams had had a bad fall. Evidently David Meynell had jumped a narrow place by the side of a gate and her horse Bobby thought that it was a bit narrow for him and made to jump the gate. As it was, he went a bit sideways and came down on top of her. It was on to concrete. Di was left sadly disabled. It was a most shocking accident.

1991-92

The Joint-Masters were unchanged except that David Meynell became the alternative Field Master – in other words, there was a job for him whenever he came out. He had already given us thirteen seasons of his life, and enjoyed himself. We have been so lucky with our Field Masters.

Martin Bluck had moved on to the Barlow as Huntsman and Robert Howarth had come home, as you might say. He had first come to the Meynell in 1983, and since then had been with the Bramham Moor as a Whip.

Hunting went very well with sport holding up right through the season. Followers may well remember the bitterly cold day when they swam the Brailsford Brook and David Barker went for an unplanned swim in the Bentley Brook.

We all attended the Rally at Stoneleigh in defence of Country Sports. A pity we have to do this. If it was not so serious it would be a good day out, seeing lots of people you know, including Robin Smith-Ryland barging his way forward so he could be interviewed on the T.V. An estimated 12,000 people turned up. Luckily, the Conservatives won the General Election and we knew we would be hunting for the next few seasons – which would just about see me out. But then you should not think of yourself. On these occasions you should think of the next generation.

Billy Foulkes was the new Chairman of the Point-to-Point, taking over from Mike Power who had done it for fourteen years. The Members Race got a few more runners this year, five, nearly six, against last year's one. Jeremy Allen did a good job in the Patrons Tent and it made a record profit. The second Bazaar held at Abbots Bromley was run by Di Monier-Williams. It was good to know she was still going to be involved in the Hunt after her awful accident. The Hunter Trial was again held at Nick Hutchinson's, with over a hundred competitors enjoying themselves. The Show-jumping evening started up again at Marchington, for that we have to thank John and Margery Snow. The Hunt Supporters' club did a tremendous lot of work – they organised a trip to Cheltenham for the races. Mick Collins organised a Sixties disco at Hanbury Village Hall. The Sponsored ride at Shooting Butts, growing in popularity, made £1400. George Shaw, and Margaret too, no doubt, ran a very good Farmers' Party at Burton Town Hall as part of their commitment to the Sheep Scheme. As the market for lamb had become more depressed they needed to recruit more sheep-walkers.

The Inter-Hunt Relay team at the Royal Show consisted of Phil Arthers, Valerie and Caroline Brown and Sarah Ward. They were second in the Best Turnout and second in the Relay to a very professional Irish Team, the East Clare Harriers.

Offal disposal became prohibitively expensive and the knackering service had to be suspended, with alternative employment being found for Stewart Rogers.

JUMPING FOR GREAT BRITAIN

I had done no show-jumping for years so the letter that came from the B.S.J.A. was a bolt from the blue. Would I like to go to Holland, all expenses paid, to represent Great Britain in the Old Riders series. (According to regulations, riders are *old* at fifty, and above). Linda and I flew from East Midlands to Schipol and were met at the railway station by two friendly *young* people and the other members of our team: George Nimmo from

Carnforth in Lanarks and John Greeves from Fife, but the other member failed to show. It was very cold and there was snow on the ground. We were taken to have a look at the show-ground, which was quite a small indoor school, before going to our hotel so that we could settle in, and then back to the show-ground to meet the horses. Whereas the other teams from different countries mostly rode their own horses, we had to ride what was provided for us. Mine was a bit of a has-been; he stopped quite badly if you were standing off too far but I did tell Linda that if I could get the horse round to my way of thinking we might go places.

How hospitable the Dutch were! We were taken to the most superb restaurant for our evening meal and there, in the team that the Russians had brought, I recognised one of them from the old days at the White city in 1962. Quite a coincidence!

The next day we had to do what we had gone to do and take our horses over the jumps. George soon got to grips with his but it took me longer. It switched on, switched off. Thank goodness the class was only a warm-up. Next there was a Speed Class. George was placed; John Greeves, who had only been riding for five years, was all right: and I rode slowly. The next day, during another warm-up class, I thought we were going better. The horse felt happy and so did I.

Before the Grand Prix all the teams had to parade, with a chap walking in front of them carrying a banner showing the name of their nation, and the music of their national anthem playing. The Dutch organisers got things just right and made a great occasion of it. There were hundreds of people. It was not the biggest place and the course was a very tricky one, but I think the excitement of it put my horse on his toes. It reminded him of his glory days and he jumped a superb clear round. Our team finished third and I got a lovely silver cup to add to my collection. What a party we had that night! George was in his kilt and made quite a hit; he was over 65 and lived life to the full. We were certainly dancing until the early hours. George made real friends with the Russians. When they were exchanging mementoes, he took a button off his coat and gave it to a Russian. There were some of George's older friends who he had known while they were living in Scotland. He had told them we were coming, so when the show had finished they picked us up and showed us round a dairy farm, a lot of stud farms, and the kennels where the drag-hunting hounds were kept. In fact we had the most marvellous time. They called in on us the next time they came to England.

Our next trip was to Moscow. We all met at Gatwick for the flight. What a dreary place Moscow Airport was. There were about three electric light bulbs to light the whole place. We stayed in this great big building where the

Army stayed or any big-wigs who came. There was a lot of snow outside but it was quite warm inside. The hotel was a tall building, and on each floor there were two people sitting at a desk. If you left your room they took the keys and kept them for you. There were six people on our floor, each sharing eight-hour shifts, and so, if you consider how many floors there were, you can understand how the Russians found work for nearly everyone.

For the jumping we were on a more level playing-field than in Holland; this time everyone had to ride Russian horses. We got a different horse each day and drew for it. Each horse had a number. We walked into the ring and drew a number out of a box and that was the number of our mount for the day – a much fairer arrangement. There were about thirty jockeys of very high calibre, three of them were Olympic horsemen. It was a pretty big school and the courses were very good but our team was just out of the money every time. Never mind. They took us around Moscow and showed us the Olympic Stadium. I bought a Russian hat from a market trader and then we were shown round Red Square. It was a lot bigger than I imagined with a steep climb to get into it. I bought some of the Russian dolls, the ones where there are a lot of dolls each fitting inside another one and a tiny one right in the middle. We had a wonderful time, including a big party on the last night. We were all given mementoes. As they had heard I was a hunting person I was given the most lovely bronze of a hunting scene. They did not have a lot but were lovely people – so generous.

Our next trip was to Berne in Switzerland. We travelled across country by train, through picture-book scenery – so clean and well tended, tidy houses with the logs stacked up outside each one, and cows in the fields with bells round their necks. This show was held in the Army centre where there was every creature comfort and amenity – show-jumping rings, dressage arenas, indoor school, loose boxes – but the competition arrangements were hard. At least we had the same horse throughout. We were given Ukrainian-bred four-year-olds to ride. George got a nice bay horse, I got a skinny chestnut, and John's was about its equal. Still, it was the taking part which mattered. We were made very welcome and lavishly entertained. They took us up into the mountains in a bus for a beautiful lunch and in the evening a marvellous dinner with a special dish, a Swiss speciality, called a fondue, which I for one had never had before. But to get back to the jumping, it was done outside. The courses were fairly big and were a bit much for our four-year-olds but we gave it our best shot. It was very hot. By the time the Grand Prix came around they were tired but we had another worry: none of us were insured. We were too old to be insured for equestrian sports. We could just imagine breaking a leg out there and having the extra expense to get us home.

Still, nothing daunted, we carried on. I jumped quite a good first round, but by the second round my little horse was tired and he stopped twice at the last part of the treble. I thought to myself, "I know I'm riding for Queen and Country but I wonder if she would mind if I retired?" – So I did. After Switzerland, with the worry of knowing we were too old to get insured, we thought we would give it best. Although we were invited to go to Poland, we decided to decline.

Linda and I had a very interesting trip to Ireland that year. We went to the Ballymeclad Kennels and saw some lovely horses. They looked well. Ballymeclad was some of the most wild and woolly country in Ireland. All around the kennels were carcasses – cows, sheep and pigs. I think the idea was to turn the hounds out and let them help themselves. I visited the place a few times, never any different, but I also bought some horses from there. One particular one this first time was Snowman, a big horse, six years old, 16.2hh, with white flecks all over him. The first person to look at him over here was Phillip Watts, huntsman of the South Notts, who was now picking up our dead stock. (As already mentioned, the Meynell had stopped picking up fallen stock, a great loss to us farmers). Anyway, Phillip liked the look of him and thought he went very well, but I think he was outside the price for Joint-Masters. It was Fiona Shepherd-Cross who wanted a horse for one of the boys and bought him to go along with Fritz and Jimmy.

A few weeks later Fiona rang again. Could I find a horse for her husband James? He would want a big horse. I had never met him and, as it happened, I had just bought a big horse from David Nicholson, who we had been dealing with for the past twenty years. I don't think David was aware, but I knew that the horse had been sent to him to sell by Angela Radcliffe, as she was then. She is now Angela Needham. (I had known Angela for many years and bought a few horses from her. She was one of the best point-to-point jockeys in the North. She used to ride for Mr Caley who I used to ride for as well. She was a good show-jumper too). This horse was a chestnut gelding, seven years old. As I had had a fall, Tim, the stable-jockey, was given a leg up. We thought that the horse looked a foreigner although it was getting more and more difficult to tell the difference. We called him Fritz just the same. When Tim took him out I was being driven around in the car and I am not a good car follower. I was there when they came trotting through Hollington, and shouted to Tim, "How are you going then?" and he shouted back, "I've had a couple of falls but he's a very good horse." When he had come to me I had a suspicion he might kick a hound. (If a horse is inclined to have a go at a hound it is as well to buy a few chickens and feed then alongside the horse). We were satisfied enough for me to ring Fiona and tell her that I had a horse that might do for James. She brought the lads down to try him and they both fell off but that did not put her off. She was pleased with him and so was James.

Next she gave me the order for one for her daughter-in-law, a cheapy to start her riding. I had heard that Martin Speed was giving up hunting and wanted a good home for a very nice bay horse he had called Bandit. I put them in touch with one another and a deal was done. Fiona sent me a very nice Christmas present and said she was sending Martin a case of champagne. I felt sure she would. However, she had bought an ex-eventer from somewhere and did not like it. She asked me find her "that very good horse". I was still travelling and looking at hunters as well as going to Ireland. In Lancashire I was talking to Ray Lucas one day (I had known him since Sarah and Tim's juvenile jumping days and Martin, his son, rode under the Senator banner). He said he had a grey horse that had won about £500 show-jumping and was still only seven years old. He had lent it to someone in Nottinghamshire and they had then decided they did not want it any more. He asked if I would go and have a look at it. If I liked it I could take it home with me. Linda and I went to have a look (in the horse-box, of course) and we both liked what we saw but could not understand why the people weren't going to buy it. We hadn't a lot to lose so we loaded up and when we got him home, went about it very quietly, rode him on the road, round the farm, jumped over the hedges, and still could not find a thing wrong with him. I thought the truth would come out when I hunted him. The meet I took him to was down at Marston-on-Dove, home of Billy Foulkes. They were only cubbing but I went off on my own and jumped a few good places, faultless. I was over the moon. I used to tell Sarah and Tim that when I pulled on my breeches and boots I was going to work. Well, this was a good morning's work. I rang Fiona that night:

"Fiona, I have found a horse for you. He's a grey and his name is Snowy River."

She told me she had just bought one.

"Sell it on," I said quite crossly. "Sell it on. Get rid of it. Give it away. Do something with it. I insist you buy this horse."

"Oh, I don't know if I really want another horse. Besides, I think I have lost my nerve as well."

"I'm not unsympathetic, but you know the best thing for you is to get it back again."

I persuaded her to come and see him. She just looked and bought him. He made such a wonderful horse for her that, from losing her nerve one moment, the following year she was Joint-Master of the Grafton. She rang me to say she was so excited. It was all beyond her wildest dreams. She often came and had a day with the Meynell. But one time she rang me it was not good news. She told me she had cancer and not too long to live. She wanted to thank me for all the happiness I had given her, especially by making her buy Snowy River. It was not long afterwards that she passed on. I had lost two very dear friends in the Grafton, first Mrs.Watt and now Fiona Shepherd-Cross. Linda and I went to her funeral and the church was packed. I thought to myself, and I don't mind admitting it with a tear in my eye, that from all the people there, of high rank and higher, I had provided Fiona with as much fun in her short life as anybody. It was a very strange feeling but she wouldn't want me to grieve too long for her. She was not that sort of person.

On the same trip to Ireland when we bought Snowman, I bought a roan horse, six years old, 16.2hh, just the right sort for Mark, I thought. When we got him home and had ridden him around the farm, Mark was quite excited. He seemed just what he was looking for. The first chance of a real test that we got was a cubbing day at Billy's and I took him along. Hounds had hardly started drawing some kale before they were running and — Pull! I could hardly hold the thing! He definitely wasn't going to suit Mark. I thought he

A few of the horses sold to the Shepherd-Cross family

would make a good Whip's horse, would be better out in front. As Phillip Watts was still coming over from the South Notts I showed him the roan. He suggested that I could take him to the coming meet of the South Notts at David Gardener's in Hazlewood (I had once ridden a point-to-point winner for David but had not seen him for years. He had just moved to Hazlewood) and let the Whip ride him. Came the day and the Whip was pleased with him. I said they should take him back to the kennels, have him vetted, and see how he settled down. (I knew John Mason would vet him because he was their Joint-Master at the time). Phillip Watts rang after they had had him for a month and said the horse was not right; he had got a leg. I pointed out that their man had vetted him, that they had kept on hunting him, and there couldn't be much wrong with him. The next I heard, he had jumped the Whip off, galloped over a cattle-grid, and broken both front legs. I would not sell them another.

Along with Snowman and the unfortunate roan we bought three more.

Kells, a black horse, six years old and 16.3hh. came from the blacksmith who lived just outside Kells. We always gave him a call; if he had nothing for us he, being a blacksmith, would know where there was

Linda riding Oliver and Mark on Kells

something that would suit us. He had a very little sand-school. Everyone in Ireland seemed to have a sand-school. Kells jumped very well, probably not the fastest ride but a good solid sort to carry 14.7. At the time, I had the roan horse in mind for Mark but when we found him not suitable Kells was the next best thing. Mark tried him, liked him and bought him. He was probably not the most exciting ride but he carried him safely.

The next horse we bought was at Doyle's, Punchestown. The one he brought out was the most lovely grey horse by Sea Crest, six years old and 16.2hh. Linda loved him although he had a touch of stringhalt behind but I remembered Cement City winning plenty of good chases at Wolverhampton and knew that a lot of racehorses have a touch of stringhalt – it is a nervous part of the body – and bought him fairly confidently. Back home, I had a word with Richard Davison, the dressage expert, and asked him if it would make a good event horse. The answer he gave was that the only problem would be with the piaffe. I hunted him, another super jumper, though he liked a buck. When we met at John Ward's one Tuesday I saw his daughter Catherine on her two feet. She explained that her horse was off the road, so I told her she could have the horse I had just bought in Ireland if she could get her father to pick him up on Friday ready for hunting on Saturday. What a Saturday we had! Catherine was saying he was the best horse she had ever had, but I must say she was giving him a great ride. He was returned in one piece.

The other horse I bought that day was from John McAuley himself. Although I had bought four horses already that day he felt sure I would buy the next one. He pulled out a nice bay gelding, 16.1hh, five years old. At that point, Linda said she was going into the house and would watch from the kitchen. I had no doubts after the show he gave, bought him, and named him Kitchener. When he arrived at home I gave him a day or two off and then hunted him at Weston Underwood. It was nothing but pleasure. Who should be out that day but Kate, the daughter of Annabel Startin who had been such a help to Linda in the Pony Club. Annabel rang that night to tell me Kate had been quite taken with the horse I had been riding and asked if they could come over and have a ride on him. They all came over, both Tom and Kate rode him, and had the idea of going eventing with him. I thought he might not fare very well with his dressage but Annabel had two good jockeys – if they couldn't sort him nobody could. They took him, did very well with him, and kept him through to his happy retirement.

We never named the next horse, a chestnut, because we did not have him long. We bought him just outside Dublin from a place that was barricaded by a great high wall with barbed wire on the top and had a speaker in the wall beside some very big gates. After we had announced ourselves they eventually opened, and we drove up this very long drive to a mansion of a place with beautiful stables. I saw what I think was one of the nicest horses I have ever seen. He looked so well. I hardly tried him and he was soon on his way to England. A few days later Peter Mellor was wanting one for the Chairman of his local pack, the Rockwood Harriers, and bought him. He told us that the Chairman was a Funeral Director and had a Wedding Car business as well. As Sarah was about to be married, part of the deal was that he should supply the cars for the wedding. What Sarah got was a very smart white Rolls-Royce. What's the good of having friends unless you make the most use of them?

1992-93

Annie Chandos-Pole gave up her part of the Mastership. She had been a Joint-Master for four seasons, though had been Mrs Annie Chichester since her marriage to James. (What a good do that had been!). She and Jane had done a wonderful job to turn the ship around after the awful politics of the late eighties. David Meynell had a bad fall that had put him out for most of the previous season.

Phil Arthers was in plaster for weeks after a bad fall towards the end of the season over some big stiff post-and-rails. Neil Seaton handed in his resignation and it was accepted, which was a shock to him after over thirty years working for the Meynell Hunt. A good follower in the job was found in Dick Woolley. There is no-one who can't be done without; some are just missed more than others. The casualty-list included Billy Foulkes with multiple injuries after a bad fall in November; Jane Walker-Okeover out of action for much of the early season; Robert Howarth, the Whip, with an injured knee that kept him out; Mick Collins who had a frightening encounter with a lorry; and David Barker who escaped serious injury in a nasty fall when jumping a gate with wire in front.

The Hunt Supporters ran another very good evening show-jumping at Marchington. A good day out again at Booth Hay where the Cross-Country Team Event took place, again thanks to Tom and Vera White. The Lamb Roast and Country Sport Evening was held again at the Kennels, where rebuilding three buttresses and doing some re-pointing was this year's contribution to the on-going maintenance and improvements. It was a very wet evening but Jeremy Allen was leading by example in organising the games. He knows one or two good games does Jeremy.

A Junior Hunt Supporters' Club was set up. Its first function was a

Disco and Karaoke Evening, followed by a Wee Willie Winkie Disco (It's amazing what young people wear to go to bed!) but the Midsummer Bronc in July was the most successful and popular. Football and rugby teams took the field, with not very startling results, until a five-a-side rugby team won a tournament set up by the Oakley Hunt. More importantly, these activities provided useful sums of money for Riding for the Disabled, the Hunt Kennels, and the Campaign for Hunting.

The Bazaar at Abbots Bromley made enough to donate £1000 each to Cancer Relief and the R.N.L.I. as well as a substantial sum to Hunt Funds. The Hunt Supporters were providing a new Hunt lorry and gave £2000 to the Fencing Fund and £1000 to the Campaign for Hunting. John Hingley agreed to take over the Chairmanship of the Hunt Supporters from Nick Hutchinson.

The Inter-Hunt Relay team made it to the second round at the Royal Show. It included two new members: Johnny Greenall and "young" Doug Hibbert who took the place of the old man of the party, with Val Eaton and Caroline Brown, team veterans. Once again, after a terrific struggle, spurred on by noisy supporters, they had to take second place behind an Irish team, this time the North Kilkenny.

On that year's trip to Ireland, I bought three: Snip, Glendower, and Clancy. Snip came from the farm next door to the Quins, by the airport, a big bay horse, 16.3hh, another one that looked like warm blood. (It is difficult to find the ideal horse with, as folk used to say, a head like a Duchess and an arse like a cook). He came over with his green book and a vet's certificate that said, "This horse is up to doing any job." That is all you ever got; yet, although I had every horse I bought over there vetted, never once did I have one failed by the vet. I must add that I never had one fail the vet over here either.

Tim's diary said, "*I was Test Pilot again, and I was very pleased with Snip.*" Mark rode him a lot. One day I saw him leading the field where there are three very big hedges with only a few strides between them. He had a grin from ear to ear for a week. Someone came to try Snip and I can't think who it was. He was dressed in immaculate breeches and boots, bowler hat, and big long spurs. After I had given him a show in the front field and jumped the hedge, he wanted a ride on him. Snip, although very kind, was a high-class horse with a lot of thoroughbred blood in him and when he felt the spurs in the middle he simply took off, jumped the rails onto the road, and was just going into Brailsford, which is one and a half miles away, before he could stop him. We jumped in the car to go after him and caught up with him standing by the roadside rather shaken. He asked whether I would ride him back as he wanted to go back in the car. It really shook the horse up as well. It shook him up so much that we could not show him to anyone in that field again. After being so frightened by those spurs he just would not settle. Luckily, it did not affect him out hunting, and that was a good job.

I sold him to a chap called Walters who tried him here but wanted a day on him. We went through the usual procedure, had him vetted, he paid me, and after that if he wasn't happy with him out hunting he could have his cheque back. He seemed pleased enough with him after he had tried him but then he told me he was buying the horse for someone else – a very dangerous thing to do. Always buy them for yourself and hope someone else likes what you like. I never heard of him again so I suppose it went all right.

Tim (Who else?) was test pilot of Glendower. He was, or is, the most lovely grey and came out of Granard Country, Longford. He belonged to an Army Officer who I never actually met as I was shown him by his wife – but I had seen the horse before. He was being show-jumped at Millstreet when he played up and put his leg through the wooden part of his loose box so that when I first saw him he had the most enormous bandage on it. This time he was all right. I never rode him or saw him ridden but I bought him. Tim hunted him and according to his diary thought him the best he had ridden. He wrote that he had shown a lot of self-discipline – meaning, I think, that he would have liked to have gone higher and wider. I was off the road at the time and Stewart Shaw came over to ride him (They don't do any good standing in the stable). From the car, I saw him jump a good wall at the top of Ilam, Thorpe Road. A very good catch jockey is Stewart; it didn't take long for him to get better. The first time I rode him was at John Ward's and decided the horse was very special. The Prince was out and I knew he was wanting a horse because Jane Walker-Okeover had said so. I went up to him. It was no great deal; he had been hunting with us for over twenty years:

"This horse would make you a very good horse, sir."

He didn't disagree, but said, "See David Barker."

I privately thought, "No thank you. I can sell my own horses."

That night when I told the family I had offered him to the Prince, they all went berserk. They had been talking about Glendower and how good he was and thought I should keep him for myself. I told them that I got my kicks out of life by riding different horses, testing their courage against mine. I thought keeping a horse for oneself was a sign of getting old and I didn't want to get old. However, I did compromise and said I would not offer him to anyone, but if anyone offered me a good price for him I would consider it.

The week after that conversation, when I was in no hurry queuing for a hunt jump, Peter Balance's horse must have run back about thirty yards and kicked Glen on the inside of his hind leg. It was not the biggest of cuts but I thought I would have it stitched, never imagining there would be any trouble. I think the vets had been to see him over the years and Glen could smell them coming. He was very difficult to stitch. They had to give him a massive injection to dope him, but he must have got some dirt in the wound as it kept flaring up and I had to take him down to Gibson's at Oakham. They got him right. Then I tried to claim off Peter Balance's insurance but they would not have it. On top of that trouble he was nearly impossible to clip. Hugh Davies would have to give him an injection, as much as he dared, and not be too far away in case he had to have a bit more. That went on for a year or two until I heard Tim Marsland could clip these difficult horses without having to dope them. When I next saw him out hunting I asked him to come over, and from that first visit Glen has got better and better so now we don't even have to put a twitch on him. I have kept him, and must accept that I am growing old, as gracefully as I can. He would probably not be the best horse I have ridden, but he is certainly very good. Di Turner even says he is the best in Europe – and she should know. She is as good a judge as you would come across.

Last comes Clancy. I named him after the village I bought him from, where was a great chemist's shop that could sell you any horse drugs at half the price of anywhere else. On its left is where Jim Cash lives (and I've bought a few horses off him in my time) while Ned Cash lives on the right. If you go between them and turn left, about half a mile down the drive you come to the biggest hireling yard in Ireland. I had been there a few times before this but had never bought anything there myself. Now I saw this horse, with a lot more quality than I had seen normally. He was a bay gelding, 16.1hh, six years old, and three-quarters bred, that jumped very well in the sand-paddock. I just rode him down the drive, found he suited me, and bought him. He came over with the other two; the quicker you can get a load together the quicker they are over, taking about a week over it, unless, of course, the sea is rough. He wasn't long coming and was very fit and well so I hunted him at the first opportunity when the hounds met at Somersal Herbert. The first fence we came to was a very substantial post-and-rails, where we just had to wait a few moments, probably hoping they would get broken, but they didn't, so it was a case of– Here goes! He jumped them in fine style (You always feel better when you get the first one out of the way) but after that – Pull! He about pulled my arms out of their sockets. When I got him home I looked inside his mouth and found he had a terrible sore there. He must have pulled before I had him. When his mouth was better I sold him to a Mr. Heber-Percy from

Gloucestershire. There, they thought what a good horse he was, but a nice jockey he was too. It makes such a difference when you are able to sell to good jockeys.

Mark had put his grey mare, the one he had hunted with the Grafton, in foal and her foal was now two years old. It was never going to get big enough for him to ride so he sent off an advert to *Horse and Hound* and some people near Belvoir Castle came and bought it. When I delivered the two-year-old to them and we put her in the stable she was very good because we had handled her a great deal. Their farm was next to Mick Toulson, who I had sold a lot of horses to, but had never been to his place. It was nice to call on him. When Mick showed me a very good sort of grey mare, I asked if he would sell her, and we had a deal there and then. After John Craven, at my request, had vetted her, I went back and fetched her from right in the middle of the Belvoir country. It looked all plough to me – it didn't compare with the Meynell where we are nearly all old grass.

When Kate Cooper had been to look at Jack, Jane Walker-Okeover's horse that had come from John Whittaker, I had put her off as he was far too big for her but she asked me to let her know if ever I came across any horse that might suit her. Now was the time. I gave her a ring and she came over and bought her, confirming my judgement of Kate and of the grey mare. How well she has done with her! She still occasionally gives me a bottle of champagne for Christmas.

I did not always go over to Ireland myself; John McAuley would ring and say, "I've seen a nice horse today. Could you do with him?" If he described the horse well I would ask him to send the horse over. That was how one horse, a near thoroughbred, arrived just before Christmas. The first time we took him out, with Tim as test pilot, was when they met at the Dog and Partridge at Tutbury, on New Year's Day. Tim was going very well on him so I said to Tim, "Let's have a bit of fun with Johnny Greenall." Off I went to tell him about this horse just arrived from Ireland, winner of a point-to-point in Ireland, by Strong Gale out of a Deep Run mare. (Actually I hadn't a clue how he was bred). Johnny said, "Oh, I must have a ride on him." To be fair, he did say afterwards that he had just about given up race-riding and he thought the horse was a bit green as a hunter. Meanwhile Tim was riding Johnny's horse, Ben, the one he had bought from Perkins, and had gone A over T at some post-and-rails and spent the next five hours at the Derbyshire Royal Infirmary with a wing up. It was Alan Edmunds that bought him, just Alan's sort. Different people like different types of horse but you an always tell a Betteridge horse. I can't just describe what it's like, but I do know it when I see it.

1993-94

We had a big change in the Mastership: Jane Walker-Okeover gave up after five years – she had always said she would do her five years – but she would still be clearing the ground at Osmaston and Okeover. (She was also having to spend more and more time being Lady-in-Waiting to the Queen Mother). I said previously what a wonderful job she and Annie had done. They were the only two who could have done it, and they had left the Meynell in far better state than when they took over. Onwards and upwards! Phil Arthers and Sue Perkins were joined by Jenny Barnes, who had hunted with both the Meynell and South Notts so she knew what it was all about. Then out of the blue came Tessa Hibbert. She had certainly come a long way since I found her the grey cob, Marble, in 1980. They were very good news, especially as their husbands supported them, and even more very good news was that Johnny Greenall was going to join the Mastership too. I wonder when he sat down to breakfast here a few years ago, when Billy Foulkes had brought him cubbing, if he had an idea he might become a Joint-Master of the Meynell one day.

Tessa Hibbert was being kissed by quite a lot of people on her appointment and I turned to Bernard and said, "You'll have to get used to

Johnny Greenall, John, Mark and Linda with Meynell hounds at home at Shuckton

201

seeing your wife kissed like that."

He said, dryly, "I'm used to it already."

We had a very wet season, but among many long and exciting runs in the record, I remember one from Brian Goodall's. I still think around Sutton is the best of the Meynell country, with never quite so many people out as when they meet at Booth Hay or Snelston.

Half an inch of snow in the morning of Point-to-Point day caused major headaches for John Fairclough, the hard-worked secretary. He had to let everyone know it was cancelled and stare at a debt that stood at £11,000 before any insurance could be reckoned in.

The Cross-Country Team Event was again very popular especially the Young Entry and Cub Hunters Classes, which were very well supported. Thanks are due again to the Whites and Potters. There was an Open Evening at the Kennels, on a wet evening, so that the Hound Judging had to be held in the Long Room. The Terrier, Lurcher, and Family Dog Show also took place at the Kennels, under Greg Mousely's management, now with assistance from his son, Richard. The Lamb Roast and Country Evening was another good night and whenever the secret is out that Guido is cooking the folk know they are in for a feast – and his riding is improving. He will tell you that if his ancestors had not built our roads we should still be living in the Dark Ages. One fine evening, Nancy Bird showed us round her beautiful gardens. The Summer Ball was again held at Top House Farm, Alkmonton. Bernard and Tessa Hibbert held a supper at their home, a very good evening. The Junior Hunt Supporters lived up to their promises and put on a total of eight very lively events.

After a lot of spit and polish we won the Best Turned-out at the Inter-Hunt Relay. Phil Arthers, a comeback, Caroline Brown, Jo Marshall and Stewart Shaw made up the team. After beating the Irish favourites from North Galway we were pipped at the post yet again, by the Bicester and Whaddon. One day we will win and make that trip to Dublin. The Hunt again benefited to the tune of £450.

I bought Kingswood from Mark Thompson from Burton-on-Trent. Tim first hunted him when they met at Dalbury Lees. It was an awful day, sleet and snow. Most of the field went home at 2.30, including Linda and me, but Tim stopped out, wanting to try the horse a bit more. Anyway, they found in Silverhills, went across Young's Farm down to the railway towards Mickleover, running for forty minutes, and over fifteen huge fences. (Tim actually took me on Sunday morning to have a look at some of them). There were eventually only six people who stayed out: Phil Arthers, Mandy Haynes, John Hingley, Trevor Brown, Johnny Weatherby and Tim. After that we had a real problem with the horse – It blew his brains and he never settled afterwards. Tim and I hunted him a few more times but he used to break out in a sweat every time he heard hounds. We knew he had won a bit at show-jumping and he could come down to a big fence, and so, to get him out and about a bit, we asked Mark if he would ride him for us at a few shows. We registered him with the B.S.J.A. (which was not cheap). Mark came over and had another sit on him. On the Wednesday we met Mark at Ling Farm. We had put the horse in for two classes at a fiver a go and with a tenner for Mark. On the Saturday we went to Walsall, again it was two classes at a fiver a class, with a tenner for Mark. The following week we did two more shows and by then I was ready to suggest to Linda it was working out on the expensive side. We had spent eighty pounds on the horse, plus the price of the diesel, and all for a measly rosette, which we had given to Mark anyway. I had to say he had made a really good job of riding him. The horse had done well enough too but had not put that sort of value on himself. That was the end of his show-jumping career with us.

Sarah and Mark came with me to Ireland, where we looked at a few horses but nothing caught my eye until we came to a place that John McAuley said belonged to a Swiss chap. It had everything for schooling horses. There was a grey horse going round an indoor school and I asked if he would he be for sale. He looked nice, just right for Sarah, so we tried him a bit more there before taking him outside. He was 16.1hh, and six years old, a bit green, but I bought him. When he arrived home with his vet's certificate, it said, "Scarred on both front legs." None of us had looked under his front boots when he was working in the indoor school. That was one horrible lesson we learnt that day: always look under a horse's boots before you buy. I certainly would not have bought him if I had seen the scars, but they weren't too bad when you got used to them. He stayed right too. In fact, we never had a moment's bother with him. Sarah evented him and got him to Intermediate. Then sold him on to Sorrel Woods for her daughter to ride in Pony Club eventing.

I have not said why I was looking for a horse for Sarah. Claire Evans-Schreiber had sent over some Americans called Sloan (she was a Thorne). The father wanted a hunter for himself and probably one for his children to take Pony Clubbing. Jessica who had given us so much fun and had been Sarah's horse for the Inter-Hunt Competition was ideal for them. Her only fault was she was difficult to catch. I told them so, but as the horses were all turned out in a paddock by the stable she just followed the rest in. I never heard from them again. I should have liked to know how she went on with them.

Back to Punchestown House, home of the Doyles where I bought a bay gelding, three-quarter bred, 5 years old, 16.2hh. I did not have him long either. We never hunted him but sold him as a potential eventer to the Hardstaff family for the girls.

1994-95

There was no change in the Mastership, which is always good news. In fact there were no changes anywhere.

It was another wet season, with few exceptional runs, but sport was consistent all through the season, thanks to David Barker's expertise. Hounds were invited to hunt for a day in the Atherstone country and the Grove and Rufford, where the popular Huntsman is "our" Roderick Duncan.

We lost two people that year who would be impossible to replace. Major Wakey Chandos-Pole, Squire of Radbourne, died. When we were hoping to rent Shuckton Manor Farm and went to be interviewed, it was the Major who asked all the questions although he had given the farm to his wife. All he wanted to talk about was hunting so it did not take us long to feel sure we would be the next tenants of this farm. Years later, he was the one who came to see us and tell us his wife wanted to sell. He advised us it would be a good buy for us as sitting tenants – a great man.

I have never mentioned it before but I was impressed when, after Annie had a bad fall and he wanted to tell us, the phone went and a voice said, "Squire here." These days you don't expect to get a phone call like that.

We lost Sir Francis Ley too, another great friend of ours who enjoyed his hunting, but I think he enjoyed supporting his wife Vidi as much. And Charlie Etches, a friend of mine for many years, died too. We had travelled the shows together, he with his Shires and me with the jumpers. He farmed at Tissington, and, luckily, his son still farms at the family home and we are still sure to find a fox there. I think they keep them in the garden!

The whole Hunt, and the puppy-walkers in particular, shared in the excitement of winning two Firsts at Peterborough: Dawdle won best unentered bitch, and Glasswork and Glucose best entered couple of bitches, with Dawdle and Dazzle gaining second couple for unentered bitches. The Kennels Clock was installed in 1876 by Smiths of Derby. The appeal for funds to repair it reached its target so that Greg and his builders and John Blackwell of English Clockmakers were able to get everything in place and working. It was ticking as well as ever. The Point-to-Point did take place but what a day! The car park was just like a quagmire. Most of the trade stands never opened because of the driving wind and rain. Jeremy Allen was again to the fore persuading people to become Patrons by getting them by the scruff of the neck! Guido did another good job on his Lamb Roast and Country Sports Evening and his riding continues to improve. Brocksford Hall where Tim went to his Prep School was the new venue for the Summer Ball. 94-95 The Junior Club had a quieter year, concentrating their efforts on the Easter Bunny Ball at Repton. I remember Tim coming back with a headache.

The other annual events continued, with varying fortunes, while a new effort was an Inter-Hunt Quiz between six teams in all. The D.N.S.Beagles came out well on top.

The Inter Hunt Relay Team at the Royal Show was made up of Val Eaton née Brown, Jo Marshall, Stewart Shaw, and Phil Arthers. They took the Best Turned Out (always there or thereabouts) and finished second to the Irish Team from the County Clare – but, at last, as the best British team we were invited to the Royal Dublin Show in August.

That year I bought a very nice horse from Norman Proffit, Frankie, a chestnut horse, five years old, 16.3hh. Tim hunted him a lot and loved him. Mark also had a good many days on him. We sold him towards the end of the season to the Hon.Mrs. Willoughby from the Middleton. Dazzle, a very good horse who came from Ireland to Tony then on to Ray Lucas, had won about £250 show-jumping. He was 16.1hh, a bay gelding with the most honest face, a lovely horse, one of my favourites. I cubbed him at Radbourne and was very pleased. Fiona King said a friend of hers was looking for a horse for their daughter. They were the Anleys from Roston. Well, I could not bring myself to sell him until I had had a few more days on him and had to say to Fiona that she could have first chance of him if I thought he was suitable. I took him out another couple of times when nothing special happened but then one day I took him to the Fountain's Farm and we had a very good hunt around and jumped some very difficult fences, very awkward. That was the day he really turned out to be very special. It was time to tell Fiona he was ready to sell and she could bring her friends over. The Anleys came, bought him, and I delivered him. He has had a good home ever since – another case of the right horse for the right person.

I saw Roland jumping at Marchington, with Mark Thompson riding him. Then I saw him tied to the horse-box so I made a few enquiries about him. He had won about £200 show-jumping. He was a chestnut gelding with white flecks on him, a white leg or two, and six years old, a very kind horse, an Irish one again. The first time we cubbed him was at Rolleston Park, with a big field out. Roland just behaved himself, Tim being very diplomatic with him. He could have boiled over. I saw Tim jump a very awkward place out of a farm-yard – only a show-jumper could have done it – and then a very big hedge with an enormous drop before hitting the Cubley-Alkmonton Road. He did go through a dizzy stage but he came a good horse. Stewart Edmonds rang one night; I had got to know him through his riding for Peter Robeson. He hunted with the Oakley and had seen the grey horse which I had sold to the Garfields going very well. Now he wanted to know if I might have one like him, for his father-in-law, Peter Jones, Huntsman of the Pytchley. (Of course we knew his son, Nick Jones, who had been whip in the Chapman era, and his daughter, Tricia, who Stewart Edmonds had married). I described Roland and suggested that he might be the right sort of horse they were looking for. He came over, bought him, and never found any reason to regret it.

A nice bay horse I sold, probably more solid than we normally sold, was to a Mr. Hignot. Although he lived in the Fernie and hunted with them, he and his daughter also hunted with the Meynell. He rode a grey. His wife came here a couple of times to try the bay horse. When she brought his daughter, they declared it suitable for Father and so they bought him.

HORSES SOLD TO DEREK RICKETS

Derek Rickets was coming up to hunt a bit now with the Meynell. He was a friend of David Barker and he was on the lookout for hunters but a hard man to deal with, kept bidding me very low. After the first two I sold him, for the third and subsequent ones I just asked him quite a lot more than I would sell it for so he would bid me and after a bit of haggling he would buy. He thought he had a good deal and I knew I had one as well. He bought Sandyman, a raw-boned chestnut horse that would not really furnish until he was probably a seven-year-old. He had been bought in Ireland, one of Mr. Quin's finds. He did not know too much about him and we did not have him long Another horse Derek had was Moonshine, who had come from Tony Maguire. I think he was the showiest horse we had ever had but he was a good jumper, a great big bay horse – must have been able to carry seventeen stone, and a big horse is difficult to find, but Derek must have already made his mind up where he was going to go and he had the right client for him. The next horse for Derek was Jamie. Now he was a nice dark bay that I bought from Paul Goddard, knowing that a lot of Paul's horses came from Tony in the first place, and that a horse from Paul would have been well hunted. (A few years before, Paul had made some country around Leek huntable, a good piece of work, and that had led to him starting up the Moorland Harriers with his partner Judith. I think he later married her. If he didn't, he should have done).

One thing, when you sell to a dealer and he keeps coming back for more you think you are doing something right.

Tim and I were off to Ireland where we bought six, but I did not realise at the time that it was going to be our last trip buying horses.

Teddy was the first we bought, a liver chestnut, five years old, 16.0hh. that came from the Derwins of Athlone. At first sight Tim did not like him – did not think he was big enough – but when I saw him jump in their sand-paddock I knew he was on his way to England. When I got him back, Stewart Edmonds was wanting another one, this time for his mother-in-law. I remember when I was cubbing him round Hilton Gravel Pits saying to Sam Jones, her grandson, "Do you think this horse will do for Granny?" Sam would be about six. He said, "I'll ring her tonight and tell her I've seen the horse she ought to buy." He must have done, and done it well, because Monica rang me that night and told me she had got a message that I had a horse to suit her. I wasn't to sell him to anyone else before she and Stewart had been over to see him. They turned up and bought him, never wanting him vetting or making a bid for him. He must have been a success. Whenever I see her she always gives me a big kiss and says, "Thank you for finding me such a wonderful pal. He's changed my life."

The second, a chestnut gelding, six years old, 16.2hh, came from a very nice farm. He gave a very good show, looked so well, and had a lovely skin on him. Paul Scott, a big friend of Sarah and Mark's wanted a day with the Meynell and we were still cubbing so I asked him to have a ride on this new horse because I had another new one to take out. I took Mac, a horse we had bought from Peter Mellor. I knew my horse was a very good jumper and we did jump some very nasty places but where I went Paul was to follow. I remember an especially bad place by Top House Farm, Alkmonton, a single iron rail about four feet high in a gateway, no ground line and we both jumped it well, as we did at another awful place by Stydd Farm, a double of sorts. Graham Nichol bought the chestnut horse and Jane Walker-Okeover bought Mac. I think that could have been the sixteenth or seventeenth horse Jane had bought off me.

Lottery was the third horse to come over, a four-year-old which I bought off Adrian Murray. (Some years before, I had bought the big bay that had been out with the staghounds from Adrian). Lottery was off for a while when we got him home, with a splint, the curse of young horses. David Campbell, the vet, always said they took twenty-eight days and he was not far away again. I never hunted him, Mark had a very good day around Kedleston and I sold him to Helen Connors, née Foulkes. She said she had a client for him. He was a nice horse.

The fourth horse was also a bay, six years old, and 16.2hh. Karen Kelly rang up and wanted a horse for a friend of hers.

I said, "I've just had some horses come from Ireland. Bring your breeches and boots and have a day on the one I think might fit your bill."

She came the day before and stayed with her mother, Mrs. Player from Ednaston We were up in the old country, top side of Ilam. He went very well for her but then she has always been a very good jockey. (I must have thought so; otherwise she would not have been riding him). We never actually had a name for him, but he was sold to some people called Hodgekinson. When they brought him up and had a day with the Meynell we saw they had taken his mane off. He looked awful, but he was their horse. I suppose they could do as they wanted with him.

The fifth, Jackpot, came from a chap who had a place in some woods where I had been a few times before but never bought anything. (I remember once when Norman Proffit and I went and he bought one we saw jumping in the car lights. I liked to have a better look at them than that – but he was a nice horse). As I said, Graham Nichol bought the second horse in the lot, the chestnut, but as he sold him on to the Berkely within a day or two, he came back for Jackpot.

The sixth, and last, came from Miley Cash who hunted with the East Galway. John McAuley seemed reluctant to take me, but I insisted. After all, I had an order from Geoffrey Fox that if I liked a horse over there I must buy it for him and so we went to see Miley Cash's chestnut. A twelve-year-old girl rode it for us and it gave a very good show. We got it home, put the saddle on it – and did it buck! After we had it on a lunge to quieten it down a bit, Tim climbed on board, a bit apprehensively I think, but he was all right. When Geoffrey sent for the horse he was very pleased with him. He was Field-Master of the Hurworth and this horse did his turn.

I have said this was my last buying trip to Ireland. I felt that now I was sixty-five I was not confident I could do these Irish horses justice. A lot of them were quite green compared to our horses and I believed I had made such a success of my dealing because I would hunt nearly every horse myself so that whenever a strange jockey climbed on their backs I would have a good idea if he or she could cope, in addition to being able to tell how good a jockey was by the hang of the leg. There are still more horses that I can write about, but they weren't dealing horses. I shall carry on hunting as long as I can. If you can walk you can ride.

Tim came home in June and said he would like to have a point-to-pointer. It came as a bit of a shock to his mother and me, but one has to go along with these things. I suppose he had got this idea from the jockeys he was meeting in his job as Bloodstock Sales Manager to Sheik Mohammed. I knew the Meynell Team was going to Dublin in August but that was the time of the next Doncaster Sales and we needed to get to them. We had to miss the Dublin Show after all! With Tim not having ridden a racehorse before we ought to buy a maiden with some experience. At Doncaster, we looked at a few but as Tim is over six feet tall we had to look for one that was tall enough. After going through the catalogue, we finally whittled it down to Lot 133. We knew he was the sort we wanted: he was called Rambling Lord and had been placed second in a Novice Chase at Kilbeggan and second in a Point-to-point. Tommy Carberry had trained him and son Paul had ridden him but we did not know this at the time we bought him. Although Tim says he picked him out, I think I did, but we were faced for a time with the problem of not being able to find anybody in charge of him.

Once home, although he looked well, we turned him out for a few weeks. When we brought him in we found we had bought ourselves a very kind horse, but a poor jumper – no confidence in himself at all. Cathy Simpson was already schooling another horse for us so we asked her to take him on as well.

The other horse was Clan Reel, a chestnut gelding by Move Off, that I had bought at the same sale at Doncaster. I had seen this horse walking round the outside ring and told Tim I was going to buy him.

"Why?" said Tim. "What do we want him for?"

"He'll make Sarah a nice Event horse."

After I had bought him, I introduced myself to the owner, Robert Goldie, who I knew from the days when I travelled Scotland with the jumpers. I told him I meant to make an Event horse out of him. He thought that would be just the job. We got him home and found he had a big jump. Although he had been placed fifth in his last run in a hurdle-race, for a six-year-old he was very laid back. Cathy was doing a good job with him, chiefly doing a lot of grid-work, not big, but building his confidence all the time. We thought Rambling Lord should do the same, but he just kept propping going into his fences. I wanted to give him a lead and asked Tim to follow me. We had a small ditch in the front field, about eighteen inches wide and six inches deep, that the Pony Club had built. I went first on Glen and heard a sickening thud behind me. Lordy had stopped at this mini-ditch and poor Tim went head-first into it. When we started to qualify him, he was the worst jumper I have ever ridden, and even Tim was going no better on him, until one day, after stopping a few times at a plain ditch by Ireton Wood, it all seemed to click. There are some lovely hedges going away from Ireton Wood. I was giving a good lead on Glen and jumped about six or seven in a row, with good take-offs and landings. We got him through his qualifying but we looked after

Tim and Rambling Lord exercising at home at Shuckton on a frosty morning - dare we dream of a p-t-p winner?

him as regards his jumping.

We pulled out two hedges to make our gallops. One was one mile three furlongs, another six furlongs, and another four furlongs. Then we knew we had the ideal place to get a horse fit. We would take him for a wander up Jim's hills. He started to look really well. I learnt an awful lot from Charlie Hall.

Come January we thought we ought to get serious with him. Tim had let Andy Streeter, who trained just outside Uttoxeter, have some good horses. When approached, Andy said "We have a few galloping on Sunday morning. Bring your horse over, and let's have a look."

We went and spent a bit of time schooling over hurdles before graduating to a couple of fences. Then we did a piece of work with one of his better horses. That left us more than satisfied with Lordy.

Our first run was at Southwell. Brian Goodall, who was bringing his good mare, Cruising, was to lead him up for us, and it had got around that we had very good gallops. We had also found him a jockey in Emma Guest. We got to the race. He was a handful when Brian led him up. They set about ten runners. Tim, in the middle, jumped about four fences, and when they came to an open ditch, Lordy put in a very awkward jump. Poor Tim fell off. – We

Tim winning on Rambling Lord at the Holderness

had got to do some more schooling.

I built just a ditch, and lunged him over that. I took him twice to Brian's for a schooling there. Then we set sail for Market Rasen and the Burton Point-to-point. We put him in the restricted. David Anker, who at the time was Huntsman to the South Wold, said he looked well, and asked me if he might win. I really had no idea. He was in at 8/1. They set off. He sailed over the open ditch. Tim rode a tremendous race on him and won by three lengths – beating some good horses in the process.

Next it was Holderness, a place where I had ridden forty-five years before for Mr Caley on First Bid. David Nicholson, from nearby Dalton Park, who had been dealing with me, both ways, for more than twenty years, led him up. I told him he would win. I told lots of people he would win. Tim rode him superbly, went the shortest way, especially round the bend turning into the straight. He won by about one length.

He was a big horse and the ground came up very hard, so we put him away. I went up to David Nick's place. He took me along to show me his new print. It looked very expensive. It was a print he had always wanted and he had bought it out of Rambling Lord's winnings.

211

We had intended Sarah would event Clan Reel, the other horse I bought that day at Doncaster, but now we thought a season's show-jumping would do him good. Sarah and Mark decided they would like to buy him and Sarah won about £350 on him, before she broke her leg on another horse. After that, she got Jo Marshall to ride him and took him to two one-day events. When he was placed second both times, Sarah was offered some good money by some Dutch people, and sold him.

We had so enjoyed our point-to-point season we decided we needed another; so off we went to Doncaster and bought Amadeus, a French gelding, seven years old, and been placed twice over fences. He was a lovely horse. I knew I would be proud of him when he was being walked round the paddock. I found I was doing most of the qualifying and missing some good hunting, but we got them both in and qualified before Christmas. I started wondering how keen Tim was and told Linda about it. One Sunday lunch-time, I put it to him: "How keen are you really on this point-to-pointing?"

He went straight upstairs, but came down a bit later. "I can't go through all that wasting."

"Fair enough," I said, "but I'm not having anyone else ride them."

On Tim's side, he had changed jobs and now worked at Doncaster Racecourse where it would be even harder for him to get himself fit. I advertised them in the *Racing Post* and sold them both in a week. I followed their careers and they were both placed.

I have done most equestrian sports and I think this one gave me as much pleasure as any of them. The people were so nice to us. And there it was – three runs, two wins. It was a pity Tim did not start point-to-pointing a few years earlier.

I would like to apologise to all the horses I have not mentioned.
If I write a sequel I will mention you all.

EPILOGUE

An old boy was on his death-bed.

His wife said," Harold, you've had a wonderful life. Hunting, shooting, and fishing. You've come through life on a first-class ticket. What would you have done different?"

"Mary," he said, "I would have hunted one day a week extra before Christmas".

He heard a holloa, and the Huntsman blowing, 'Gone away'.

His wife knew there would be nothing more.

But was it to be the last Gone Away of them all?

John and Glendower jumping a "proper" Meynell hedge

Printed in the United Kingdom
by Lightning Source UK Ltd.
106982UKS00002B/64-330

9 781905 237418